POPULAR EDUCATION: ENGAGING THE ACADEMY

International Perspectives

Edited by

Jim Crowther, Vernon Galloway and Ian Martin

niace
promoting adult learning

Published by the National Institute of Adult Continuing Education (England and Wales)

21 De Montfort Street
Leicester LE1 7GE
Company registration no. 2603322
Charity registration no. 1002775

promoting adult learning

NIACE has a broad remit to promote lifelong learning opportunities for adults. NIACE works to develop increased participation in education and training, particularly for those who do not have easy access because of barriers of class, gender, age, race, language and culture, learning difficulties and disabilities, or insufficient financial resources.

NIACE's website on the internet is **www.niace.org.uk**

Cataloguing in Publication Data
A CIP record of this title is available from the British Library

ISBN 1 86201 209 1

Typeset by Kerrypress Ltd, Luton, http://www.kerrypress.co.uk
Printed by Latimer Trend, Plymouth

Contents

Notes on contributors

Dan Baron Cohen is a writer, community educator and cultural activist. He has spent the past twenty years developing community-based methods of sustainable cultural action with dispossessed and excluded communities, co-founding and working towards a cultural method of self-determination with Frontline: Culture & Education in Manchester and Derry. In 1994 he re-entered university teaching as a senior lecturer in drama at the University of Glamorgan, UK, but in 1999 he chose to return to full-time activism, collaborating with the landless, indigenous and trade union movements in Brazil in search of a cultural pedagogy of self-determination.

Bob Boughton teaches adult and workplace education at the University of New England, a regional university in Australia. Prior to taking up this position in 2002, he worked for two decades as a development worker and adult educator with indigenous people's organisations in central Australia. He can be contacted through the School of Leadership and Professional Development, Faculty of Education, Health & Professional Studies, University of New England, Armidale, NSW, Australia, 2351. Email: durn@ozemail.com.au.

Bríd Connolly is a lecturer in the Department of Adult and Community Education, National University of Ireland, Maynooth, County Kildare, Ireland. She began her career in adult and community education twenty years ago in women's community education, with which she is still closely associated. Her research interests include the role of educators in social change, and, in particular, bringing critical pedagogies developed in community education into the academy.

Jim Crowther is a founder member of the International Popular Education Network. He is the co-editor of *Popular Education and Social Movements in Scotland Today* (1999), *Powerful Literacies* (2001) and *Renewing Democracy: An Educational Source Book* (2002). He is a senior lecturer in adult and community education at the University of Edinburgh where he has worked for the last twelve years. Before that he organised adult literacy work and was a trade union activist. His current research interests include the politics of lifelong learning, learning in social movements and critical literacy.

Maria Clara Buena Fischer is a Brazilian researcher in adult, popular and vocational education. She works at the University of UNISINOS (Universidade do Vale do Rio dos Sinos/ Rio Grande do Sul, Brazil) where she teaches and researches in the postgraduate education programme on issues related to education and social exclusion. She has worked with social movements and workers' cooperatives to support them in the process of legitimising their experiential knowledge, and has published several articles related to these issues.

Claudia Flores-Moreno is a Mexican research student currently finalising her PhD thesis on the micro-politics of popular schools at the Institute of Education, University of London, where she also completed an MA in 1999. After studying pedagogy in Mexico City in 1994, she became involved with a Mexican NGO working on popular education and citizen networks. Her early experience as a researcher helped to stimulate her interest in the engagement of the academy with popular education.

Griff Foley is a research associate of the Centre for Popular Education, University of Technology Sydney (UTS). He was formerly an associate professor of adult education at UTS, where he established the Masters degree in adult education, the Aboriginal adult educator professional education programme, and the Centre for Popular Education. He has a long-standing interest in learning in social action, and in the professional education of adult educators and other learning facilitators. His publications include *Learning in Social Action* (1999), *Understanding Adult Education and Training* (2nd edition 2000), *Strategic Learning: Understanding and Facilitating Organisational Change* (2001), *Dimensions of Adult Learning: Adult Education and Training in a Global Era* (2004), as well as papers on informal learning in community organisations, workplaces and social action; the political economy of adult education; adult learning in social movements; self-directed learning; the history of education; and the dynamics of learning groups. He is currently managing a native revegetation project on Australia's east coast, and writing about the informal learning of unpaid ('voluntary') workers.

Vernon Galloway is a lecturer in the Department of Higher and Community Education, University of Edinburgh. His main interests lie in adult and popular education. He previously worked as an adult educator in communities in and around Edinburgh developing popular approaches to educational practice. He is a director of the Adult Learning Project in Edinburgh and the Scottish Civic Forum and is a consultant to the Adult Learners Forum in Edinburgh. He can be contacted by email at vernon.galloway@ed.ac.uk.

John Grayson is Senior Tutor and has taught social history and community development at Northern College, England since 1986. After study at Cambridge and Sheffield universities he has spent his career in adult education, first in trade union and community-based programmes with the Workers Educational Association and then in residential adult education. He has been a Labour Councillor, and still is a union and community activist in housing and anti-racist struggles. In recent years he has written a history of the tenants movement in the UK, *Opening the Window* (1996), edited a survey of community development in European coalfield communities, *Rich Seam* (2002) and contributed to a history of Northern College, *Northern College: 25 Years of Adult Learning* (2004). He is currently developing work on citizenship, and a programme of courses and actions with local activists, refugees and asylum seekers around the theme of 'combating racism'. He is also writing a history of community organisations in civil society.

Jonathan Grossman lectures in the Department of Sociology at the University of Cape Town. His work focuses on the lived experience of the working class and processes by which workers survive and collectively challenge and change the conditions of exploitation and oppression forced upon them. He has published in areas of working-class organisation, action, education and history. Forthcoming publications deal with youth and the struggle for socialism in South Africa and World Bank thinking, higher education and workers. He is currently working on the development of health and safety training with domestic workers and work around 'new social movements' and the working class. He welcomes engagement with others committed to developing collective understanding and action around these issues. Email: Grossman@humanities.uct.ac.za.

Paula Guimarães has been a researcher at the Unit for Adult Education, University of Minho, Portugal since 1992. She has been involved in several research teams, mainly in projects concerned with the study of informal education processes and adult education and training policies. Unit for Adult Education, University of Minho, Rua Abade da Loureira, 4700-356 Braga, Portugal; Tel +351 253601284; Fax +351 253618372; Email: pco@uea.uminho.pt.

Rennie Johnston is a freelance researcher/practitioner in lifelong learning, community development and community-based research. He previously worked at the University of Southampton New College where he was Co-ordinator for Research and Development, worked with a range of community groups and social movements and organised and taught courses in lifelong learning and community studies. He is co-author and editor, with Pam Coare, of *Adult Learning, Citizenship and Community Voices* (2003). He is an active member of the ESREA (European Society for Research in the Education of Adults) Network on Active Democratic Citizenship, a co-founder of the International Popular Education Network and has written widely on adult learning for citizenship as well as on community education and experiential learning.

Liam Kane previously worked as a language teacher in Latin America and as a development education worker for Oxfam in Glasgow, Scotland. He is Senior Lecturer in Modern Languages/Adult Education in the Department of Adult and Continuing Education, University of Glasgow. He researches and teaches on popular education in Latin America and is the author of *Popular Education and Social Change in Latin America* (2001).

Sue Mansfield is a feminist educator and researcher working in the Department of Community Education at the University of Dundee, Scotland. Prior to this she was a practitioner working in the north-west of England in the field of community-based adult education and is still active in the voluntary sector supporting emancipatory educational action with women. She has a special interest in the development of critically reflexive co-inquiry methodologies with particular reference to the use of auto/biographical approaches as a way of exploring the discourses that shape community education practice. Her current research interests centre on the development of co-inquiries with women practitioners and learners, exploring how they make sense of and draw meaning from their professional and personal life experiences with particular reference to the value that they and those around them place on these accounts. This includes developing the use of storytelling and building narratives not only as part of an emancipatory curriculum but also as part of the research process.

Ian Martin is Reader in Adult and Community Education at the University of Edinburgh, Scotland, UK. He has written extensively on the politics of adult education, lifelong learning and citizenship, and is co-editor of *Community Education: An Agenda for Educational Reform* (1987), *Education and Community: The Politics of Practice* (1992), *Popular Education and Social Movements in Scotland Today* (1999) and *Renewing Democracy in Scotland: An Educational Sourcebook* (2002). He is a member of the editorial boards of the Scottish journal *Concept*, the *Journal of Adult and Continuing Education* and the *Journal of Postcolonial Education*, and a founding member of the International Popular Education Network.

Barbara Merrill is a senior lecturer in the Centre for Lifelong Learning, University of Warwick, UK. She is the academic co-ordinator of 2+2 social studies degrees for adults and the foundation degree in community development. She has been involved in several European and national research projects looking at class and gender issues in the experiences of adult students in further and higher education. Her other research interests include community-based learning, citizenship and biographical methods. She is currently Chair of SCUTREA (Standing Conference on University Teaching and Research in the Education of Adults), a member of the Steering Committee of ESREA (European Society for Research in the Education of Adults) and co-ordinator of the ESREA Access Network. She is co-founder of the International Popular Education Network.

Michael Newman is Australian and worked in the fields of community and adult education for some thirty-five years in both the UK and Australia. He was a community outreach worker in inner London, the Warden of the Working Mens College in London, Secretary of Workers Educational Association in Sydney, a national trainer in the Australian Trade Union Training Authority and a senior lecturer in adult education at the University of Technology, Sydney (UTS). He has written a number of books dealing with adult learning and social action. These include *The Poor Cousin: A Study of Adult Education* (1979), *The Third Contract: Theory and Practice in Trade Union Training* (1993), *Defining the Enemy: Adult Education in Social Action* (1994) and *Maeler's*

Regard: Images of Adult Learning (1999). He has recently retired but remains an honorary associate of UTS and continues to write.

John Payne is a writer, researcher and community activist. From 1999 to 2001 he was a part-time Senior Research Fellow in the School of Continuing Education at the University of Leeds, UK, and he continues to collaborate with his former colleagues Cilla Ross and Keith Forrester on a number of projects. He makes regular contributions to educational journals. His most recent books have been published by Five Leaves Press, an independent publisher in Nottingham, *Journey up the Thames: William Morris and Modern England* (2000) and *Catalonia: History and Culture* (2004). Correspondence is welcomed. John Payne, Mortimer House, 9 Vallis Way, Frome, Somerset BA11 3BD, UK. Email: JHPayne777@pop3.poptel.org.uk.

Lídia Puigvert is an associate professor in the Department of Sociological Theory, Philosophy of Rights and Methodology of Sciences at the University of Barcelona, Spain. Her studies in education are informed by gender issues, especially concerning women who belong to disadvantaged social groups, particularly ethnic minorities. She is the co-ordinator of the European research network on Popular Education and Women. She has contributed to various projects at European and state levels, including a research and technological development project called *Workaló: The Creation of New Occupational Patterns for Cultural Minorities: The Gypsy Case*. She has published in *The International Handbook on Lifelong Learning*, written the Preface to Ulrich Beck's *El Normal Caos del Amor* (1998), *Participación y No Participación en Educación de Personas Adultas en España: Un Enfoque Comunicativo y Crítico en Investigación* (1998), and *Aportaciones de Paulo Freire a la Educación y las Ciencias Sociales* (1998).

Ralf St. Clair is Scholar-in-Residence at the Canadian National Literacy Secretariat, and a Research Associate at Simon Fraser University, Vancouver, Canada. He has twenty years experience in community-based adult education in Scotland, Canada and the United States. His research interests include adult literacy education, methodology, community adult education, and critical curriculum studies.

Amélia Vitória Sancho has been a researcher in the Unit for Adult Education, University of Minho, Portugal since 1979. She has also been a trainer of adult educators, teaching subjects related to adult education in general and adult education pedagogy in particular. Unit for Adult Education, University of Minho, Rua Abade da Loureira, 4700-356 Braga, Portugal. Tel +351 253601284; Fax +351 253618372; Email: avitoria@uea.uminho.pt.

Rosa Valls is Professor of Education Theory and History at the University of Barcelona and is a research fellow in the Centre for Research on the Education of Adults (CREA). Her extensive research has focused on the analysis of educational change and social participation. Her most recent work includes *WORKALO: The Creation of New Occupational Patterns for Cultural Minorities. The Gypsy Case, Brudilla Calli: Gypsy Women Against Exclusion, ETGACE. Educating* *for Governance and Development Programme.* She is the author of numerous publications including: *Las Voces de las Personas Participantes en los Movimientos de Educación de Personas Adultas en el Siglo XXI* (2000), *Las Comunidades de Aprendizaje* (2000) and *Learning Communities: Informational Society for All* (1997).

Astrid von Kotze's work in adult education began as a member of an experimental theatre company that created and performed political plays in apartheid South Africa. This led her to participate in various forms of cultural activism within the trade union movement. Since the 1990s she has been engaged in processes of participatory learning/teaching with community-based development practitioners in southern Africa, particularly in the field of disaster risk reduction. Her research interests are in popular education. She is employed in the Community Development Programme at the University of KwaZulu-Natal, Durban, South Africa

James Whelan is a lecturer and researcher at Griffith University's Faculty of Environmental Science in Brisbane, Australia, where he convenes the postgraduate Environmental Advocacy course and associated community-oriented workshops and internship scheme (http://www.environmentaladvocacy.org). His doctoral research identified and evaluated strategies for education and training for environmental advocates. He is leader of the Coastal Cooperative Research Centre's Citizen Science research theme (http://www.coastal.crc.org.au), a suite of projects focusing on participatory resource governance and social learning. He has combined his academic and advocacy interests as a board member, volunteer and action researcher with several social movement groups. As an environmental advocate, he has worked with the Queensland Conservation Council and The Wilderness Society, campaigning on air pollution and sustainable transport, air toxins, tropical rainforest conservation and wilderness conservation.

Introduction: Radicalising intellectual work

Jim Crowther, Vernon Galloway and Ian Martin

This book shows how university-based teachers and researchers in different parts of the world choose to use their work to support popular struggles for greater democracy, equality and social justice – and to do so at a time when all the demands being made upon them are, seemingly, towards institutional *dis*engagement from social and political action. The argument is that universities are, at one and the same time, privileged and contradictory places in which academics, whatever the pressure and constraints they encounter, still enjoy a high degree of relative autonomy. Perhaps this applies most where it may seem to matter least: in the more marginal areas of the academy's activities, such as university departments of adult education and lifelong learning, where it may still be possible to make a distinction between the particular job we are paid to do and the wider work we choose to undertake. As this book demonstrates, politically committed academics can choose to use this relative autonomy in different ways.

In arguing for the social and political engagement of university teachers and researchers, it is necessary to challenge and change many of the current trends in intellectual and institutional life: the hegemony of technical rationality and the new managerialism, the construction of higher education as a competitive market place, the commodification of knowledge and research, the ubiquitous common sense of individualised models and modes of learning and achievement, and the vacuity of much fashionable postmodern theorising which cuts radical education off from its roots in social purpose and political change. This book is therefore about the radicalisation of intellectual work. It advocates this as an important, necessary and urgent task – and shows how it can be done – at a time when universities are being drawn inexorably away from social and political engagement. In our view, the time is ripe for some dissonance and dissent – and for dissident voices to be heard!

The politics of popular education

Popular education, as the term is used in this book, is essentially an answer to the question: Whose side are we on? It unambiguously takes the side of those social interests and movements which are progressive in the sense that they are concerned to challenge inequality, exclusion and discrimination and to be part of the broader struggle for democracy and social justice. Like all educational terminology, popular education is subject to a range of competing interpretations which reflect a variety of historical traditions and cultural contexts. So it is as well to be clear about what is meant here.

The Popular Education Network, with which most of the contributors to this book are directly or indirectly associated, is an informal international network of university-based teachers and researchers which meets in conference every two years (see www.neskes.net/pen). Membership of the network is open and free to all who are willing to subscribe in general terms to the following statement of intent:

Popular education

Popular education is understood to be popular, as distinct from merely populist, in the sense that it is:

- rooted in the real interests and struggles of ordinary people
- overtly political and critical of the status quo
- committed to progressive social and political change.

   Popular education is based on a clear analysis of the nature of inequality, exploitation and oppression, and is informed by an equally clear political purpose. This has nothing to do with helping the 'disadvantaged' or the management of poverty; it has everything to do with the struggle for a more just and egalitarian social order.

The process of popular education has the following general characteristics:

- its curriculum comes out of the concrete experience and material interests of people in communities of resistance and struggle
- its pedagogy is collective, focused primarily on group as distinct from individual learning and development
- it attempts, wherever possible, to forge a direct link between education and social action.

Linking the local and the global

Although the term 'popular education' has come to be associated with relatively recent developments in Latin America, it has strong resonances with many traditions of radical adult education. Popular education seeks to connect the local and the global. In every context it proceeds from specific, localised forms of education and action, but it deliberately sets out to foster international solidarity by making these local struggles part of the wider international struggle for justice and peace.

The purpose of the Popular Education Network

In the short-term, the purpose of the network is to:

- bring together university-based teachers and researchers with an existing interest in and commitment to popular education
- forge active links and solidarity at both national and international levels.

In the longer-term, the network seeks to:

- catalyse action by linking local activists, workers and politically committed academics
- produce and provide educational resources for social and political action
- reassert and reinvigorate adult education's role as an integral part of progressive social movements.

The point to emphasise is that this statement is intended to be uncompromisingly political and partisan. The implicit theoretical base is a materialist political economy. This requires an essentially modernist analysis of late capitalism that links the major social divisions of power in class, gender and 'race' formations. In this sense, popular education seeks to take the side of and be in solidarity with particular collective identities and interests – and it stands against others. In practical educational work it may be necessary to deploy such a modernist rigour with a postmodern sensibility – showing, for example, how cultural identity is related to structural position – but what must always be maintained is that popular education is essentially and fundamentally a political project. In this respect, the danger of technicism – of reducing purpose to process – is precisely that this depoliticises popular education. This is why it is essential that practical pedagogy in popular education is systematically theorised, and that its theory is ideologically justified.

Education, understood as a dialectical process, is constituted of contradictory interests and intentions. Thus, in Paulo Freire's terms, it embodies simultaneously the potential both for 'liberation' and 'domestication', transformation and reproduction. No neutral position is possible. It is true, of course, that no education is ever neutral in the sense that it always reflects particular values and serves particular interests. What is distinctive about popular education is that it is quite explicit about its political purpose and the ideological commitment that informs this. Crucial choices must therefore be made in answering the question: Whose side are we on?

Popular education starts from the real and systematic inequalities and injustices that currently exclude many people from anything but a nominal notion of citizenship. One way in which popular education must be 'popular' is in listening to and articulating those voices which have been silenced and excluded from the public business of civic and political life. Much is to be learnt in the common struggle for majority rights from specific struggles for minority rights. Above all, what a genuinely inclusive popular education has to address is the reality of *un*popular issues. The struggle for the rights of minority and marginalised groups is an integral part of the wider struggle for social justice.

In some important respects, popular education seeks to reverse the ways in which education usually works. For example, it derives its curriculum primarily from people's interests, aspirations and lived experience rather than the expertise of the teacher, the demands of the discipline or the imperatives of policy. In this sense, it is a 'bottom-up' as distinct from 'top-down' process. It is worked *up* from the concrete experience of 'knowing subjects' who, as citizens, have a particular, equal and indivisible political status. The curriculum is constructed, partly at least, from the intellectual and cultural resources as well as the social and political interests they bring with them. They are social actors – not empty vessels, deficit systems, bundles of need or, indeed, primarily agents of production or consumption. Moreover, their educational interests and aspirations are shared and collective. This is the starting point because it is what they have in common as citizens. Learning is essentially about making knowledge that makes sense of their world and helps them to act upon it, collectively, in order to change it for the better.

Engaging the academy: voices and choices

If education is understood as a dialectical process, it is also necessary to recognise that politically committed educators are dialectically positioned 'in and against' it. This is, perhaps particularly and increasingly, the case in universities today. The contemporary academy – certainly in the rich world – is a hotbed of market ideology orchestrated by the dictates of the new magerialism. In the era of academic capitalism university knowledge has become a commodity, and the successful academic is now a trader in the educational market place – as the proliferation of pygmy professorships and the sprouting of cloned journals of academic entrepreneurialism bear testimony. One consequence of this is that there is simply not enough intellectual and political argument going on in the academy – at least the kind of argument that can make a difference to most people's lives. An urgent and distinctive task of popular educators in the academy is therefore to develop new arguments and re-invigorate old ones – for instance, arguments about unfashionable things like equality and justice. By bringing together relatively isolated individuals *in* the academy, this book assembles a set of arguments *against* the dominant discourse of the academy.

The contributors suggest a variety of ways in which the contradictory positioning of university-based teachers and researchers can be harnessed to the politics of popular education through different kinds of social and political engagement. Politically committed academics can help to show how different types of action have different effects and consequences, thus elucidating the grounds for making strategic choices. Perhaps one of the most important contributions of the academy is in developing theoretical analysis to clarify, inform and synthesise popular action – simultaneously making visible some of the key contradictions and conflicts of interest that lie at the heart of much academic work. In this respect, history and historical consciousness are important. Popular education is strengthened by research which seeks to excavate silenced, repressed or discounted histories of radicalism and to reconnect them with today's struggles. This is also a reminder that certain kinds of adult education and adult learning have always been an integral part of progressive social movements. In this sense, politically committed academics need to see their work in history – and to see themselves as exercising agency within historical processes.

In one way or another, all the contributors to this book address the same context of globalisation – or, better, globalising capitalism and the neoliberal restructuring regimes which are invading and colonising the lives of more and more people across the globe. As capital goes global, it undermines the sovereignty of the nation state and, simultaneously, exerts similar pressures everywhere to maximise profit and cut back on public expenditure. The same processes are at work in the logic of the globalised market system and its familiar euphemisms, whether accomplished through the 'modernisation' of welfare states in the rich world or 'structural adjustment' programmes in the poor world – the costs of which, in both contexts, are primarily borne by those who can afford them least, mainly poor women. This has both common and differential effects, as the chapters of this book demonstrate, but these effects are always systematic rather than random.

One such effect is seen increasingly in the role of education, particularly adult education and lifelong learning, in preparing 'flexible' workers for risk and uncertainty. A key purpose of the currently dominant version of lifelong learning is to act as an agent of the 'conservative modernisation' by means of which collective welfare structures are being actively dismantled and individuals remoralised for the brave new world of entrepreneurial citizenship – to thrive if they can, and to survive or go to the wall if they cannot. A crucial contribution politically engaged academics can make in this context is to expose the politics of policy in order to show, in both their teaching and research, that democracy is not the same thing as the market, and to reassert – and, if necessary, help reconstruct – collective interests and solidaristic identities in the face of pervasive processes of individuation and social atomisation.

The subtitle of this book is 'International Perspectives'. Its contributors come from ten different countries around the world – in order of appearance in the text: South Africa, Australia, Scotland, USA, Portugal, Spain, Brazil, England, Mexico and Ireland. This is a rich and unique collection of international voices, all of which seek to engage with various aspects of the same global context but do so in different and distinctive ways. Many of the authors draw directly on research and case material derived from their own practical educational and political experience. In this respect, one important aim of the book is to reverse the usual flow of know-how and expertise by showing what the rich world can learn from the poor world, with its more socialised and genuinely civic traditions of popular action, as well as what the academy can learn from social movements.

Much is now being made of the notion of 'choice' in the rhetoric of public policy. One may perhaps pause to ask whether most people would really choose to be customers rather than citizens. Several contributors seek to turn the idea of choice around by emphasising the extent to which academics still have the opportunity to express their own agency in the choices they make about the kind of work they do and who they do it with. There is still scope in the contemporary academy, whatever its preoccupations and pressures, for defining and choosing different – indeed, subversive – agendas, and re-establishing the connections between the personal and the political in intellectual work. Moreover, it is always necessary to recognise that professional choices are essentially political choices, and that political choices are ultimately moral choices.

Spaces and resources

Popular education, as proposed here, is best understood as a distinctive kind of political commitment and the attitude of mind that accompanies it. Consequently, it is not confined to particular educational sites. As the role of the state changes – as in the current restructuring and privatisation of welfare – so new spaces for popular education are opened up in the reconfigured relationship between the state, the market and civil society. This presents an opportunity to move into the spaces created by the contradictions and unintended outcomes of policy. Popular education often operates in this gap between the intentions and outcomes of policy. It may also be that popular education has much greater potential in the formal contexts of, for instance, schooling and organisational development than its advocates and practitioners have been willing to recognise in the past. The more general point, however, is that there is both the need and the potential to create opportunities and spaces for popular education in all aspects of academic work: teaching, research, training and consultancy. In this respect, many of the contributions to this book show that where there's a will, there's a way.

In popular education, what counts as knowledge and understanding is actively constructed in the creative encounter between the expertise of the teacher and the experience of the learner, each role conferring a distinctive kind of authority. This, surely, is what Marx meant when he said, 'The educator must himself be educated'. Pedagogy is a matter of principle and purpose rather than mere technique. Methods of teaching and learning must therefore be developed and deployed in ways which enable the teacher to learn and the learner to teach. The idea of a pedagogy which generates such dialogical knowledge is liberating in two senses: first, because it claims that knowledge itself can be emancipatory and that what counts as knowledge is contestable; second, because it suggests that alternative and sometimes subversive ways of knowing and acting can be liberated through teaching and other kinds of educational work.

One of the crucial questions that arises is the epistemological distinction and relationship between the formalised and codified knowledge of the academy and other forms of knowledge and knowledge production – for example, the knowledge embodied in indigenous languages and traditions, the knowledge derived from lived experience, and the 'knowledge from below' of exploited, oppressed and marginalised peoples. Some of the papers in this book argue that a genuinely deliberative democratic process must be based on a dialogue of such knowledges – something that is deeply subversive of the academy's traditional assumption of its own legitimacy in defining what counts as worth knowing.

In all of this it is, of course, necessary to accept – as any systematic political economy requires – that education is a necessary rather than sufficient condition of social, economic and political change. Nevertheless, it does have an essential part to play – not least in providing both theoretical and practical resources for change. It is in this sense that a commitment to *praxis* must remain at the core of the relationship between popular education and the academy. And *praxis* in popular education – whatever its difficulties in the context of the academy – must be not only about learning in order to act but also learning from action, even when it fails.

Engaging the academy in popular education will always be a struggle which has to be fitted in – often squeezed in – among all the other things academics are expected to do. To exploit academic autonomy in a purposeful way, it is necessary to engage dialectically with the opportunities and constraints of the academy. There are always new spaces to be opened up and new connections to be made. This process is much more creative and congenial in the company of others, which is one of the reasons for the Popular Education Network – and for this book.

Part One

Popular Education: Values, Contexts and Purposes

Chapter 1

People's Education and the Academy: An Experience from South Africa

Astrid von Kotze

The central focus of this chapter is on the challenges facing popular education in the 'new' South Africa. In particular, what happens to the popular education movement, so important in the struggle for freedom and democracy, in the post-liberation context of neoliberal state social and economic policy? As inequalities between black and white, rich and poor go unchallenged, what can university-based educators do? How should they respond? The author draws on her own experience of social and political engagement to suggest ways forward.

Two worlds of knowledge and action

The University of KwaZulu-Natal, Durban Campus, is situated on top of a hill, overlooking the harbour and the city. 'On a clear day,' we used to say, 'you can see the class struggle down there in the valley.' If you work in the docks and let your eyes trace an avenue of palm trees going up the hillside, you see the citadel of learning with its tower in the clouds – remote, distant, inaccessible. Sometimes, individuals from up there go down, and in the last few years, groups of workers have also found their way into the tower. But on the whole, the academy and labour represent different worlds and trade in different currencies of knowledge.

This chapter looks at different ways in which university adult education has engaged (with) the principles of popular education in the recent past in South Africa.[1] It is a tentative attempt at tracing and understanding the changing relationship between universities and sections of civil society, notably social movements, within the context of shifting socio-political dynamics. I suggest three phases. In the 1980s, popular education was overtly oppositional and directed against the apartheid regime and capitalism. Through the actions of individuals the academy became involved without necessarily having taken a decision to get involved. In the early to mid-1990s until after the government of national unity had taken over in 1994, popular education was supportive of what had previously been the opposition movement. One could argue there was the potential of a meaningful relationship with the academy, resulting in a moral and epistemological commitment of higher education to organised sections of civil society. However, since the mid-1990s and the introduction of the Growth, Employment and Redistribution (GEAR) policies, which have caused an ever-growing chasm between rich and poor across racial divides, popular education is again in opposition mode, directed primarily against the economic policies of the state. The universities have responded to policies dictated by fiscal rather than educational considerations by redirecting their emphasis to serve the dictates of the market. They have interpreted 'popular education' as access to competency-based studies that hold out the promise of individual advancement rather than social and economic change.

People's education for people's power

When I joined the university as an academic in the early 1980s, I was working in the trade union movement, assisting workers with shaping their experiences of exploitation and oppression as workers, as black, and sometimes as women into plays, praise poems, stories, songs and artworks. Workers' acts of reclaiming and controlling their creativity were both self-conscious resistance to dominant culture and another strategy for advancing the larger struggle against oppression. As a collectively drafted document explained: 'we are a movement which announces a real democracy in this land – where people like you and me can control for the first time our productive and creative power' (von Kotze, 1988: 64). Participants in the workers' cultural group wanted 'to create space in our struggle – through our own songs, our own slogans, our own poems, our own artwork, our own plays and dances' (DWCL, 1986: 60). By then, unionised workers all over the country had begun to perform in public spaces, at union meetings, shop steward seminars, in church halls and at mass rallies – wherever people met to organise, mobilise and inform. After the performances songs re-linked the reality of the story to the immediate present, and the workers engaged with the audience in debates around the causes of their misery, drawing parallels between the story and the audience's lived experience. Collectively they analysed and interpreted the conditions of their situation, and suggested alternatives and solutions. Despite the overtly educational dimension of this work, neither I nor the participants thought of this as adult or popular education, but rather as political activism.

In South Africa, popular education was part of 'People's Education for People's Power', an idea born out of the 1985 education crisis and deeply embedded within the larger political struggle against apartheid and capitalism. In many ways, 'people's education' was consistent with the definition of popular education that informs this book: that is, it was rooted in the real interests and struggles of ordinary people; it was overtly political, and it was committed to progressive social and political change (Crowther et al, 1999). The slogans revealed the inspiration derived from popular struggles in Latin America and, in particular, the writings of Paulo Freire, whose *Pedagogy of the Oppressed* was a banned book that was passed from hand to hand in the Black Consciousness movement of the 1980s. Like popular education elsewhere, people's education was both a political and an educational strategy: a cause around which to mobilise and organise for the larger struggle against apartheid, and a means of learning through action and charting a path towards a future alternative. The subject matter was diverse, ranging from issues affecting workers as trade union members, to health, women, literacy and agricultural development.

While people's education was focused mainly on schooling, it included a broader perspective on lifelong education, with the key principles of 'non-racialism, democracy and participation of students and parents in education structures' (Motala and Vally, 2002: 181). It called for an end to any education that 'divides people into classes and ethnic groups', that is 'essentially a means of control to produce subservient, docile people', that 'indoctrinates and domesticates' and that is 'intended to entrench apartheid and capitalism' (SASPU, 1986).

For many academics like myself, our practice in popular education was rooted primarily in being political comrades and activists, rather than educators or researchers. A history of working on collectively defined projects with a common purpose had established the basis of trust. Accumulated trials and triumphs in creating and performing plays, music, art and writing forged a solidarity that was inspired by a passionate belief in the possibility and necessity of change towards social and economic justice, and expressed in mutual care and caring. But the regard for what each had to contribute, based on different knowledge and ways of knowing, had to be constantly renewed. As a white middle-class woman, I felt I had to prove my worth to working-class movements both through my actions as a cultural facilitator and by demonstrating respect for and, eventually, knowledge of local cultures and customs, by participating in fellow activists' lives in times of joy and sadness.

While control of the cultural work remained firmly in the hands of the collective will, it was acknowledged that my academic background allowed me to contribute information and interpretations that were beyond the scope of workers' experiences. I saw my role as building processes of critical dialogue, initiating creative projects, offering another perspective, creating moments of playful or analytical experimentation in the search for other ways of telling a story, questioning, reviewing and reworking what was always perceived of as a production for public performance and discussion. All the work was considered a contribution to the struggle, 'because, even if we are culturally deprived as workers, we demand of ourselves the commitment to build a better world' (DWCL, 1986: 69).

The link between this work and the academy was incidental and instrumental. The university provided access to resources such as books, materials for making pamphlets, telephones and safe spaces for meetings and rehearsals. Beyond sporadic rhetorical acts and through performing rituals that confirmed its commitment to the rule of law and academic freedom, both of which were seriously undermined by the apartheid regime, the university did not enact a supportive relationship to social movements. Generally, activist academics went about their political business knowing that this work was not deemed part of an academics' job description, but the nature of their employment with its flexible time schedules afforded the opportunity to get on with it.

However, when the apartheid regime declared a state of emergency in June 1986 as a way of further repressing counter-insurgency and protests, the doors of the academy were forced open. Activist-academics brought grass-roots organisations, unions, support agencies, literacy programmes, community health advocacy units and the like *physically* into the space as a way of securing them a base for operating safely. As political attacks and assassinations escalated, the university provided an important sanctuary for social action initiatives linked to the struggle. Projects were generally funded by outside (international) donors and the university finance division provided some of the book-keeping infrastructure. Physically, projects were squeezed into a corner office in some corridor; organisationally, they functioned much like non-government organisations. Ideologically, they were informed by the interests of poor people, women, workers.

Academics in a variety of disciplines began to work in two ways: on the one hand, they developed ways of valorising experiential knowledge; on the other, they attempted to popularise formal disciplinary knowledge and make it accessible to people who were excluded from university study. As a result, non-formal adult education programmes abounded: Street Law (a project on 'practical law' that taught people how to understand and use the justice system), shop stewards' courses, workshops in meeting skills and basic financial management for community-based organisations, industrial health and safety courses, literacy classes, drama and writing workshops and the like were run both on and off campus. All saw themselves as part of serving and supporting the struggle against the apartheid regime.

University adult education and popular education

Most of the initiatives took place outside the normal operations of the academy. But as Millar has pointed out (1993: 150):

> University-based adult educators – in contrast to academics in mainstream education departments servicing the schooling system – found their field of practice authorised by The Struggle – as alternative education with the capacity for social transformation. They operated with considerable legitimacy in the project world of small organisations with a field of practice lying between educational and organisational work – a field that maximised their process and strategic skills. Such engagement ensured the flow of donor funding into university departments of adult education: they were resourced, in fact, through demonstrated distance from the university.

In 1990 I left my job in a mainstream academic department and was hired by the more marginal Centre for Adult Education at what was then the University of Natal to design and run a new programme for community activists. These were in the main people who continuously applied for formal university study in adult education but were rejected because they lacked the requisite entrance qualifications for university study. The 'Certificate in Adult Education' and other such initiatives (Walters and Loza, 2000) were new in so far as academics' time spent preparing, organising and teaching was recognised as a legitimate activity. For me it was the first time that my work as an activist did not require ducking and diving and looking for gaps in which to sneak in popular education.

The course attracted students who, in the main, were black adult activists working in voluntary organisations, trade unions, non-government organisations, support agencies and movements like the workers' initiative who used performance culture for education and mobilisation. Most of them had found themselves in positions of educational leadership as a result of their organisational abilities, rather than specific demonstrated skills as educators and trainers. Often their only experience of education had been schooling in the Bantu Education system; real learning, for them, happened outside institutions in the 'school of life'. They were organic intellectuals, articulate leaders who had a wealth of understanding of how the dynamics of power and interest are played out. What they may have lacked in terms of academic reading and writing skills, they made up for with their understanding of 'how society works'.

The experiential knowledge of participants became the core of our curricula, and the philosophy of popular education replaced hierarchical formal teaching. Much of the process of learning and teaching drew on local oral cultural traditions. This also meant foregrounding various aspects of the struggle. For example, a session might begin by emphasising the importance of local, indigenous knowledge systems, and in the process raise the issue of ancestors. A woman might protest against the fact that there are no female ancestors and no rituals around praising and celebrating her fore-mothers. This would lead to an exploration of the need to restructure the new society more generally, and to highlight the women's struggle as an important component of the overall struggle for social and economic justice and equality.

There was a great emphasis on process as we worked in what I came to call 'construction sites of knowledge': production processes reminiscent of drama workshops that demanded collectivity, connectedness, creativity and criticality. Drawing on different perspectives, participants analysed strategies and rehearsed arguments, made sense of the South African situation by contextualising the local struggle within larger socio-political, economic and environmental developments, constructed new meanings and understanding and formulated clear ideas and suggestions that would inform future action. For a moment, the possibility of epistemological transformation of university courses seemed real. The classroom interactions prefigured possibilities of changed power relations between educators and students, book-based imported knowledge and local oral knowledge, across disciplines, based on shared interests and common purpose.

Participants valued the time out from the harsh realities of daily struggles, and a space dedicated to reflection, critical investigation and creative imaginings. Studies were not formally accredited; they were recognised by social networks and NGOs, but not by government departments and private sector employers. At the time this did not matter as the underlying purpose was to further the aims of progressive movements – not to get individual accreditation for personal mobility. Participants' commitment to learning together was high: frequently, factory workers arranged to go on night shifts in order to attend classes during the day, and NGO employees dodged political violence during the height of the KwaZulu/Natal civil war on their way to the university. In many cases, participants attended classes at the university with the expressed and financial support of their organisations. In return for time off to study, they could be expected to feed whatever they had learnt back into the work of the organisation and in this way to multiply their personal learning. The slogan of 'each one, teach one' was taken seriously as a way of practising accountability.

At strategic moments, the university presented this course and the students on it proudly as examples of the institution's 'commitment to community outreach', 'upliftment of disadvantaged communities' and the will to transform what used to be an almost exclusively white institution. The trend to Africanise curricula and initiatives to create access to members of marginal and previously excluded communities signalled a shift in thinking that reflected the larger political transformations in the country. Many of the new ANC-led members of the government that came into power in 1994 had been nurtured in the mass movement, and the methodology (not the politics!) of popular education was cited as useful for future programmes of action: just as people's education had been employed to help dismantle apartheid, it could be mobilised for the work of building democracy and civil society. Activist academics and students participated in voter education campaigns and train-the-trainers workshops for census workers. In the classroom, women and gender issues, racism and economic exploitation were debated hotly as obstacles to equity and the building of a truly democratic society.

Incorporate or corporate

By 1997, two years after the promise that the economic framework of the Reconstruction and Development Policy (RDP) would reverse the fortunes of people through a radical redistribution of land, access to jobs and loans and education and training, it was replaced by GEAR. GEAR has often been described as South Africa's own home-grown structural adjustment policy because it encourages an export-led, market-driven, internationally competitive economy through the reduction of tariffs on imports and participation in various trade agreements. GEAR came with measures for accelerated repayment of loans and drastic cuts in public spending – including spending on education and training beyond basic schooling, and, in particular, adult basic education and community education.

Changing funding policies and lack of foreign donor support, the exodus of leadership into the ranks of government and the private sector combined with blatant opportunism and corruption changed priorities as new opportunities presented themselves. In addition, the sense that the democratically elected government would take over many of the functions previously performed by non-governmental organisations led to the collapse of a wide range of NGOs and support agencies. Furthermore, as Maslamoney suggests (2000), civil society became depoliticised. Many of the old leadership within and outside universities moved away from direct contact with communities into national and local government, or into lucrative jobs in the private sector. The empowerment experienced as a member of a social movement was power *with*, rather than power *over*, people. Now that particular individuals and groups participated more fully and effectively in the political functioning of the new order, they became part of that system: 'By gaining power, they have a stake in maintaining that power. In other words, they buy into the larger configuration of power relationships and become co-opted' (Schapiro, 1995: 41).

Units and organisations that had found refuge in the university were given a choice: be incorporated into mainstream academic work, or corporate, that is, join the market place outside the academy and become independent self-financing bodies. Generally, organisations that survived into the late 1990s did so only by succumbing to the pressure to adopt more cost-efficient management systems, cut staffing, engage in operations of scale, and deliver tangible development outputs. Alternative courses such as the 'Certificate in Adult Education' were subjected to sustained pressure to professionalise by offering a university-recognised qualification which would be linked to the emerging National Qualifications Framework. The formalisation of these courses has had an inevitable impact on curriculum. They are no longer designed in consultation with and in response to the expressed interests and needs of movements, action groups and organisations but in submission to the pressures of outcomes-based education and defined in keeping with competencies that respond to market-driven imperatives. Where we were once called upon to assist the process of transition from capitalism to socialism in the interests of all, we are now expected to prop up the new order through 'empowerment programmes' that prepare the few to be good capitalist entrepreneurs. Students are meant to conform to generic entrance criteria and pursue a pre-designed course of modules within a set programme – and pay the high fees demanded for university study. In order to afford mobility, the courses must equip them with the academic literacy that will enable them to study further. The profile of participants reflects these changes: currently, participants seeking admission to university adult education have personal life trajectories and as 'portfolio shifting' individuals they attend university study with aspirations for professional advancement (Gee, 2000).

Meanwhile, the language of popular education was (and is) still used as if the meaning of terms rooted in opposition politics has remained the same in neoliberal times. In 1999 the then new education minister, Kadar Asmal (1999), outlined the key priorities for education as guided by the principles of 'participation', 'social empowerment' and 'empowerment partnerships'. Educators were/are in danger of becoming what Brecht (1967) called 'instructors in the school of sharks'.

Engaging the academy: the way forward?

Not surprisingly, conditions of disaffection and deprivation have generated the emergence of new grassroots struggles in opposition to what Desai has called 'the frontlines of the establishment's "undeclared war" on the poor' (2000: 7). As the gap between the rich and the poor increases, so does the determination of the poor, the landless and the sick: 'Civil society is now beginning to move from a sense of powerlessness to a situation in which it is tentatively but increasingly asserting itself' (Motala and Vally, 2002: 189). Impromptu plays performed by members of the Treatment Action Campaign (TAC) inform about ways of tackling the stigma associated with HIV/Aids; songs learnt on the march or picket line help to mobilise support for the campaigns of the Landless People's Movement; discussions are rehearsals for people to argue about the link between the lack of social grants and economic globalisation. In the university, former activist academics remember old responses to repressive policies and acts, and try to find the space for working as political allies or activist educators. They work to invent new ways of engaging what is now the academy in a democratic country with the struggles of people from popular movements.

I want to sketch five ways in which like-minded colleagues in current university adult education can try to help students and movements to build crucial knowledge and skills to improve this new democracy. All of them involve going outside established epistemological frameworks and political relations, listening to dissidents naming their own reality (often in their own home language, *isiZulu*) and collectively creating a counter-hegemonic voice. All have the purpose of facilitating change.

First, through research. The fight against poverty and capitalism, against environmental degradation and the AIDS pandemic is now fought at a more geographically localised level. We can research, and encourage students to research, with people and groups engaged in struggles. The nature of this research requires that we become members of the communities of practice that we are studying (Hart, 2000). Often, as investigations and participation fuel anger and passion, students realise that they themselves are implicated in the injustices out there, and so they begin to take a stand, both as researchers and as citizens.

Second, through teaching. By taking the decision collectively to translate complex theories into accessible ideas that allow us to rethink and reconnect we model democratic ways of knowledge production. By being more inventive, more subversive and more determined to function – by acting, as Eich (1973) put it, as 'the sand, not the oil, in the works of the world' – we can kindle the passion that fuels action. By asking questions that smoke out agendas and scrutinise conflicting interests, as opposed to simply positing them as part of 'diversity' and 'stakeholder positions', we can help students to build understanding of how social control is maintained and changed. In this way, they may begin to discuss how education at university should be designed so that it serves the interests of people rather than those of corporations, of life rather than commodities.

Third, through community-based learning. Universities have old-established assumptions about where knowledge is located, and sending students (and ourselves) out into communities requires them to seek and recognise it in often quite unexpected places. Observing how two organisations with very different racial and class-based histories come to work together around a common project helps them to discover that you learn democracy by acting democratically. Asking people on the ground how to formulate and design the text for a pamphlet about the local community resource centre where they can get advice and support in order to access social justice teaches them respect for other literacies. Through engaging with civil society students learn about how power dynamics and interests really play themselves out. This is not the kind of knowledge totted up in shopping lists of 'module competencies': it is the kind of knowledge that helps to question, to challenge and to re-make.

Fourth, through support. Like academics elsewhere, we are called upon to increase the number of fully paid-up students for whom the university can claim full-time-equivalent points and money, to upscale publication quotas in accredited journals, and to compete for prestigious and lucrative research funding (Crowther, Martin and Shaw, 2000). And yet, we also have the freedom to research and write in support of progressive social action initiatives, instead of channelling our creative energies solely into refereed journal articles. As in the past, we can still respond to requests to support popular campaigns by running workshops and preparing learning materials and information in ways that are accessible to English-second language learners.

Fifth, through direct action. When the academy threatens to abandon its social responsibility agenda by clamping down on our little freedoms of space and time, we can say no. We can act with and on behalf of those sectors of society that are excluded from the citadel and invite them in. And we can act in opposition to forces that entrench patriarchal, hierarchical and authoritarian ways of working and decision making. We can also go outside the safe walls of the institution and align ourselves with movements, directly.

Conclusion

How will the real interests of the poor be both reflected and supported in the academy? As academics we are expected to teach, to do research and interpret findings, to decipher trends and help make policies. We have a choice. We can choose to do our work so that it props up the global forces that benefit elites. Or we can raise the questions and develop the analyses that challenge those forces. I believe that universities have the duty to generate knowledge that does not serve greed, accumulation, exploitation, oppression, patriarchy and racism, but rather knowledge that is informed by values of mutuality, connectedness and respect.

Living and working as an activist-academic with one foot in popular education and the other in the world of the academy creates peculiar tensions and excitements. We may dodge and dive competing agendas and expectations in order to find that space that allows us to live with integrity, contributing to the struggle for social justice, and along with others, becoming more fully human in the process. Recently, my university has merged with another one that was historically designated 'Indian', and is now in the process of reinventing itself as 'The Premier University of African Scholarship'. We have a chance to make this a different place – epistemologically and politically. Many of us draw on a common history of activism and we can bring that experience to bear on our decision making bodies and processes, teaching and research, and on policies. We might model a way that redirects funding to collective forms of research and publishing, to active engagement in unearthing and valorising progressive indigenous knowledge, to work more democratically with students and communities outside. It is now our job to insist that the new university does not simply function as an organ of the state, but allocates resources to work that is explicitly aligned to a social justice agenda. This is our chance to choose.

Acknowledgements

I would like to thank Jill, Ari and the WWIP (Women's Writing in Progress group) for constructive feedback on drafts of this paper. Sections of it are based on a presentation delivered together with my colleague Linda Cooper, University of Cape Town at the Popular Education Network Conference in Edinburgh in June 2000. I gratefully acknowledge her contribution.

Note

1. As a white woman I have studied and worked in a university that in terms of racial policies was designated for 'white' students. Since the early 1990s, the University of KwaZulu-Natal (UKZN) has changed dramatically, and the majority (83 per cent) of students are now of African and Indian ancestry. In this paper, 'academy' refers primarily to 'historically white' universities like my own institution, although there are considerable parallels to the work of colleagues at the University of the Western Cape, a historically 'Black' university (see Walters and Loza, 2000).

References

Asmal, K. (1999), 'Call to action: mobilising citizens to build a South African education and training system for the 21st century', *Adult Education and Development*, 53, pp. 7-33.

Brecht, B. (1967), *Gesammelte Werke Bd 12*, Frankfurt: Suhrkamp.

Crowther, J., Martin, I. and Shaw, M. (eds) (1999), *Popular Education and Social Movements in Scotland Today*, Leicester: NIACE.

Crowther, J., Martin, I. and Shaw, M. (2000), 'Turning the discourse' in Thompson, J. (ed.) *Stretching the Academy. The Politics and Practice of Widening Participation in Higher Education*, Leicester: NIACE, pp. 171-85.

Desai, A. (2000), *The Poors of Chatsworth: Race, Class and Social Movements in Post-Apartheid South Africa*, Durban: IBR & Madiba Publishers.

DWCL (Durban Workers Cultural Local) (1986), *Black Mamba Rising*, Durban: Culture and Working Life Publications.

Eich, G. (1973), *Hoerspiele*, Frankfurt: Suhrkamp.

Gee, J. (2000), 'The new capitalism: what's new?' in *Working Knowledge: Productive Learning at Work* Conference Proceedings, Sydney: University of Technology.

Hart, M. (2000), 'Adult education and the political allegiance of universities', *Convergence*, 33(3), pp. 25-41.

Maslamoney, S. (2000), 'Youth and the small screen: I see, therefore I am: the portrayal of youth on TV', *Development Update*, 3(2), pp. 160-9.

Millar, C. (1993), 'University-based adult education and the field of practice: a South African case' in Miller, N. and Jones, D. (eds) *Research: Reflecting Practice*, Proceedings of the 23rd Annual SCUTREA Conference, Manchester: University of Manchester, pp. 148-50.

Motala, S. and Vally, S. (2002), 'People's education: from people's power to Tirisano' in Kalaway, P. (ed.) *The History of Education under Apartheid 1948-1994*, Cape Town: Pearson Education South Africa, pp. 174-94.

SASPU National (Newspaper), 18 February 1986.

Schapiro, R.M. (1995), 'Liberatory pedagogy and the development paradox', *Convergence* 28(2), pp. 28-46.

von Kotze, A. (1988), *Organise and Act. The Natal Workers Theatre Movement 1983-87*, Durban: Culture and Working Life Publications.

Walters, S. and Loza, F. (2000), 'Township learning: adult education within a South African university', *Convergence* 33, pp. 41-55.

Chapter 2

Popular Teaching, Popular Learning and Popular Action

Michael Newman

This chapter develops a conceptual framework which clarifies different types of social action and the implications of each for teaching and learning. The author makes a distinction between conventional action, confrontational action and violent action. He goes on systematically to examine what these kinds of action involve and to assess their potential consequences in moral, political and strategic terms. Perhaps the essential contribution the academy can make is to clarify the basis on which moral choices are made that further the struggle for social justice.

Action

In popular education we learn in order to act, and act in order to learn. We could argue that we achieve our full humanity when the two activities of learning and social action fuse into one. People, Paulo Freire (1972: 61) says, are built 'in word, in work, in action-reflection'.

To practise popular education, then, we need to form an understanding of action, identify the kinds of action available to us, and consider the implications of engaging in each kind. Dalton (1996) and McAllister (1992) write about participation in the affairs of the state. Both talk of 'conventional' and 'unconventional' participation. McAllister then breaks up the unconventional category into legal protest, semi-legal protest and radical protest. But there are problems in the concepts of participation and protest. Participation can imply acceptance of the *status quo* and has a potentially counterproductive, good mannered feel about it. And protest has negative or reactive connotations, since we are normally resisting *someone else's* initiative. Drawing on Dalton and McAllister but changing their terminology, I would like to propose three categories of action: conventional action, confrontational action and violent action.

Conventional action enables us to participate directly and peaceably in the affairs of our community, society and state. It involves activities such as voting, taking part in elections as campaign workers, entering into communal activity, making contact with politicians and officials through letter-writing, email, phone and meetings, organising petitions and lobbying, and engaging in consumer boycotts, lawful demonstrations and lawful strikes. In this kind of action the people involved are intent on making changes within the existing structures, and not with altering the structures themselves. When middle-class people, for example, take to the streets to protest against government changes to the public education system, they are not challenging the existing order, since in many other respects they are an integral part of that order. As Dalton (1996) points out, these kinds of modern demonstration are often carefully managed, with people being bussed to pre-arranged meeting points and kept in order by marshals provided by the protesting organisations themselves. Moreover, if we accept Max Weber's definition of power as 'the exercise of one's will *despite resistance*' (1968: 53, my italics), then these kinds of disciplined demonstration can actually confirm the authority of those in control. The demonstrators provide a manageable form of resistance while those in control make a public display of their power, either by ostentatiously rejecting the demonstrators' demands or by magnanimously acceding to them.

Confrontational action is what it says. It takes on those in control more openly and directly. It involves strategies designed to disrupt or distract, such as hacking into a corporation's website and redirecting browsers to an activist website, invading a meeting, blockading a road, and holding demonstrations or strikes which have *not* been coordinated with the authorities. So environmental activists will picket a uranium mine, block an underwater outlet from a chemical works, or dump waste outside a company headquarters. And peace activists will scale and write the words 'No War' on one of the sails of the Sydney Opera House. The consequences of confrontational action are uncertain. Activists may occupy a building not knowing whether the police will arrest or simply eject them.

Violent action crosses the line. It involves damage to property and violence against people. So students or workers in some countries take to the streets, and literally do battle with the police or armed services. Taking such action involves flagrantly breaking the law, or confronting authorities who will offer little leniency if the activists are detained. Taking such action is physically dangerous, and involves stepping across both legal and, even more importantly, serious moral boundaries.

Popular educators aim to help people play their parts as subjects in social history. They use processes which may, if effectively applied, *impel* people into action. So an educator bringing together people from a community affected by the dumping of dangerous industrial waste will help them gather information and analyse the social, economic and political circumstances that permitted the dumping of the waste to occur. In all likelihood this process will lead to a call for action to prevent further dumping. Now the educator and the learners will need to consider carefully what action is available to them and what are the possible outcomes of that action. In particular, the educator will need to help the learners examine the implications of moving from one kind of action to another.

There are no easy responses to these challenges but there are stories to tell, of people who have used the different forms of action effectively and of people who have crossed the lines from one kind of action to another. When two hired killers came into Wilder, a town in Tennessee, USA, in 1933 to kill his unionist friend, Myles Horton, the activist educator and founder of

Highlander, helped a group of strikers decide whether or not they would kill the killers. In recounting the story, Horton made the point that since the authorities were not ready to protect the miners' leader, non-violence was not an option. The decision was between the violent death of one person or the violent death of two. 'Of course, any person in their right mind would be for non-violence over violence if it were a simple choice,' Horton said, 'but that's not the problem the world has to face' (1990: 39-41).

Griff Foley tells of activists in Australia who, in an otherwise non-violent anti-logging campaign in the 1970s, broke ranks and took action in a way that endangered the lives of the loggers. The challenge for the non-violent activists in that campaign (and for anyone hearing the story after the event) was that the actions of these mavericks swung the campaign in the environmentalists' favour (Foley, 1999).

And elsewhere I recount the story of a friend who used educational and industrial action in the early 1990s to combat the use of child labour in brick kilns in an area of north Pakistan. At a crucial moment, when the release of a number of children from their virtual slavery was under threat, my friend's comrades kidnapped the son of a kiln owner. They used the child as a bargaining counter to get the campaign back on track (Newman, 1999: 167-9). Kidnapping is repugnant. It must, short of murder and rape, be the most complete assault on a person's rights. But the labour from which my friend and his comrades saved a whole group of children is also repugnant.

Sites for education and action

Since popular education involves acting on our social, economic and political world, we need to develop an analysis of the world which will enable us to locate our teaching and learning effectively within it. Do we locate our educational action in a community context, an industrial context, or a corporate context? Do we locate our work within a particular social class, an ethnic group, a group defined by gender, or a group defined by sexual preference? Do we work with people with different kinds of disadvantage?

The concepts of 'the system', 'civil society' and 'the lifeworld' can help us make some of these decisions. The term 'the system' can be used colloquially but it is also used in critical social theory to describe the processes of exchange that make up the economy, and the political and administrative controls that make up the social and political structures within which we all live. It is that combination of money and power which dictates much of our lives (Habermas, 1984; 1987). 'The system' is sometimes used synonymously with 'the state', but it is a more comprehensive concept and includes transnational corporations, multinational consortia, and other facets of power and exchange which transcend individual political systems such as the International Monetary Fund and the World Bank.

The system is an object of study and a site for action for popular educators. We can help ourselves and our learners analyse it and its multiple manifestations. We can identify the ways the system affects people's lives. And we can decide on the kinds of action which will make changes to ourselves, to the ways we exist within the system, and to the system itself. This kind of popular education requires educators and learners to address issues of global, regional and national political economy. We can find examples in trade union education when activists come together to examine the system and identify ways to further their members' interests within it.

'Civil society' is a more localised idea, and refers to that pattern of relationships and groupings we enter into as we seek to manage and fulfil our lives. There are different emphases in the definitions. Frank Youngman (2000) sees civil society manifested in reasonably formalised organisations like professional associations, trade unions, employers' federations and religious bodies or in social movements like peace campaigns and environmental movements. Jodi Dean (1996: 221) argues that civil society comprises 'the institutionalised components' of our lives which 'preserve and renew cultural traditions, group solidarities, and individual and social identities'. Eva Cox (1995) describes civil society as those familiar community groupings with democratic, egalitarian and voluntary structures such as sporting clubs, craft groups, local environment associations, some ethnic and religious groups, playgroups, and neighbourhood centres.

Cox's vision of civil society is constructed on trust. She distinguishes between financial, physical, human and social capital, and argues that for the first three forms of capital, excessive expenditure will lead to their depletion. So if we spend money profligately, we will have less. If we chop down the forests without replacing them, we will degrade the environment. If management exploits its employees, this will lead to burnout, ill health and a loss of the accumulated skills and knowledge the employees possess. However, in the case of social capital, the more we spend, the more we amass. The more we base our relationships on trust, the more trusting all the parties become and the more trust we create. This vision of civil society becomes an alternative to the system. It is another, perhaps ultimately more important, arena in which to act out, and give meaning to, our lives.

This concept provides an attractive location for popular educators to work in. We can aim to bring people together to examine ways of building and affirming local associations and groupings in which they can accumulate social capital. But a civil society constructed on trust is an essentially humanist vision, and it may also be useful to look for 'harder' versions. Antonio Gramsci (1971) described civil society as being made up of organisations such as schools and universities, state bureaucracies and the church. He described these institutions as ramparts shoring up the state, promoting and reinforcing its hegemonic control. Gramsci drew a distinction between 'a war of manoeuvre' and 'a war of position'. In a war of manoeuvre, armies join battle and seek to win through the strategic movement of their forces. In a war of position, forces gain entry to the ramparts and fight from within. Gramsci, writing from prison during the Fascist regime in Italy in the 1930s, argued that we need to see the organisations which make up civil society as sites for struggle. Activists need to gain entry to them in order to disrupt, deter and alter their policies and practices. Because these organisations promulgate the ideas and authority of the state, this kind of action has the potential to bring about significant change.

Popular educators can make use of this more structural, less benign, concept of civil society. We and our learners can examine organisations such as large NGOs, public institutions, private enterprises, the print, electronic and internet media, training organisations and cultural and arts organisations which may constitute modern versions of Gramsci's ramparts of the state. We can seek to establish the degree to which they and other organisations might be used to challenge or counter hegemonic control. We can plan strategies based on infiltration, provoking and managing change, persuasion and possibly even subversion.

A third form of civil society is to be found in social movements. Structured social movements like the churches, semi-structured social movements like the indigenous peoples' movement, and unstructured movements like the vast collection of people combating the spread of the HIV/AIDS virus and caring for the sufferers, can all bring about considerable change. All provide dynamic sites for popular education. We and our learners can analyse social movements and evaluate their actions. We can help forge alliances between movements. We can form social movements of our own. And we can join existing movements, helping their members link learning directly to struggle. Just as corporate trainers seek to turn working organisations into learning organisations, and lifelong educators try to turn suburbs, towns and cities into learning communities, popular educators can help turn social movements into learning movements. There are many examples of popular education practices associated with the environmental movement. There are independent activist-educators who go to the point of conflict in a campaign, to save a rain forest, for example, and offer training in forms of action, resistance and self-protection. There are environmental organisations which run discussion groups, information campaigns and web sites with databases and interactive features such as forums and chat rooms. There are semi-formal or formal courses designed to bring people together to plan ways of preventing rather than abetting environmental degradation.

No single concept of civil society need take precedence. Our aim should be to create a society where we can accumulate trust, work inventively within the structures of the state, and act collectively to bring about social justice.

'The lifeworld' denotes the almost infinite number of shared understandings upon which we build our lives and base our interactions with others. It is made up of those convictions and assumptions which we take for granted. Habermas (1987: 131) talks of a 'vast and incalculable web of presuppositions', the countless givens we draw on when we make meaning of events and when we judge people's actions and utterances. For the most part, the lifeworld remains unexamined. But it is possible to take a segment of our lifeworld, bring it into the foreground, and consciously examine it. The rest of the lifeworld, however, remains unquestioned, continuing to provide the frameworks within which we think and the background against which we act. For popular educators and our learners, therefore, the lifeworld can be both a subject for examination and a resource to draw upon in the course of making that examination.

Learning

Popular education involves learning in order to act. Learning is a tool, and we need to understand the various ways it can be used. Jack Mezirow (1981; 1990), drawing upon Habermas's (1972) discussion of 'knowledge constitutive interests' describes three 'domains' of learning which he originally designated as instrumental learning, learning for interpersonal understanding and learning for perspective transformation. These ideas have been taken up by others, and the terms 'instrumental learning', 'interpretive learning' and 'critical learning' have become reasonably current.

We engage in instrumental learning in order to deal with our environment. We learn about cause and effect, and how to solve problems by commonplace logic. In the world of academic disciplines, this kind of learning would be found in subjects such as geology and physics. In the worlds of technical and informal education, this kind of learning would be found in practical, skill-based courses. In our everyday lives, this is 'how-to' learning. We need to be careful, however, not to think of instrumental learning as simply to do with the physical environment. We can also engage in this kind of learning to deal with the legal, economic or political environment. The learning is instrumental if our interest in learning is to control and manage that environment as if it were inanimate, as if the people who inhabit that environment were objects.

Popular education is concerned with action and so will usually involve instrumental learning. A popular educator engaging with street kids, for example, will need to teach (and will probably learn) a range of very practical, very instrumental survival skills.

We engage in interpretive learning in order to understand the human condition. It is the learning about what people are, how they organise themselves and how they relate, about symbolic interaction and the social construction of meaning. We learn to solve problems by talking things through, by seeking consensus, and through reflection and insight. The 'rules' governing interpretive learning are different from the rules of instrumental learning. In the world of academic disciplines interpretive learning would be found in the descriptive social sciences such as sociology and anthropology, and in history, literature and theology. In the world of informal education this kind of learning would be found in communication skills and 'personal growth' workshops and liberal adult education courses. In our everyday lives this is learning about living as social beings.

Popular educators make considerable use of teaching and learning in the interpretive domain, and we find a rich variety of examples in the work of cultural activists. These are the educators and activists who make use of the arts, who perform, or encourage performance, with the aims of making people think, and raising their moral and political consciousnesses.

Critical learning helps us examine ourselves and our culture. It helps us understand what 'makes us tick'. We learn to solve problems by adopting a form of self-reflection. In this kind of learning we foreground segments of our lifeworld. We tease out the ideas, values and ideologies we have constructed our lives on and set about changing those which no longer suit us. Again the 'rules' are different. Critical learning is a political act. It helps us see through ourselves and so become better at seeing through others. It makes us much less susceptible to hegemonic control. In the world of academic disciplines this kind of learning might be found in the critical social sciences such as psychoanalysis, the critiques of ideology and the philosophy of science, and in some forms of cultural studies. In the world of informal education this kind of learning might be found in courses and workshops that involve a reflexive examination of social and cultural norms. In our everyday lives this is the learning we do every time we try to separate out 'truth' from 'ideology'.

Critical learning holds a privileged place in the discourse of popular education. This comes about because of the prominence of Freire (1972) as a theorist in the field, and in turn because of the central place he gives to 'conscientization' in his thinking. But critical learning can also occur at chance moments, or as a part of another activity. A popular educator, confronted with an unthinkingly racist comment during a community discussion, instead of asking 'Why do you think that?' might ask 'Where does that idea come from?' and conduct a discussion on how thoughts have histories. A popular educator training a group of young people to play football might find an opportunity to speculate with them on the manufacture of the ball they are using.

Control

Popular education is concerned with learning to identify, use and resist various kinds of social control. We exercise and experience control through physical force, institutional control and control by ideas. Physical force is the most obvious. There are uses of physical force which we can claim to be benign. We hold back a child at the edge of road. We corral people at a pop concert for their own safety. We incarcerate people who are a danger to themselves and to others. And there are malign uses. We are pushed around, and we can push others around. We smack the child. There is domestic violence. A street gang menaces us. We lock boat people up. An oligarchy employs murder by roving hit squads. Terrorists strike, killing thousands. One country, or a 'coalition' of countries, invades another, killing uncounted thousands more. Physical force is easy to identify, and in a sense it also easy to understand. But control by physical force rarely occurs spontaneously. Behind most manifestations of physical force is an organisation – a ministry, political party or corporation, a family, that street gang, the tactical response group of the police, a government or governments.

In most cases physical force is an expression of institutional control. Institutional control encompasses both coercion and consent. All of us submit to institutional control, and often do so willingly. We give up a range of freedoms in exchange for the membership, services and security those institutions provide. We abide by the rules of the local sports club in order to use the club's facilities. We run with a gang in return for a sense of belonging. We submit to the laws of the land in return for the services and security the state provides us.

Physical force and institutional control are closely related. Some institutions, such as the penal system or a health department, make overt use of physical force. They lock people up. Other institutions make use of the threat of physical force. We keep up our repayments for the loan on a house out of a fear of eviction if we default. Physical force in actuality or in the form of menace underpins many social relationships. And since social relationships are formalised in institutions, such as the family, the club and the workplace, we can interpret institutions as structured embodiments of physical force.

The third kind of social control is control by ideas. Just as physical force and institutional control fold over into one another, so do institutional control and control by ideas. Institutions are made up of people, structures, rules, procedures and property. But they are also constructed on sets of values and ideologies, which those institutions espouse, promote, and in some cases seek to make dominant. If a class or group or an institution succeeds in making its ideas the dominant ones in society then that class or group or institution achieves control. Its ideas become embedded in public utilities, private corporations, the churches and the education system which make up part of the structure, the ramparts, of the state. The ideas become uncontested, accepted as common sense and therefore in need of neither justification nor explanation. They enter the collective lifeworld, and control is achieved by consent. If developers can get people who are living in the path of a proposed freeway to say 'You can't stand in the way of progress', then they will not need the courts or the police to move the occupants out of their houses. The occupants will move of their own accord.

It would be tempting to suggest a simple match of learning to control, and propose that we respond to physical force with instrumental learning, to institutional control with interpretive learning, and to hegemonic control with critical learning. But the different forms of control fold over into each other, and the exercise of power will almost always involve all three. So our response will need to be multi-layered. We will need engage with learners in all three domains of learning, locate that learning in a combination of social sites, and employ a combination of different kinds of action.

The popular educator in the academy

How do we teach popular education from within the confines of the academy? We can teach about different forms of action. We can provide an analysis of the different social sites where popular education might be located. We can teach the different domains of learning. And we can teach different kinds of social control. These concepts do not match perfectly so they are not offered as a framework, but as concepts around which discussion can be built.

But I believe the university teacher has two further responsibilities. The first is to teach choice. Rick Turner, the South African philosopher, wrote:

> Human beings can choose. They are not sucked into the future by stimuli to which they have to respond in specific ways. Rather, human beings are continually making choices. They can stand back and look at alternatives. Theoretically they can choose about anything. They can choose whether to live or to die; they can choose celibacy or promiscuity, voluntary poverty or the pursuit of wealth, ice cream or jelly. (Turner, 1980: 8)

I would argue that popular education is about teaching choice, about helping ourselves and others understand that we do have choices, and about helping ourselves and others develop the necessary capabilities to make those choices.

But what kinds of choice? I would argue that the second responsibility is to teach *moral* choice. Horton had the greatest respect for his learners. He got them to tell their stories, and used those stories as the curriculum. He got people to talk, to share and to work together to make meaning from their lives. And he got his learners to make their own choices.

> . . . [E]ducators should try to help people make conscious decisions at every point: long and short range decisions, small decisions, decisions that affect only a few people and those that affect many. All of them are important. (Horton, 1990: 138)

Yet Horton's commitment to the principle of people taking responsibility for their own decisions did not stop him from sharing his own vision. When he felt it would be useful he intervened, offering his own analysis, ideas and moral viewpoints (Peters and Bell, 1987).

I believe that the university teacher should do the same. We should share our vision. In my case, then, I would like to promote the idea of responding to an attack with thoughtfulness rather than revenge. I would like to encourage our learners to look for reasons for hatred and violence and where possible address those reasons through humanitarian means. I would want them to look long and hard at the people who wield power, and make informed decisions about who are our friends and who are our enemies. And I would like encourage them to work with the friends, and to look for ways of talking those enemies round, countering the effects of their actions and, at the end of the day, disempowering them.

References

Cox, E. (1995), *A Truly Civil Society: 1995 Boyer Lectures,* Sydney: ABC Books.

Dalton, R. (1996), *Citizen Politics*, New Jersey: Chatham House Publishers.

Dean, J. (1996), 'Civil society: beyond the public sphere' in Rasmussen, D. (ed.) *The Handbook of Critical Theory*, Oxford: Blackwell Publishers.

Freire, P. (1972), *Pedagogy of the Oppressed*, Harmondsworth: Penguin.

Foley, G. (1999), *Learning in Social Action: A Contribution to Understanding Informal Education*, London: Zed Books.

Gramsci, A. (1971), in Hoare, Q. and Smith, G.N. (eds), *Selections from the Prison Notebooks of Antonio Gramsci*, New York: International Publishers.

Habermas, J. (1972), *Knowledge and Human Interests*, Boston: Beacon Press.

Habermas, J. (1984), *The Theory of Communicative Action*, Vol 1, Cambridge: Polity Press.

Habermas, J. (1987), *The Theory of Communicative Action*, Vol 2, Cambridge: Polity Press.

Horton, M. (1990), *The Long Haul*, New York: Doubleday.

McAllister, I. (1992), *Political Behaviour: Citizens, Parties and Elites in Australia*, Melbourne: Longman Cheshire.

Mezirow, J. (1981), 'A critical theory of adult learning and education', *Adult Education*, 31(1).

Mezirow, J. (1991), *Transformative Dimensions of Adult Learning*, San Fransicio: Jossey-Bass.

Newman, M. (1999), *Maeler's Regard: Images of Adult Learning*, Sydney: Stewart Victor Publishing.

Peters, J. and Bell, B. (1987), 'Horton of Highlander' in Jarvis, P. (ed.) *Twentieth Century Thinkers in Adult Education*, London: Croom Helm.

Turner, R. (1980), *The Eye of the Needle: Towards Participatory Democracy in South Africa*, Johannesburg: Ravan Press.

Weber, M. (1968), *Economy and Society: An Outline of Interpretive Sociology*, New York: Bedminster Press.

Youngman, F. (2000), *The Political Economy of Adult Education and Development*, London: Zed Books.

Chapter 3

Ideology Matters

Liam Kane

This chapter reasserts the political nature of popular education. It argues, in particular, against the tendency to reduce popular education to a range of participatory methodological techniques. Through understandable concerns to promote progressive approaches, popular educators often fail to address the explicitly ideological nature of their work. Drawing on experience of popular education in both Latin America and Scotland, the author examines how ideological factors influence educational practice and what this means for working both inside and outside the academy.

In their excellent review of the first international conference of the Popular Education Network, von Kotze and Cooper (2000: 22-3) state that the 'pre-conference information had been unequivocal about the commitment to a particular vision of popular education', but that they were surprised to discover that:

> the explicitly political and social purpose which framed the conference proposal and which was restated unambiguously in the opening session seemed to be interpreted in such different ways. We were unsettled by the wide range of conceptualisations of popular education that emerged in some of the presentations and papers.

I share the authors' unease, but no longer their surprise: at most popular education events I attend, whether in Europe or Latin America, the story is similar and 'popular education' is interpreted in a myriad of ways. Given the multi-lingual/cultural nature of the conference, at times, perhaps, the problem was semantic: I concluded, for example, that the Norwegian usage of 'popular education' translates better into UK English as 'liberal adult education'. But linguistic discrepancies aside, I agree with von Kotze and Cooper that 'in future, it will be important to confront these diverse – and sometimes contradictory – understandings directly'.

The problem, in my view, is that through a concern to promote progressive methodologies (as opposed to 'banking education') and the emergence of authentic 'subjects' of change, popular education movements rarely address, explicitly, the ideological aspect of their work. By 'ideology' I refer to the particular set of ideas and beliefs – political, cultural, philosophical – held by a group or individual (the educator) and used to interpret the world (Storey, 1998; Hindess, 1997).

In an attempt to confront such diversity of understandings, and drawing on experiences from Scotland and Latin America, this paper examines how popular education practice is affected by ideology, and considers, in conclusion, what this means for the academy.

The role of ideology

Ideology matters. It is a fundamental principle that for education to be authentically 'popular' it should have a political commitment in favour of the 'oppressed'. In practice, however, the concept of political commitment – as well as that of the 'oppressed' – has proved to be vague and open to many ideological interpretations: the ranks of popular educators have been swelled by Catholics and atheists, social democrats and Marxist revolutionaries, feminists and *machistas*, nationalists and internationalists, with many and varied hybrid combinations (see Kane, 2001: 149-52 for examples from Latin America). There has been surprisingly little discussion about how such an assortment of bedfellows can supposedly engage in the same activity. While this may be rooted in a commendable desire to avoid the traditional in-fighting of the left, I think it also constitutes a theoretical weakness in popular education and a source of confusion to anyone trying to grasp the dynamics of a popular education movement.

But why, it might be asked, should such ideological diversity make any difference? After all, other fundamental aspects of popular education include:

- a recognition that learners, as well as educators, possess important knowledge
- a methodology which asks open-ended questions, encourages people to think and act for themselves – rather than having solutions forced upon them – and promotes 'dialogue' between educators and learners.

Surely this non-manipulative, learner-centred approach relegates the importance of the educator's opinions to a cameo role in the educational process? What does it matter whether popular educators are Marxists, nationalists or social democrats when their job is not to promote their own ideas but to encourage others to become authentic 'subjects' of change? Though there is a certain logic in this line of questioning, I believe it has serious flaws.

First, take Freire's notion of 'critical consciousness' (Freire, 1972). If educator-activists aim to develop this faculty in learners – and they themselves are supposed to possess it already (leaving aside, for the moment, the question of how they are meant to have acquired it) – then their only way of recognising critical consciousness is through their own particular ideological construction of what this actually means. But what counts as 'critical consciousness' for some could be 'naïve consciousness' for others. Freire, as well as Marx and Gramsci, talked of how oppressors try to present inequality as a natural phenomenon and argued that the role of education is to unveil the ideological manipulation behind the dominant, hegemonic ideology. But in Latin America, if someone currently believes there is no alternative to the right wing economic doctrine of 'neoliberalism' and that 'democracy' is the key to progress, socialism now being a utopian dream (see Castañeda, 1994), does this constitute 'realism' or could it be a lack of 'critical consciousness'? In 1999, the UK and US governments claimed that their rationale for going to war in Yugoslavia was humanitarian. This was accepted by many people on the left who presumably claim to possess a degree of critical consciousness. In examining the different class interests involved, however – information not readily available in the mainstream press – others argued that an acceptance of the humanitarian rationale showed a complete lack of critical consciousness. This is not the place to rehearse their respective arguments (see Chossudovsky, 1996; Chomsky, 1999): the point is simply that the understanding of what constitutes critical consciousness, a basic concept in popular education, is something which can vary dramatically in accord with more generalised political-ideological beliefs.

Second, while popular education seeks to 'problematise', rather than present solutions, and the methodology is one in which educator-activists encourage discussion and analysis by posing questions rather than giving speeches, it is an illusion to think that questions are inherently more ideologically independent than statements. This was powerfully illustrated for me when, after a state ban on any mention of homosexuality in schools, a gay rights group in the US leafleted pupils to 'ask about lesbians': all day long teachers had to answer the question, 'Please, miss/sir, what's a lesbian?'. As they interact in any group discussion, the questions occurring to educators will depend on how they happen to see the world in the first place. Although these questions should be open-ended, they do have a great deal of power to suggest what people should be thinking *about*. When I attended a popular education workshop in Nicaragua for people who had been traumatised by Hurricane Mitch, the participants took part in a simulation exercise in which different groups held different degrees of power. In the debriefing session, it was clear that different educators instinctively tended to ask different types of questions, some leaning more towards 'structural' political questions, some more towards the 'personal'. In the current Scottish context, working with a group in an area of urban deprivation, one educator might be inclined to ask, 'What can the new Scottish parliament do to bring about change? What can we do to make sure it happens?'; another could ask, 'Do you think the parliament has the power to bring about real change? Should we put any effort into lobbying the parliament, or should we concentrate on other activities?'; yet another might ask, 'Whose interests does/will the parliament seek to defend? How will it behave if big business flexes its muscles?' These are different kinds of questions, each prone to push the discussion in different directions. The three educators could be highly-skilled practitioners with a genuine political commitment to social change: inevitably, however, their different ideological positions inspire a diversity of questions which are likely, in turn, to lead to different educational experiences for learners.

Third, while dialogue, as opposed to knowledge-transfer, is at the heart of popular education methodology, what any educator-activist actually says in the course of a dialogue must have some influence on its outcome. There will be times when educators are called upon to explain and state clearly what they think of the subject being discussed and while this should not be presented as objective truth, but rather a contribution towards a collective search for understanding, it should affect what people are going to think *about*. In the workshop in Nicaragua, as well as the questions they asked, educators also contributed their own interpretations of what the simulation game represented. The extent to which anyone might agree with the educator's views is one thing, and will depend on a number of factors – the way in which this connects with the learners' experience, the credibility accorded to the educator, the strength of views of the learners themselves, and so on – but it is inescapable that the different ideological orientations among educators are bound to result in different experiences for the learners. It matters, then, what the educator happens to think.

But the dynamics of any dialogue cannot be reduced to a formulaic exchange of views – between educator and learners or among learners themselves – in which dispassionate human beings rationally select the best bits of each argument and weave them into a whole new personal philosophy. Dialogue involves argument, debate and passion in which people are likely to start by defending their current view of the world until they are persuaded to think or feel otherwise. And herein lies the contradictory role of the popular educator. On the one hand, educators aim to encourage independent critical thinking; on the other, in the midst of a collective investigation into the best way to bring about change, they will endeavour, naturally, to recruit people to their own particular point of view. Even though they may be open-minded, if they have strong, well substantiated views, what they might really want, ideally, is that learners become independent critical thinkers and then, of their own volition, arrive at the same conclusions as themselves! This tension – though it can be creative – is particularly evident in organisations with both a campaigning and an educational wing. Recently, for example, Friends of the Earth Scotland (FoES) has been running an exciting popular education programme on the theme of environmental and social justice (see Samson and Scandrett, 1999). What this has shown is that the unpredictability of the educational process can clash with the campaigning imperative to encourage people to take specific forms of action if particular negative developments are to be averted. Sometimes the particular ideological bias or content of the educator's contribution is obvious, either in the educational materials they use or in their own personal or institutional identity (religious activists, feminist popular educators, NGO personnel or party political members, for example); sometimes it will be more subtly embedded in the details of their everyday practice. In either case, learner-centred methodology notwithstanding, Freire is surely right to have claimed that to a greater or lesser degree, all education is directive: in assessing in which particular direction, a consideration of the educator's ideological orientation is of primary importance.

Finally, though popular education respects the value of 'popular' knowledge, only an educational practice rooted in what the Latin Americans (Núñez, 1993: 56) call *basismo* – roughly translated as 'grassrootsism' – would expect popular movements, purely from their own experience, to come up with the best ideas for taking their struggle forward. Popular education has to bring 'popular' and scientific, academic or 'systematised' knowledge into contact – what Ghiso (1993) calls a 'dialogue of knowledges' – to maximise the potential of education's contribution to change. Educators have a key function in determining to which particular 'systematised' knowledge a group will be exposed – through their own views, the educational materials they select or the people and resources they bring into contact with the particular group or organisation. And though in popular education new knowledge should be presented for analysis, discussion and possible rejection – not for uncritical consumption – it matters very much, I believe, what this new knowledge happens to be. Whether it comes wrapped in a technicist, religious, feminist, Marxist, social democrat, nationalist or environmentalist (etc.) ideological package, it will undoubtedly have a variable, though not deterministic, effect on the educational outcomes.

Ideology v methodology: an analytical framework

Putting the educator at the centre of the picture, Diagram 1 illustrates my understanding of how questions of ideology relate to the practice of popular education in Latin America.

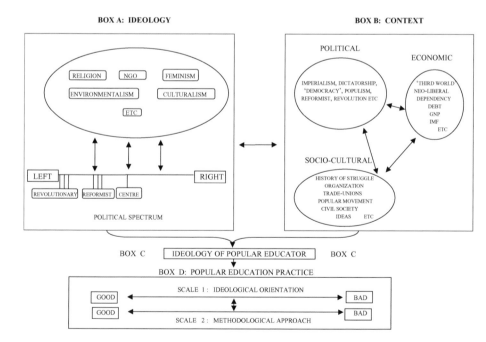

The line at the bottom of *Box A: Ideology* represents the political spectrum, from far right to far left. Anyone to the right of centre is really at odds with the fundamental precepts of popular education. Although they may genuinely feel for those who suffer hardship, whatever their explanation for its existence, it does not include the belief that the system is basically designed to favour those who control it: the notion of a 'right wing popular educator' is a contradiction in terms. The ranks of popular educators are undoubtedly filled by those from the left – although, as we have seen, this too incorporates a wide range of beliefs. The bottom line, however, is that all of them see the system as unjust and poor people as the victims of oppression; the differences lie in the analysis of what needs to be done. But the picture is more complex than finding a position on a standardised line of political affinities. Many other ideologies, from nationalism to the ethos of a particular NGO, can cut across this line, at any point, interacting with more traditional forms of political identification and resulting, at the end of the day, in a myriad of different ideological outlooks.

Box B: Context shows ideological orientation not as an abstract phenomenon but as dialectically linked to a specific social context. This context has political elements (from Pinochet's dictatorship to the Cuban or Nicaraguan revolutions to Scottish devolution), economic elements (such as the degree of crisis or interference by the International Monetary Fund) and socio-cultural elements (like the strength of the popular movement), each having an influence on the other. In revolutionary Nicaragua, for example, the Sandinista government was constrained by outside interference and economic crises; when it lost the elections in 1990, however, the new government of Violeta Chamorra, in turn, was restricted by the continuing strength of revolutionary grassroots organisations. Different ideologies spring from different contexts: the early days of revolution in Nicaragua and Cuba inspired great hope that radical change was possible whereas, currently, the apparent triumph of neoliberalism has led many to abandon radical politics altogether. But ideology also influences, as well as responds to, the social context; indeed, ideas *are part of* the context. The ideologies of the Landless People's Movement in Brazil (Stédile, 1997), the Zapatistas in Mexico (Harvey, 1998), the traditional Church, liberation theology, the media and so on – all make significant but differential impacts on the context, while at the same time having to respond to it.

Box C: Ideology of Popular Educator shows that, having distilled his or her own views from a complex interaction between a multiplicity of ideas and a particular social context, the popular educator duly sets off to work. Whatever form this personal distillation of ideas takes – and it will vary widely from person to person – it will unavoidably influence the individual educator's practice.

Box D: Popular Education Practice shows that in any popular education practice the educator has both an ideological and a methodological contribution to make. In one sense, these contributions are completely unrelated, running in parallel (hence the parallel lines of Scales 1 and 2): regardless of their ideology, educators could be highly or poorly skilled in methodological terms. In another sense, since learners experience this practice in its totality, they are also inter-connected (hence the arrows between the lines). However, in assessing the value of any particular practice of popular education we should distinguish between the educator's ideological orientation and his or her application of methodological procedures. What merits 'good', 'bad' or 'somewhere-in-between' on the ideological Scale 1 depends on who is doing the judging: social democrats would be likely to give Marxists a 'bad' and *vice versa*, though other values – feminist, nationalist, environmentalist, religious etc. – will cloud the issue. In methodological terms (Scale 2), people who try to manipulate or abuse their power or go on ideological rants would be down towards the 'bad' end; those who start from people's specific concerns, promote genuine dialogue, use appropriate and imaginative pedagogical techniques and contribute their knowledge without trying to dominate would be up towards the 'good' end. An outside evaluator could well judge an educator to be 'good' on one scale, and 'bad' on the other.

Conceptually, I believe that this distinction between the ideological and the methodological is extremely important, though mostly absent, in discussions and debates about popular education. First, the two are frequently lumped together. In Latin America, Marxist popular educators have often been accused of being 'over ideological' when, in fact, I suggest, they are no more or less ideological than Christians, social democrats or anyone else: the target of such criticism should be the educators' bad *practice,* if they are being manipulative, not their *ideology* – although there would be some logic to the argument if the (mistaken) interpretation of Marxism is that it is inherently manipulative *per se*. (By contrast, the same accusation is seldom directed towards the many popular educators attached to the radical church or liberation theology who are clearly, but paradoxically, promoting a particular message as well as stimulating critical thinking.) But anyone, of whatever ideological orientation within the limits already defined, could engage in good or bad practice: social democrats, Catholic activists, revolutionary socialists – all have the potential to be exemplary or woeful practitioners of popular education. If the purpose of critique is to point to deficiencies in practice with a view to making improvements, that is all to the good; if it is to discredit a particular ideological viewpoint, then the critique should move to different terrain altogether, to the purely ideological-political, and leave popular education, temporarily, to the side.

Second, if, as I have argued, it does have an effect on the educational process, then ideology must matter. Educators have to take it seriously, constantly re-evaluating their thinking and being conscious of the role ideology plays in their work. This can raise problems. In certain contexts – El Salvador, for example – if there are strong political rivalries, the promotion of explicit, ideological debate could be delicate and run the risk of being counter-productive. Nor would it be appropriate, normally, for educators to declare their beliefs at the start of a project: their motives could be easily misinterpreted. Suitable timing is required. In any general discussion or analysis of popular education, however, at some stage the question of ideology should, if possible, be dealt with openly and honestly so that the educator's position is clear and political-ideological debate can be distinguished from discussions about the quality of educational practice.

Practising what I preach, then, I describe myself as a *socialist* popular educator (see Kane, 2001: 144-9 for a fuller explanation). While others, too, link popular education with socialism (von Kotze and Cooper, 2001; MST Setor de Educacao, 1996), some highlight, instead, descriptors such as *religious* or *spiritual* popular education (García, 1993; McIntosh, 1999), anti-racist or *intercultural* popular education (Subirats, 1993) or *feminist*, even eco-feminist, popular education (Walters and Manicom, 1996; Nicholas, 2001). The use of such qualifiers is rare – and not unproblematic, since they too are labels which are open to (mis)interpretation – but they become necessary if we are to make sense of the multiplicity of practices now identifying themselves, generically, as popular education.

A note on popular education in Scotland

While my argument often focuses on popular education in Latin America, I feel the same points apply to Scotland, and elsewhere, too. I see considerable ideological diversity in the contributions to Crowther et al's (1999) seminal account of popular education in Scotland, for example, or among the views expressed by the members of the Popular Education Forum for Scotland. Popular education with a reformist, revolutionary, religious, nationalist, 'culturalist' or 'economistic' bent – it's all there in Scotland too, though Scandrett (2001) usefully reminds us that ideology can be eclectic. Encouragingly, however, it is an issue we have started to tackle and is now being discussed and debated both through the pages of the journal *Concept* (11: 2 & 3, 2000), and in active Forum events. I am hopeful we can achieve greater conceptual honesty and clarity – without splitting into sects – and recognise diversity where it exists, disagree when necessary and improve our practice in the process. Eventually, I suspect, we will have to address the (potential) relationship between popular education and political parties. The recent growth of the activist-based, as opposed to purely representative, Scottish Socialist Party will surely provoke this – another dimension of popular education crying out for closer examination (but see Damasceno, 1988).

Relevance to the academy

The discussion so far has been generic to autonomous popular education movements, presupposing a climate in which open discussion is possible. Those of us working in universities seem to agree that we too have considerable intellectual freedom, certainly compared to most adult educators working for the state (see Moir, 2001). While it may not be astute to shout our radicalism from the university rooftops – for there is certainly increasing pressure to succumb to narrow, vocational objectives – in my experience the rhetoric of 'academic freedom' still allows us, mostly, to be honest about what we think. In that respect then, with regard to our work as educators, the discussion of popular education and ideology is equally relevant to academics. Our role is to use our relative autonomy to develop critical consciousness amongst our students, both through posing questions – and making explicit their ideological underpinnings – and, more generally, by exposing students to a range of ideas and literature which is often ignored or not seen as relevant to the dominant instrumentalism.

Two further areas of particular relevance should be mentioned: first, though it is almost a shibboleth that popular education deals with both theory and practice simultaneously, there is no doubt that the contribution universities can make to popular education movements leans more towards the theoretical than the practical. To that extent, analysing, clarifying and synthesising the relationship between popular education and different ideologies is a task well suited to university-based popular educators and one which hard-pushed activists will find difficult to pursue.

Second, in our own university teaching, when making our ideology explicit we also have to account for the question of institutional power. Understandably, acquiring good marks/grades is the prime motivation of most students, and research suggests that learning processes are often subverted towards this end (Entwistle et al, 1992). It would be the antithesis of popular education if students felt that regurgitating the views of their teachers was the road to success. Three suggestions for addressing this issue are:

- Make it clear that while you, the teacher, will be open about your views – in order *not* to manipulate students' thinking – this bears no relation to the criteria for marking assignments. Having examined these criteria with students, emphasise that you can award a good grade to something you disagree with, and *vice versa*.
- Openly 'problematise' with students the issue of institutional power, recognising that in their shoes you too might be suspicious of a teacher's ability to be dispassionate when marking assignments.
- As a useful exercise, put students in groups, with a copy of the grading criteria and a selection of past essays to assess. Students award the essays a grade and explain their decisions; you then tell them what grade the essays actually received. This exercise helps make the grading process explicit; if at least one essay contains views with which the teacher obviously disagrees, but in terms of the criteria it receives a good grade, then this can inspire students' confidence in our ability to refrain from prejudice: they can then feel secure about freely pursuing their own line of enquiry.

In conclusion, then, I believe that popular education movements everywhere should consider more explicitly the role of ideology in their work. This is a task in which the engagement of the academy should have something distinctive to offer. But academics also need to do this for themselves: whether writing papers, teaching students or setting up international networks, the more explicitly we can address questions of ideology, the less confusion will surround the multiplicity of practices purporting to be popular education.

References

Castañeda, J.G. (1994), *Utopia Unarmed: The Latin American Left after the Cold War*, New York: Vintage.

Chomsky, N. (1999), *Kosovo Peace Accord*. http://www.zmag.org/chomsky/articles/z9907-peace-accord.html.

Chossudovsky, M. (1996), *Dismantling Former Yugoslavia, Recolonising Bosnia*. http://www.communist-party.ca/english/html/yugo_chossud.html.

Crowther, J., Martin, I. and Shaw, M. (eds) (1999), *Popular Education and Social Movements in Scotland Today*, Leicester: NIACE.

Damasceno, A. (1988), *A Educação como Ato Político Partidário*, São Paulo: Cortez.

Entwistle, N., Thomson, S. and Tait, H. (1992), *Guidelines for Promoting Effective Learning in Higher Education,* Edinburgh: Centre for Research on Learning and Instruction, University of Edinburgh.

Freire, P. (1972), *Pedagogy of the Oppressed*, Harmondsworth: Penguin.

García, P.B. (1993), *Libertação como plano e sonho de Deus e de homens: Uma experiência de educação popular em área rural*, Cadernos De Educacao Popular 21, Petrópolis: Vozes/Nova.

Ghiso, A, (1993), Cuando el saber rompe el silencio . . . Diálogo De Saberes En Los Procesos De Educación Popular, *La Piragua: Revista Latinoamericana de Educación y Política*, 7, pp. 32-6.

Harvey, N. (1998), *The Chiapas Rebellion: The Struggle for Land and Democracy*, Durham & London: Duke University Press.

Hindess, B. (1997), 'Ideology' in Mautner, T. *The Penguin Dictionary of Philosophy,* London: Penguin, p. 266.

Kane, L. (2001), *Popular Education and Social Change in Latin America*, London: Latin American Bureau.

McIntosh, A. (1999), 'Liberation theology in Scottish community empower-ment' in Crowther, J., Martin, I. and Shaw, M. (eds) *Popular Education and Social Movements in Scotland Today*, Leicester: NIACE, pp. 205-15.

Moir, S. (2001), 'I want to be a popular educator but ma boss winna let me!', *Concept,* 11(3), pp. 31-2.

MST Setor de Educacao (1996), *Princípios da Educacao no MST*, Sao Paulo: MST.

Nicholas, V. (2001), 'When the personal become the educational: towards an ecofeminist popular education', *Concept*, 11(3), pp. 29-30.

Núñez, C.H. (1993), Permiso Para Pensar . . . Educación Popular: Propuesta Y Debate, *América Libre,* 2, pp. 46-61, Buenos Aires: Liberarte.

Samson, S. and Scandrett, E. (1999), 'Environmental citizenship and environmental justice: Friends of the Earth Scotland's Catalyst Project', *Concept*, 9(2), pp. 26-7.

Scandrett, E. (2001), 'Popular education and ideology: a response', *Concept*, 11(2), pp. 15-16.

Stédile, J.P. (1997), *A Reforma Agrária E A Luta Do MST*, Petrópolis, Brazil: Vozes.

Storey, J. (ed.) (1998), *Cultural Theory and Popular Culture: A Reader*, London: Prentice Hall.

Subirats, J. (1993), El Enfoque Conceptual y Metodológico de la Educación Popular y Bilingue, *La Piragua: Revista Latinoamericana de Educación y Política*, 6, pp. 66-7.

von Kotze, A. and Cooper, L. (2000), 'Popular Education Network Conference: Engaging the Academy, Edinburgh, June 2000', *Concept*, 11(1), pp. 22-3.

Walters, S. and Manicom, L. (eds) (1996), *Gender in Popular Education: Methods for Empowerment*, London/New Jersey: Zed Books.

Chapter 4

University Faculty and Popular Education in the United States

Ralf St.Clair

The main focus of this chapter is on the role of academics as public intellectuals. Drawing on first-hand experience and the distinctively North American tradition of popular education, as exemplified in the work of Miles Horton and the Highlander Folk School in Tennessee, the author examines the connections and contradictions between popular education and politics in the United States. He argues that public intellectuals have an important contribution to make in terms of sustaining the democratic argument for education for social justice and political change.

This chapter presents a personal perspective on the role university faculty can play in popular education in the United States. On the basis of twelve years' work and study in North American community organisations and universities, I believe faculty have valuable knowledge and experience to contribute to education within, and for, social change. I see academics as having a duty to strive for the position of public intellectuals so that the intellectual capital they have accrued can be made available to the widest possible range of people – particularly those who are marginalised and oppressed by the structures of capitalist society. The privileges of academic life are meaningless if they are not used as a means to stand alongside those who are denied privilege and help to ensure their voices are heard.

Most of this discussion refers to education faculty, particularly in adult education, but many aspects of it also apply to instructors in other disciplines. Over the years, educational connections between universities and social movements have been developed and maintained by faculty from social work, public health and urban planning, among many others. As Apple reminds us, 'all "academics" – be they in physics, nursing, sociology, literature, cultural studies, law, medical school, and the list goes on and on – are first and foremost educators, *teachers*' (Apple, 1993: 13). As educators, academics have a vital role to play in popular education, social movements and the struggle for social justice.

Throughout this discussion I use the example of the best known and longest lived popular education project in the United States – Highlander Folk School in Tennessee. Highlander is an outstanding example of what is possible, and also has a lot to teach us about the issues arising from education for social change. I examine two issues in particular. The first is the relationship between popular education and politics in the United States – in effect, the way popular education is constituted as a contribution to the maintenance of the democratic ideal. The meaning of, and justification for, popular education and social movements in the US is bound up with understandings of what a democratic society should look like and how a democratic people should act. The second is the role academics can play within this tradition, and what they can offer the process of education for social justice. I situate this discussion within Korpi's (1978) notion that social change depends upon marginalised groups developing sufficient organisational capital to justify a claim to power. The potential contribution of faculty arises from their training in the organisation and dissemination of knowledge, a key activity in building and sustaining critical agency among collectives.

This chapter argues that there are real possibilities for the involvement of academics in popular education, and that they have a significant role to play in developing the potential for change. The space to work imaginatively and creatively is there – but we must choose to use it.

Highlander and Myles Horton

In talking of popular education, I follow the definition offered by Hamilton and Cunningham (1989: 443):

> Popular education must establish and specify relationships between knowledge and power. Its goal is to transform social reality into a more democratic state by confronting dominant and dominating institutions through the creation of opposing knowledges – through the celebration of many indigenous cultures and the writing of many histories of and by the people.

Popular education is a process of cultural transformation, of questioning the hegemonic assumptions shaping and constraining our activities within society. It is a means to collect and reinforce the narratives not usually heard, a way to value the diversity of experience and knowledge. More significantly still, popular education makes these resources available as the raw fuel for social change. Both the feminist and civil rights movements began in a process of mutual storytelling, of discovering the common experiences of oppression. As previously invisible experiences are named and noted, the new awareness creates tension and finally action. Popular education creates impetus and energy by making the contradictions of society visible, and by giving people a means to learn from each other and to formulate what has to be done.

Social movements and associated popular education endeavours have had a significant influence on the social fabric of the United States. Among the most successful efforts in recent years have been the women's movement's efforts to get both sexism and gender issues into public discussion, and the Civil Rights movement, centrally concerned with the living conditions of African-Americans. The Gay Rights movement has also made slow but steady progress in the face of staunch opposition from the Christian Right. These movements have brought about major changes in policy and practice, including the introduction of anti-discriminatory legislation in employment, increased minority presence in legislative bodies, and less stereotyped media representation. Popular education has been a significant strategy in the creation of awareness, support, and pressure for change at local and national level.

It may be helpful to consider one example of popular education in some detail, and there is no better candidate than the Highlander Folk School of Tennessee. Highlander is one of the longest lived and most active examples of popular education for social change in the world, and has supported a number of social movements. The school, originally situated in a borrowed house, was established by Myles Horton in 1932. Horton was born in rural Tennessee and grew up with a strong ideal of social justice – and a sense of how far the United States was from that ideal. As a young man, Horton spent a great deal of time in the North, including Union Theological Seminary in Chicago, and also travelled to Denmark to learn about folk high schools. His critical approach to US society appears to have been driven by a background of poverty, involvement with unions and Christian socialism (Horton, 1990).

Over the last seventy years the school has played a critical role in two major social movements, the first of which was the labour movement of the 1930s. The South has never been receptive to organising activity, and Highlander's involvement on the side of labour led to death threats and violence, including one armed stand-off between Horton and three men sent to shoot him. The second movement was even more controversial. Highlander had been involved in literacy education for African-Americans since the mid-1930s, and by the 1960s the school was central to the Civil Rights movement. Participants included Martin Luther King and Rosa Parks, who helped to end legal racial segregation in the South by refusing to move from the 'White Only' section of a public bus in Selma, Alabama. Though the school has played a less high profile role in US affairs since the late 1960s, it remains extremely influential, and several adult education graduate programmes in the United States offer students a chance to travel thousands of miles to visit Highlander.

One of the most striking aspects of Highlander is the similarity between the methods advocated by Horton and the pedagogy of Paulo Freire (1972). Both emphasise the value of the experiences accumulated by oppressed people, and see reclaiming this experience as a central element of education for social change. Staff at Highlander spend a great deal of time interacting informally with communities, identifying both the critical issues and the local leaders with the potential to address them. An important part of the Highlander philosophy is the belief that educators do not have to know all the answers: 'The best teachers of poor and working people are the people themselves. They are the experts on their own experiences and problems' (Horton, 1990: 152).

One area of divergence between Freire and Horton is in regard to the use of academics. In Freire's approach academic sociologists and political scientists play a crucial role in the creation of knowledge concerning 'generative themes'. Horton is a lot more sceptical about the value of abstract learning, as when he recounts the story of being visited by college students who presented theoretical ways to address pressing issues. He told them: 'I appreciate all your erudition, all your knowledge and contributions, but maybe we'd better let the people who are going to be back home taking care of this problem discuss it, because they're the ones who are going to have to work it out' (Horton, 1990: 186). Highlander remains committed to the most important principle of popular education: the belief that people are capable of understanding, and working to improve, the conditions of their lives. Academic teachers can be inspired by, and supportive of, the work of the school, but are regarded as outsiders if they are not directly involved in the struggles of marginalised groups.

For academics committed to social change, whether located in adult education or elsewhere, Highlander remains a powerful example of what is possible with courage and determined engagement. Highlander also demonstrates the important role education can play in realising the ideal of democracy, functioning both as an arena for discussions about democracy and as a means to model democratic structures capable of generating social change.

Democracy and social change

The first lesson to be taken from Highlander is the importance of the democratic ideal to popular education in the United States. Whereas in European traditions social transformation can be grounded in socialist or communist perspectives, the US remains cautious about such overt collectivism. The response is to articulate the discourse of possibility within a more individualised discourse of democracy.

The notion of democracy has lain at the heart of politics in the United States since the establishment of the nation, though the form of that ideal and the group of people invited to participate in it has changed over time. De Tocqueville's (1956: 55-56) comment, written in the early 1830s, remains pertinent:

> In America, the principle of the sovereignty of the people is not either barren or concealed, as it is with some other nations; it is recognized by the customs and proclaimed by the laws; it spreads freely, and arrives without impediment at its most remote consequences.

Dewey, by far the most influential educational philosopher in the history of the US, was interested in the relationship between education, democracy and society. He saw democracy as significant on many levels beyond the political:

> A democracy is more than a form of government; it is primarily a mode of associated living, of conjoint communicated experience. The extension in space of the number of individuals who participate in an interest

so that each has to refer his own action to that of others, and to consider the action of others to give point and direction to his own, is equivalent to the breaking down of those barriers of class, race, and national territory which kept men from perceiving the full import of their activity. (Dewey, 1916: 87)

Dewey consistently emphasised the essential links between the form of society and that of education. His vision of a 'learning society' included 'decentralisation of authority, democratisation of the workplace, redistribution of wealth, strengthening of civil liberties, and the representative organisations essential to dissent and the distribution of power' as necessary elements (Mezirow, 1995: 64). Dewey also argued that 'the concept of education as a social process and function has no definite meaning until we define the type of society we have in mind' (1916: 97). With a strong democratic ideal in the United States, it makes sense that the social concerns of democracy are often represented within the educational process. Many of the most significant school reforms of the twentieth century – progressivism, free schools, multiculturalism – were centrally concerned with educational equity as a prerequisite to participation in the democratic political process. Similar arguments have been used to rationalise policy and funding commitments to adult education, whether at the level of literacy, English as a Second Language or adult entry to post-secondary institutions. Connections between social and educational forms are widely acknowledged, and the idea that education has a central contribution to make to the political and moral future is common.

Yet it would be a mistake to assume that the centrality of the democratic ideal leads inevitably to an informed and involved populace. Democracy can all too easily collapse into individualism by obscuring the structural aspects of society. In fact, De Tocqueville worries about the possibility that democracy might lead to individualism by throwing each person 'back forever upon himself alone, and threatens in the end to confine him entirely within the solitude of his own heart' (1956: 184). When commonality breaks down, the barriers Dewey talked of – race, class and territory – reassert themselves. Meaningful democracy requires constant assertion against the effects of global corporations, deep-seated ethnic differences, economic and cultural imperialism, and many other threats. In modern societies democracy is always an imperfect, partial and unfinished form of social organisation, a process rather than an end, needing to be reinvented and renewed continuously (Resnick, 1997).

The idea of democracy remains powerful within educational theory in the United States. Giroux (1992) uses the idea of radical democracy – derived from the work of Chantal Mouffe – to represent a social form that recognises the interests of many different groups and their attempts to create a more inclusive society. Fraser talks of the possibility of a 'transformed, democratic-socialist-feminist, participatory citizenship' (1989: 137). Apple (1993) has written extensively on the need to develop and maintain democratic education in an increasingly conservative era. The conversation about the role of education in democracy continues with a great deal of energy and interest, and a meaningful form of democracy is understood as far more complex and hard to attain than previously believed. In addition, recognition of issues of cultural reproduction and social hegemony in education has also opened common ground between critical curriculum theorists and popular educators (Hamilton and Cunningham, 1989), leading to a more nuanced understanding of the part education can play in the creation of a democratic society truly rooted in social justice. Education for democracy has evolved into a radical and powerful idea requiring the informed and critical participation of citizens.

While Myles Horton can be placed alongside those calling for a more radical approach to democracy, he was also aware of the limits of the argument. Ultimately, he saw world revolution as a necessary step towards substantial democracy:

> What I understand now is that you can have democracy in voting, democracy in the workplace, and a democratically chosen union, but unless you deal with world capitalism – transnationalism – the decisions you make are going to be very limited . . . you aren't allowed to make decisions concerning what is most important. (Horton, 1990: 171)

In many ways, the state of democracy in the US reflects Horton's comments, with the reality of its actual political form having been consistently disappointing. The current Bush administration, for example, is one of the least responsive to popular will in the history of the country. Nonetheless, the ideas of democracy and of citizen participation in the institutions governing everyday life still carry a great deal of weight in political and popular discourse. The Bush administration has framed even its more extreme legislative and imperial endeavours within democratic rhetoric. This does not speak to the emptiness of the democratic ideal, but rather to the importance of that ideal to the people and the governance of the US. There is a huge gap between the ideal and the reality of the democratic political process, and that gap provides an arena for popular education. The vitality of the democratic ideal at the heart of society depends upon the continual education and involvement of individuals and groups currently excluded from the exercise of power. It is here that we find both the justification for popular education and social movements in the US, and the outline of a role for academics.

A role in popular education

The second lesson from Highlander is about the role educators can play within social movements. The fundamental principle of popular education – the value of local knowledge and problem solving – suggests there is little room for outside experts. Academics, as educators, do have a responsibility to be involved in the efforts of excluded groups to gain representation, but not as respected sources of specialised knowledge. I see the contribution of educators as facilitators of an educational process led by, and responsive to, the interests of social groups engaged in the struggle for justice. Rather than experts, academics become co-creators of fora for marginalised groups to exercise their right to participate and to prepare for effective involvement in social affairs.

In contemplating a role for academics it is critical to realise that education on its own does not create social change, but responds to the degree and type of movement in society as a whole. As Heaney (1992: 6) points out:

> Foremost among the lessons of Highlander is that adult education is critical, but never the decisive factor in achieving social and political goals. Essential to successful action is the presence of a dynamic political apparatus – a collective, a union, a people's organisation through which collective energy can be collected and focused.

In essence, education follows organisation. We can understand more about the interaction of these two elements by considering the way change occurs in an advanced capitalist economy such as the US. Power, for the purposes of this discussion, will be considered as the ability to bring about change – or resist it. The dominant interests in capitalist society have a great deal of power due to their control of economic and cultural resources, but their power is not unassailable. Other groups can gain power and use it to change the structures of society, as the Civil Rights movement showed. Yet this was not accomplished by seizing control of economic and cultural resources, but through the creation of what, following Korpi (1978), I call 'organisational capital'.

Korpi's interest lies in the achievements of working-class people and movements in Sweden throughout the twentieth century. He considers various forms of capital as resources for the exercise of power in a market economy, including organisational capital arising from collective action. He points out that such power resources are far harder to mobilise than those based on economic capital or control of the means of production, and are generally limited to defensive moves or attempts to limit the incursions of economic capital. Economic capital remains privileged, but certain social conditions enhance the value of organisational capital. In the case of organised labour in Sweden, high employment, social security systems designed to increase the mobility of workers, and publicly controlled pension funds have all helped to increase the power resources of the workers. His analysis further suggests that organisational capital can arise from inclusive action, where sheer weight of numbers provides political power, or from exclusive action, where specialists can influence policy by threatening to withdraw their particular forms of expertise from the processes of production. I believe this approach to social change can contribute to understanding the role of academics in popular education.

Organisation occurs when groups of people become aware of the oppressive nature of the circumstances they share and are prepared to act in order to change them. The first stage in raising awareness depends on the development of forms of knowledge that recognise and value the experiences of the oppressed. The second is a cultural context supporting the possibility of change. Viewing culture as a selection of strategies available for application in any particular situation, the key consideration is that there are viable actions open to members of the oppressed group when they become aware of their oppression. If there is no answer to the question 'What can we do about it?' oppressive circumstances will perpetuate themselves through the justified apathy and acceptance of the oppressed. Only where there are options to be exercised and strategies to be taken up, can resistance, and eventually social change, occur. Understanding and action are co-implicated in the formation of social movements.

The contribution of popular education is to bring together knowledge of the present circumstances and the possibility of change. As educators, academics have skills and experience to contribute to this process. Research and teaching are centrally concerned with organising knowledge and placing it within a cultural context which gives it meaning, and academics have usually received many years of training in the creation of ways of looking at the world. Education is a cultural act (Giroux, 1992), reflecting and reforming the values and possibilities open to those participating. Where involvement in popular education differs from the more traditional work of academics is in the derivation and ownership of the knowledge to be transformed. The knowledge base within popular education does not come from studying the work of other academics but from the experience of the people involved, making it essential for academics to work with, and on behalf of, oppressed social groups. The cultural capital of the academy, with all the credibility and status this implies, must be put at the disposal of the people who, as Horton put it, 'are going to have to work it out'.

On this basis I remain uncomfortable with academic involvement in popular education when viewed primarily as an arena for research, even though the increasing credibility of participatory methods appears to offer a way to strengthen organisational capital and conduct systematic inquiry into how it is generated. The difficulty lies in finding a way to engage in research with marginalised groups without, on some level, reifying the notion of the academic as a disinterested and all knowing outsider. The essential paradox is that of the participant-observer, where to perform well in one role involves abdicating the other to a greater or lesser degree. For whom is the researcher speaking in conducting the analysis, and how can the benefits of research possibly be balanced between a well paid, high status professional and a group, for example, of immigrant manual labourers (Alcoff, 1991)? To contribute meaningfully to popular education, academics have to step away from the outside researcher role, putting their skills and resources on the table along with everybody else. This can often be difficult, but it is essential if we are to follow Horton and work alongside those who want to create a better world.

In practical terms, some of the aspects of building organisational capital to which academics can contribute are grant finding and application writing, publicity, recruitment and history building. The last aspect is one of the most interesting, as historical and cultural awareness are among the most important elements in allowing any movement to sustain and renew itself, contributing to the feeling of mission and possibility. Social movements often have a high turnover of activists and volunteers, but involved academics, who have a strong commitment to social action, are in a good position to record the story of the organisation. An excellent example is Tom Heaney's (1992) involvement in *Universidad Popular* (UP) over the last thirty years. UP has helped to strengthen the Hispanic community in Chicago's Humboldt Park district through education ranging from English as a Second Language to youth groups. Heaney's role has been as a founding figure, historian, grant writer, board member and face-to-face activist. As an academic and a popular educator, he has striven to make the financial and cultural resources of the university available to those traditionally excluded from it, demonstrating very clearly the part I have suggested academics can, and must, play in the continuation of popular struggle.

One challenge to the involvement of academics in popular education is that we are in a period when social movements appear to be less effective than at other times, and it is easy to argue that progress has stopped. Ten years ago, for example, many universities had affirmative action policies designed to ensure that where two candidates for employment had equal qualifications the benefit was given to the member of a minority group. Similarly, there were systems in place to recruit minority students aggressively. Due to a series of lawsuits, these policies have now been rescinded, leaving universities unable to address minority issues explicitly in hiring and recruitment – often presenting a significant barrier to innovative work. In Texas, for example, there is a huge Hispanic population widely recognised as experiencing discrimination in education, but the state universities cannot mount a comprehensive campaign to recruit Hispanic students and support them through higher education.

However, progressive change continues to accrue, and new social movements are springing up constantly. Recent protests at World Trade Organisation meetings have brought together huge numbers of different people around issues ranging from genetically modified organisms to working conditions. Concerns are expressed about issues ranging from child or sweatshop labour to the exploitation of women in the sex trade. The large and powerful social movements of the late twentieth century seem to have opened the door for others to follow. Even in a period with relatively slow movement towards social justice the rumblings of revolution persist. Academics have a responsibility to help those rumblings rise to a clamour.

Closing thoughts

My argument has been that academics have a vital role to play in popular education – not as experts or teachers, but as collaborators in the fight for change. Using the example of Highlander, I have shown how popular education can be located within the attempt to create meaningful democracy in the United States, and have outlined the kind of contribution academics can bring to what is, in the end, a very practical form of education. The key point is to realise the amount of privilege accruing to academics, and work out how to use this in the service of those without privilege. A discourse of possibility can be created by university faculty prepared to get off campus and out among the people who can then use the kind of resources academics have to offer as a means to bring about change. As academics, we have a great deal to give – and even more to learn – as we work towards the activist academy.

References

Alcoff, L. (1991), 'The problem of speaking for others', *Cultural Critique*, Winter, pp. 5-32.

Apple, M. (1993), *Official Knowledge: Democratic Education in a Conservative Age*, New York: Routledge.

De Tocqueville, A. (1956), *Democracy in America*, New York: Penguin.

Dewey, J. (1916), *Democracy and Education*, Toronto: Free Press.

Fraser, N. (1989), *Unruly Practices: Power, Discourse and Gender in Contemporary Social Theory*, Minneapolis: University of Minnesota.

Freire, P. (1972), *Pedagogy of the Oppressed*, Harmondsworth: Penguin.

Giroux, H. (1992), *Border Crossings: Cultural Workers and the Politics of Education*, London: Routledge.

Hamilton, E. and Cunningham, P.M. (1989), 'Community-based adult education' in Merriam, S.B. and Cunningham, P.M. (eds) *Handbook of Adult and Continuing Education*, San Francisco: Jossey-Bass.

Heaney, T. (1992), 'When adult education stood for democracy', *Adult Education Quarterly*, 43(1).

Horton, M. with Kohl, J. and Kohl, H. (1990), *The Long Haul: An Autobiography*, New York: Doubleday.

Korpi, W. (1978), *The Working Class in Welfare Capitalism: Work, Unions and Politics in Sweden*, London: Routledge and Kegan Paul.

Mezirow, J. (1995), 'Transformation theory of adult learning' in Welton M.R. (ed.) *In Defense of the Lifeworld*, Albany: State University of New York, pp. 39-70.

Resnick, P. (1997), *Twenty-first Century Democracy*, Kingston: McGill-Queen's University Press.

Chapter 5

Popular Organisations and Popular Education in Portugal

Paula Guimarães and Amélia Vitória Sancho

Portugal, for historical and political reasons, suffers from relatively low levels both of participation in adult education and of formal educational achievement. European Union funding has been used to address this problem, mainly through programmes of functional literacy and work-based learning/training. Little attention has been paid, however, to political literacy and the process of learning for and from social action. This trend and the impact of state-funded activity have eroded the role of popular associations in providing people with educational experiences of democratic life. Drawing on local research, the authors argue for an alternative form of popular education grounded in people's lived experience.

Introduction

For the last twenty-five years Portugal has been facing important changes in its educational, social, political and economic sectors. In the adult education field, and especially in popular education, this period has been marked by several steps forward which have then been reversed. In spite of some progress achieved, the situation concerning adult popular education is far from satisfactory. According to Lima (2001: 4), 'areas of big need still remain, and for historical and political reasons, Portugal suffers from low educational and qualification levels compared with other European countries.' One can certainly find educational activities for adults, most of them as a result of European Union (EU) programmes. However, very few of these activities are 'popular' in the sense of the promotion of radical forms of education towards empowering citizens and involving a pedagogy of conscientization, learning and social action. This is the conclusion we must draw from the research we have conducted at the University of Minho which informs this account.

In historical terms, this imbalance between popular education and other forms of adult learning and training is related to the efforts implemented by the state to promote the latter. For instance, the period from 1974 to 1976 was especially interesting in terms of popular education, and important steps were taken to fight high illiteracy rates and low levels of cultural, social and political participation within Portuguese civil society. This phase included political backing for several initiatives which sought to combine literacy programmes and other formal activities with non-formal actions of social and cultural intervention and community education (Melo and Benavente, 1978). There was also a strong desire to link schools to challenging unequal social structures by the development of educational processes based on the resolution of local problems and dialogue among educators and learners. In addition, there was the intention of developing the educational dimension of social practices, relating education and the acquisition of knowledge and 'know-how' to informal learning based on democratic practices. These times were especially meaningful even though they were characterised by paradoxes. As Silva (1990) noted, there were contradictory elements underpinning the relationship between the state and social initiatives.

The importance of popular education in this early phase was clear at both local and regional levels. There was a great deal of public support for organisations of the people such as workers' commissions, trade unions and popular associations – the latter being non-governmental organisations that provide several kinds of social, cultural, recreational and sports activities, among other things, for people of all ages and are able to make contracts, protocols and agreements with the state. In 1979 a national plan for adult and popular education, *Plano Nacional de Alfabetização e Educação de Base dos Adultos* (PNAEBA) (Ministério da Educação, 1979), aimed to reduce illiteracy rates that were high when compared to other European countries (around 30 per cent in 1979) and to promote popular education. These objectives were to be implemented by formal educational activities and to be articulated with other public resources and instruments to support social initiatives. With the PNAEBA, there was a clear intention of integrating formal and popular education since it was considered that schools alone could not solve adults' everyday life problems.

The PNAEBA did not get sufficient political support to be fully developed. The first phase was timidly implemented after 1980 and then it was abandoned in 1985, owing to administrative and political resistance. The existence of a centralised and interventionist state led to a decrease in adult education activities through a lack of funding and qualified human resources as well as the absence of a national institute for adult education that could promote and coordinate activities (Lima et al, 1988). In this sense, the 1980s were characterised by the withdrawal of support, both political and financial, for popular education (Silva, 1990).

After 1986, when Portugal became a member of the EU, adult education faced major changes that re-emphasised the move away from popular education, although some official documents were produced referring to the need to develop this field (Lima et al, 1988). There was a clear intention of articulating basic education activities with labour and local cultural patterns, by the combination of training based on professional and technical content and traditional teaching subjects, in courses for personal and social develop-ment relevant to labour dynamics and economic activities (Silva and Rothes, 1998).

From 1986 to 1996 no major steps were taken to support adult and popular education. Instead, the pattern became clear with the reinforcement of second chance education and training for the labour market. Popular associations and adult education lost out in favour of schools. As civil society in Portugal had had a difficult emergence, there were no strong social movements that could persuade public authorities to promote adult education and democratic practices. Social and educational interventions did not have priority in national policies, and there were no programmes or systems of public support for initiatives implemented outside schools.

Throughout the 1990s the situation did not reveal any important changes, except for the decreasing importance of adult education, although some efforts were made at a political level to develop a national agency for adult education. This eventually occurred in September 1999 with the establishment of a national agency for adult education and training, *Agência Nacional de Educação e Formação de Adultos*. However, this agency was closed down in 2002 and the responsibility for its work was transferred to the General Directorate of Vocational Training. So far several actions have been promoted, mainly initiatives that are providing formal certification for adults such as the validation and certification of prior learning and education and vocational training courses. In spite of these efforts, a policy is urgently needed to re-invent adult and popular education.

This short history of adult and popular education in Portugal helps to frame the difficult relationship these fields have had with the state. Its low level of involvement has meant that civil society has to carry the burden of providing other forms of welfare, especially education, implementing initiatives with very little resources or support from the state. Even if we cannot find many studies related to initiatives promoted by non-governmental organisations (for an exception, see Lima and Erasmie, 1982; Lima, 1984), the recent establishment of an impressive number of these institutions suggests the retrenchment of public educational and social provision (Guimarães, Silva and Sancho, 1998).

One has to bear in mind that Portugal is characterised by a strong state, a weak market and a civil society that is simultaneously weak and strong – weak because it is atomised and fragmented in its organisation and influence compared with other EU countries and strong in terms of domestic spheres (family structures, networks of solidarity and neighbourliness) that can compensate for gaps in a welfare state that never really existed (Santos, 1994). In this context, the state has an important role in the development of popular education due to the fact that the popular associations seem to be developing adult education actions in which participation lacks political engagement.

However, we can still find some initiatives that stress the possibility of exploring activities rooted in the lived experience of people that are concerned to promote democracy through popular participation. We consider that there is an important potential in these forms of education promoted by popular associations. Even if some activities clearly favour a vocational approach, others also focus on the everyday life of people in communities and could be considered elements in the 'democratisation of democracy' (Lima, 1996) as we discuss below.

The research project

The University of Minho's Unit for Adult Education has an unusually long and rich experience in the study of adult and popular education in Portugal, especially in the northern region. Bearing the above problems in mind, a research project was undertaken which aimed to identify and to analyse educational processes initiated by adults in different social and cultural areas. To achieve these goals, the Popularly Initiated Adult Education Project 1997 – 2002 (PIAE) was established with the support of two other higher education institutions, the University of Linköping in Sweden and the University of Cork in Ireland, funded by the Socrates Programme of the European Union. The main objectives of the research were the identification and analysis of non-formal education as well as innovative ways of devising, initiating and carrying out training in which participants do the organising themselves or, at least, play an active role in various ways such as selecting goals and contents, creating or adapting learning methods and strategies, producing their own materials and establishing working and assessment rules (Guimarães, Silva and Sancho, 1998).

This research led to a national inquiry into popular associations; a *forum* in which 48 institutions presented innovative adult education activities; and the development of several case studies (Rocha, 2000; Silva, 2000; Sancho, 2000; Rothes, 2000).

Data gathered showed that associations were in many cases the result of local group practices consisting of people with political, social, cultural or educational roles at a local level that wanted to face new educational and social challenges made up these groups. Popular associations were mostly non-profit making associations and private charitable institutions, founded after 1986 and structured by a board of directors, a fiscal department and a general assembly. Due to their nature and structure, these organisations were in many cases spaces of socialisation and active participation for their most motivated members. For instance, organisational problems, needs and decisions were discussed and the implementation of solutions was the result of discussion and debate revealing the importance of a democratic hidden curriculum in informal learning processes (Afonso, 1989).

These institutions organised different kinds of adult education activities like training, teaching and community development as well as leisure initiatives. Local authorities, mostly town halls, and especially the EU programmes and the Portuguese Employment and Vocational Training Institute, supported the development of these activities. It is possible to identify the importance these institutions now give to community development programmes which are pragmatically conceived and less politically understood because funding is regulated by the EU or the state. This diversity of sources showed a disorganised form of welfare provision owing to a lack of an integrated adult education policy, and therefore emphasised the EU policies centred on the development of individual learning and skills.

Due to the importance of the EU today, most non-governmental organisations created after 1986, and even those that existed prior to this period, revealed a managerialistic tendency. The majority of associations had volunteer board members and paid animators and technical advisors as well as in-house training staff. In some situations paid external training staff joined activities as voluntary participants. In fact, one could notice an emergent tendency to have quite complex popular associations in terms of social and formal structure, especially in the larger organisations. In some cases, their members saw these organisations as enterprises providing social services for clients and were even eager to initiate processes associated with modern managerial practices such as the commodification of welfare provision (Lima, 1996).

The majority of associations had educational programmes reflecting the particular aspects of social or cultural change they wanted to promote. Courses, projects, competitions, theatre, music and, in particular, vocational training were achieved with the purpose of raising awareness and developing specific skills. Emphasis was put on combining theory and practice. The aims were the development of skills and attitudes for the workplace. These institutions were responsible for the definition of goals and contents, together with other institutions or with learners. Most of their objectives were defined pragmatically in relation to a perceived need rather than related to a politically motivated aspiration (Guimarães, Silva and Sancho, 1998).

As a result, the expected outcomes of the initiatives were modest in terms of popular education. The decision-making process was centralised in institutions themselves, most of them in their boards of directors. Neither learners nor educators were very active in the management of popular associations and these institutions seemed much more oriented towards empowering vocational training consumers rather than empowering citizens (Lima, 1996). In this sense, a radical transformation of social reality was not aimed for and popular education did not seem to be a clear or explicit goal in activities promoted by most of the associations we studied.

As we have already mentioned, this research showed two relevant trends in non-governmental organisations' activities in terms of the development of popular education: first, the decreasing impact of this field; second, an emphasis on a vocational curriculum in adult education initiatives. In addition to the inquiry we undertook, case studies were developed in order to analyse the pedagogical disposition and the participation of learners in the definition, management and evaluation of initiatives. From these case studies, we briefly discuss three examples which are of potentially wider interest due to innovations in pedagogical terms or in their conception and promotion of popular participation in the everyday life of people in communities, although they cannot be defined in terms of radical social action.

The first case study is the Cloth, Ceramics, Wood and Glass Decoration and Painting Course. This training programme was the result of cooperation between a popular association located in Esposende, in the north of Portugal, and the local committee for adult education. It was meant to teach people to paint and to decorate materials like cloth, ceramics, wood and glass but also to train them in basic art competencies. The forms of pedagogical work included demonstration, experimentation and individual work. Practice was promoted; educators and institution's representatives were mentors.

Innovative features of training were based on the heterogeneous nature of the participants, the importance given to their active participation and the non-formal structure of the course. The learners were all women, aged from 16 to 65, with different backgrounds – teachers, factory workers, housewives and farmers. Some were related to each other. They participated actively in practical areas of training and in subjects related to culture and life in society.

Whilst the training did not include a critical or reflexive component, it was not intended to introduce social changes and did not have explicitly educational goals other than training. It was, however, conceived and implemented specifically by and for adults. Although pragmatically conceived and developed, this initiative represents one of the most common activities for adults since the end of the 1970s. Even if it is not the best example of popular education, it is considered a good start to motivate people for further actions in the future (Sancho, 2000).

The second case study is the Child and Youth Animator's Training Project. This was a course organised as part of the Popular University Project of a popular association located in the town of Viana do Castelo, also in the north of Portugal, to respond to needs identified in earlier action-research projects. The main aims were to promote the creation of educational spaces, to learn how to develop educational and leisure activities for (and with) children, youngsters and adults, and to learn how to participate in social and cultural terms.

Active pedagogical methods were used in order to promote participation and socialisation among learners and educators. Flexibility of space and time was a relevant dimension as well as curriculum – especially the possibility of adjusting content to learners' needs. As in the previous case, this course reflected a different understanding of local problems and an innovative solution based on local community resources (Rocha, 2000).

However, the importance of these non-formal aspects was less expansive due to constraints imposed by the EU programme that funded the initiative. This funding, based on a lifelong learning policy that stresses personal choice, individual responsibility, the open market and, in the words of Boshier (1998), the establishment of an 'ideology of vocationalism', led to the decline of popular education, which previously had been one of the most relevant fields of action of this popular association.

The third case study, the Black Sheep Course, was established in 1991 by a popular association located in Oporto as a history of free thought course. Sessions were about people who expressed their differences from mainstream culture and values and were opposed to tyranny and dogmatism – 'black sheep'. It ran in thematic cycles drawn from Portuguese cultural life and the work of persecuted people like Virgínia Castro Almeida, Francisco de Assis and Teixeira de Pascoaes. But other themes were also covered. Besides training sessions, learners, most of them retired women or long-term unemployed people, were involved in organising exhibitions and animation activities such as festivals and other public events.

The main aims were the establishment of a 'free school', where people could choose subjects they wanted to study and communicate their learning experiences to others. To promote these goals, educators were encouraged to foster relationships between young and old participants in order to avoid forms of social exclusion based on age. The methodological approach was innovative. To begin with, the training provided was very formal but, as it developed, it became less so and included several kinds of active and experiential pedagogical activities in addition to didactic instruction. The overall approach taken was based on reflection, experimentation and innovation. The pedagogical methods developed promoted learners' participation, teamwork and socialisation. It was a strategy denoting flexibility, since the curriculum was supposed to be adapted to the learners' needs (Rothes, 2000). However, in spite of these non-formal aspects and the lack of financial constraints, it cannot be said that this initiative was aimed to promote social and cultural transformation.

As already mentioned, our enquiry led us to conclude that nowadays more than ever popular associations are developing important forms of welfare provision which the state does not offer, many of them funded by EU programmes. Our case studies showed that the kind of adult education activities developed were pragmatically conceived, a fact that is clear in initiatives supported by both the EU and the Portuguese state (and reinforced by their funding rules) and were not systematically grounded in adults' social and political needs and interests. In addition to the constraints on resources, recent governments in Portugal seem to be pursuing a conservative modernisation of adult and popular education. As a consequence, the democratisation of the state and the empowerment of civil society in terms of the practice of democratic citizenship and the active involvement of social movements are the object of multiple contradictions. Much of this activity does not promote political engagement at all (Lima, 1996: 42). Accordingly, we would argue that there is an urgent need to stimulate more innovative and radical forms of adult and popular education which can foster democratic practices in these non-governmental organisations.

Concluding remarks

In the thirty years since the end of dictatorship it has often been said that popular associations are fundamental to the promotion of democracy and active citizenship in Portugal. Indeed, Afonso (1989) defined them as 'democratic associations for development'. These organisations have strong traditions in popular education and have been considered unique spaces for the promotion of civic participation as a process of socialisation towards democracy (Lima, 1996). However, during the relatively short period of democracy in Portugal they themselves have changed in significant ways. The original establishment of these institutions was mostly the result of popular initiatives, and they were therefore seen to be strong instruments in the promotion of democracy (Norbeck, 1984). In these 'late modern' times, however, they are facing new challenges. Apart from the historical lack of funding and technical resources, one of the main problems faced relates to promoting the democratic participation of people in local communities and ensuring the continuation of their involvement. Reviewing their practices in the light of the changing relationship between the state and civil society, Lima argues that 'most popular associations now appear to be facing a crisis' (2001: 3).

In this context, we can say that popular associations in Portugal today are confronting a difficult period, trying to find different ways of adapting themselves to these new times. The PIAE research project also leads us to reassert the importance of popular education and participation for demo-cratic citizenship. On the other hand, most of the activities identified in our research consisted of various kinds of training and there was clear evidence of a gradual conversion of broadly based education into rather narrow forms of productive activity and the reinforcement of the market (Santos, 1994). Popular associations were developing partnerships, mostly with the Portu-guese state (both central administration departments and town halls) or the EU by applying for financial support from international programmes. Negotiation represented one of the most important tasks in popular associations' activities and, as 'new enterprises', they needed to understand market rules to survive and consequently had to engage 'professionals' instead of enthusiastic volunteers. This process has consolidated the shift away from popular participation in these associations.

The sheer volume of financial resources involved in EU programmes is having a detrimental effect in many respects. As Hake (1999: 58) argues, the European state and its neoliberal policies may result in

> the weakening of the welfare state, the deregulation of markets, a focus upon 'start qualifications' for young adults entering the labour market, shifts towards market principles in the provision of continuing educa-tion and training for adults, together with the emphasis upon responsi-bility for education and training'.

In this context, the Portuguese state is now expecting civil society to fulfil many of the tasks previously understood as functions of the welfare state that it is unwilling or unable to provide. By contrast, and for those who still believe in an engaged popular education as it existed in the early years of democracy in Portugal, recent changes in adult education seem to be highly questionable and problematic. As Lima argues, 'especially in a country consolidating democracy ... everything that does not represent a strong political will towards educating for the democratisation of democracy should simply be considered insufficient' (2001: 17).

References

Afonso, A. (1989), 'A sociologia da educação não-escolar e a formação de animadores/agentes de desenvolvimento local', *Forum*, 6, pp. 73-92.

Boshier, R. (1998), 'Edgar Faure after 25 years: down but not out' in Holford, J., Jarvis, P. and Griffin, C. (eds) *International Perspectives on Lifelong Learning*, London: Kogan Page, pp. 3-20.

Guimarães P., Silva, O. and Sancho, A. (1998), 'Educação/formação de adultos nas associações', *Forum*, 24, pp. 47-110.

Hake, B. (1999), 'Lifelong learning policies in the European Union: developments and issues', *Compare: a Journal of Comparative Education*, 29(1), pp. 53-69.

Lima, L.C. (1984), *Inquérito às Autarquias Locais do Distrito de Braga – Uma Perspectiva Sócio-Educacional*, Braga: Universidade do Minho/Unidade de Educação de Adultos.

Lima, L.C. (1996), 'The democratization of democracy: a south European view on European democracy and citizenship education' in Timmer, J. and Veldhuis, R. (eds) *Political Education: Towards a European Democracy*, Maastricht: Instituut voor Publiek en Politiek/Bundeszentrale für politische Bildung, pp. 38-44.

Lima, L.C. (2001), 'Portugal' in Jarvis, P. (ed.) *Perspectives on Adult Education and Training in Europe*, Leicester: NIACE, pp. 178-89.

Lima, L.C. and Erasmie, T. (1982), *Inquérito às Associações do Distrito de Braga*, Braga: Universidade do Minho/Unidade de Educação de Adultos.

Lima, L.C., Lucas, E., Matos, L., Melo, A. and Mendonça, A. (1988), *Documentos Preparatórios III. Reorganização do Subsistema de Educação de Adultos*, Lisboa: Ministério da Educação/Comissão de Reforma do Sistema Educativo.

Melo, A. and Benavente, A. (1978), *Educação Popular em Portugal (1974-1976)*, Lisboa: Livros Horizonte.

Ministério da Educação (1979), *Plano Nacional de Alfabetização e de Educação de Base dos Adultos*, Lisboa: Secretaria de Estado dos Ensinos Básico e Secundário/Direcção-Geral da Educação Permanente.

Norbeck, J. (1984), *Associações Populares para o Desenvolvimento*, Lisboa: Ministério da Educação/Direcção Geral de Educação de Adultos.

Rocha, M. (2000), *Novos Espaços em Educação Popular. A Formação de Animadores Infanto-Juvenis*, Universidade do Minho/Unidade de Educação de Adultos. Unpublished report.

Rothes, L. (2000), *As Ovelhas Negras. Universidade do Autodidacta e da Terceira Idade*, Universidade do Minho/Unidade de Educação de Adultos. Unpublished report.

Sancho, A. (2000), *Uma Experiência Pedagógica Inovadora em Contexto Associativo: Estudo de um Caso em S.Bartolomeu do Mar*, Universidade do Minho/Unidade de Educação de Adultos. Unpublished report.

Santos, B. (1990), *O Estado e a Sociedade em Portugal (1974-1988)*, Porto: Edições Afrontamento.

Santos, B. (1994), *Pela Mão de Alice: O Social e o Político na Pós-Modernidade*, Porto: Edições Afrontamento.

Silva, O. (2000), *Nas Margens de Dentro: Um Projecto para Desempregados*, Universidade do Minho/Unidade de Educação de Adultos. Unpublished report.

Silva, A. and Rothes, L. (1998), 'Educação de adultos' in Silva, A., Rothes, S., Correia, L., Caramelo, J.A., Vaz, J.C., Costa, H.M. and Praia, J. (eds) *Estudos Temáticos III (A Evolução do Sistema Educativo e o PRODEP)*, Lisboa: Editorial do Ministério da Educação, pp. 17-104.

Chapter 6

Popular Education and the Academy: The Problems of *Praxis*

Rennie Johnston

The central concern of this chapter is the relationship between rhetoric and reality in popular education. Its aim is to examine the connections between learning and action in order to clarify and promote more meaningful and effective praxis in popular education. Drawing on a survey conducted with an international sample of university-based popular educators, the author shows how the aims and claims of popular education are translated into a variety of educational practices in different national and institutional contexts.

This chapter seeks to ground and critically explore the *praxis* of popular educators. It aims to tease out the issues and implications for our *praxis* of the broad understanding endorsed by the contributors to this book that popular education is (see Crowther et al, 1999):

- rooted in the real interests and struggles of ordinary people
- overtly political and critical of the *status quo*
- committed to progressive and political change in the interests of a fairer and more egalitarian society.

This account draws on responses from a small, purposive sample of university-based popular educators from across the world who were asked to identify and reflect on the roles that they play in relation to social movements or community groups. It then links their responses to existing literature on adult and popular education work with social movements with a view to exploring how a 'normative professional' (Kunneman cited in Dekeyser, 2001) can productively and satisfactorily interact with popular movements. It concludes by tentatively identifying some key issues and questions for further investigation and debate as a way of mapping, illuminating and evidencing popular education *praxis*.

Clearing the ground

The discourse of popular education is full of rhetoric. Of course, this is neither unusual nor, necessarily, a bad thing. All movements need to be clear about what they stand for and what they aspire to, as a basis for engaging with and influencing other like-minded people. But rhetoric is inevitably decontextualised and needs to have some real inter-relationship with practical action; otherwise, it is in danger of becoming merely empty rhetoric. A notion of popular education which is committed to progressive and political change needs to be able to demonstrate how this commitment is translated into actual practice and how it impacts on the work of our social movement partners. While, like my fellow contributors to this book, I am committed to the aims and aspirations of popular education and am involved in ongoing debates about the nature and direction of popular education and in attempting to theorise it, I am still sometimes frustrated by my limited ability to translate this into sustained and meaningful practice on the ground.

This raises the whole issue of *praxis* which is a key concept for popular educators. Originally a Greek term meaning informed and reflective action guided by a moral disposition to act truly and justly (Carr and Kemmis, 1986: 33), *praxis* has been adopted and re-worked by, amongst others, Marx, to mean a unity of theory and practice (McLennan, 1976: 92) and Gramsci, as the relationship between human will and economic structure (1986: 403). However, the most famous and meaningful reference for popular educators is Paulo Freire's definition of *praxis*: 'reflection and action upon the world in order to transform it' (1972: 28) which resonates strongly with the statement of popular education's aims quoted at the beginning of this chapter. My concern here is to investigate, clarify and problematise *praxis* in popular education by examining the practice of a small number of university-based academics who are committed to the principles of popular education, and to link this both to their own observations and to a range of existing literature about popular educator engagements with social movements and community groups.

Talking to popular educators: the sample

After a pilot attempt with two friends and colleagues, I wrote to another eleven people I knew who were involved in popular education across the world, sending them a copy of the outline for this chapter (including the particular understanding of it summarised at the beginning of this chapter). I asked each person to:

- identify and briefly describe a popular/social movement or community group which they were working with/had worked with in the last three years
- document and reflect on exactly how they engaged with this group/ movement in the first instance
- document and reflect on exactly what they did in their engagement with the group/movement: what role/s they played, what tasks they undertook, and what learning they promoted/supported
- document and reflect on exactly how they influenced any outcomes for the group/movement
- share/identify any other relevant thoughts, key developments or issues.

The sample reflected my own circle of contacts from a range of different national/cultural contexts and was not meant to be representative of university-based popular educators as a whole. There are obvious dangers in drawing any firm conclusions from such a small selection of respondents. Nevertheless, it may be interesting, illuminating and suggestive to examine their responses to my questions and connect these to wider issues. Of the thirteen people initially contacted, eleven responded positively to my questions. Of these, five were female and six male, six came from across Europe and five from further afield: Australia, South Africa, North America and Latin America. I will now summarise their responses to each question and, where appropriate, comment on them and link them to key issues in the popular education literature.

Types of social movement

In the literature on social movements, broad distinctions are drawn between 'old' and 'new' social movements. Essentially, old social movements (for example, trade unions and churches) are seen to be more rooted in tradition, and more centrally organised with a defined membership and specific aims. In contrast, new social movements (for example, environmental groups, consumer groups, groups coalescing around issues of gender, race, sexuality, disability and age) are seen to be more knowledge-based and issue-orientated, to be acting in the defence of the public realm and people's autonomy as citizens (Jarvis, 1997). It is interesting to note that the types of social movement identified by my respondents can be broken down into six predominantly old and five predominantly new social movements. Old social movements involved a school board in Scotland, a national association of adult education in Ireland, two regionally-based trade unions in North and Latin America, and two national trade union organisations in South Africa and Latin America. New social movements included: a disabled people's movement in Scotland, a group campaigning on homelessness issues in England, an animal rights organisation in Belgium, an older people's organisation in Poland and an ecumenical movement for social justice in Australia involved in environmental action, aboriginal rights and fair trading between nations.

This balance between old and new social movements might reflect historical and temperamental differences – there is a long tradition of old social movement engagement with adult educators in both formal and informal learning situations (see Fieldhouse, 1996; Walters, 1997) while an important part of the *raison d'être* of new social movements is to take responsibility for their own learning activities (Newman, 1995; Jarvis, 1997). It may also point to the fact that, despite a growing contemporary focus on the growth of new social movements (Dekeyser, 2001; Crossley, 2002), old social movements are still very much active, influential and important across the globe.

First engagement

Notwithstanding the small sample, it is still instructive to see how and why the different university-based popular educators became engaged with their identified social movement in the first place. Of the five working with new social movements, four became involved primarily through personal contacts, three through past students and one through her own children. Only one became connected as a direct result of university work. In contrast, of those involved with old social movements, only two did this through predominantly personal contacts, while the other four were either elected, invited or assigned, at least in part, because of their professional role, although in each instance personal reputations and commitment were key factors in the engagement or relationship with the social movement. What is apparent from the responses to my questions is that a vital feature in the work of this group is the importance of their own social capital, personal reputation and networks and 'street credibility' as a basis for meaningful engagement with social movements and community groups outside of the academy.

While it is sometimes difficult to tell whether respondents' engagement with social movements was primarily personal or institutional, it is even more difficult to disentangle who made the first move. Some respondents were clearly approached by social movements, particularly in the case amongst old social movements, others actively sought out social movement partners while in some instances, the main impetus and motivation for first engagement was unclear. Not surprisingly, this mixed picture of initial contact directions is also mirrored in popular education literature. There are instances of educators seeking out social movements, in the way that Foley (1999) in Australia set out to document, analyse and promote the work of such movements, as well as in a more existential way, for example, where radical South African educators have sought to make common cause with key social struggles as 'activists in search of social movements' (Cooper and von Kotze, 2000). In Latin America, with its long tradition of popular education, the relationship can often be more structured, with organisations like the Mexican Institute of Community Development, for instance, organising regular training workshops for activists from a variety of social movements (Kane, 2001: 72-89). There are also examples of social movements specifically seeking out the services of educators – for example, in the way that the Gorgie Dalry Adult Learning Project, Edinburgh looked to engage with academics in analysing and adapting the methods and ideas of Paulo Freire to a specifically Scottish context (Kirkwood and Kirkwood, 1990). Finally, there are examples in the literature of longstanding collaboration between popular educators and social movements which serve to generate a range of joint initiatives on learning and action, as has been developed in the work of the Centre for Research in the Education of Adults (CREA) in Barcelona (Merrill, 2003).

Roles for popular educators

This was the central focus of my enquiry. It was also the most complex in terms of responses. My respondents' main roles were in research, training and strategic or policy development. Of the eleven respondents, seven were involved in research activities, ranging from a relatively informal organisational evaluation to the development of a specific organisational review, more technical/methodological assistance in development programmes, assistance in preparing research bids and active involvement in publications. This does raise the question of exactly what kind of research engagement the popular educator might have with social movements or community groups. The rhetoric of popular education would seem to favour more interventionist, 'hands-on' action-oriented research in its explicit aim to forge a direct connection between education and social action – for example in the work of Cadena (1991) in Latin America, Wildemeersch (1992) in the Netherlands, Newman (1995) in Australia and Martin (1999) in the UK. However, a key contribution from popular educators might also be to embark on a more intensive attempt at documenting popular education practice, where Dekeyser's (2001) more distanced but valuable academic analysis can be usefully complemented by a more 'engaged solidarity', chronicling the processes and struggles of popular education in practice as in the work of Foley (1999), Crowther et al (1999) and Kane (2001). In this way, popular education *praxis* can be better understood, promoted and built upon.

My respondents' research engagement sometimes proved to be problematic – in two instances, their investigative academic research was disregarded, even countermanded, when it came up against entrenched power structures and vested interests, in one case of the local state and in the other of a trade union hierarchy. The problematic nature of this research engagement raises important questions of 'ownership' and accountability. In the past, the research work with community groups of Wildemeersch (1992) in the Netherlands and Zacharakis-Jutz and Flora (1997) in the USA both identified problems in making the research process and outcomes fully democratic. Indeed, Wildemeersch noted the fact that his research with local people, nothwithstanding his emancipatory intent, at times became 'infected' by academic rather than popular considerations, a situation very similar to the experience of one of my respondents.

One way of ensuring democratic ownership of research and a central focus in the rhetoric of popular education is the practice of participatory research. A very useful reference point here is the past work of Budd Hall and the International Participatory Research Network who have identified key questions about developing participatory research *with* social movements: who initiates the research? who defines the problem? who conducts the analysis? who uses the results and, ultimately, who benefits? (IPRN, 1982). However, in this context, it is salutary to note a developing critique amongst some disabled people's organisations that in more recent times participatory research is becoming more professionalised and can easily slip into a more 'liberal' practice of research (Walmsley cited in Martin, 2001) where concerns with process and participation supersede the more 'political' aims of 'emancipatory research'. This critique may reflect our increasingly complex and diverse (discursive) world, appearing, as it does, to be concerned with re-interpretations and assumed differences between the changing discourses of 'participatory' and 'emancipatory' research. However, it still highlights a vital research problem for popular educators: how to derive research from the concrete experience and material interests of people in communities of resistance and struggle, and link this to the political aims of popular educators?

A key factor here is to ensure that the 'voice' of popular movements is accessed, heard and responded to. Popular educators may well recognise at a rhetorical level that:

> ... voices forged in opposition and struggle provide the crucial conditions by which subordinate individuals and groups reclaim their own memories, stories, histories as part of an ongoing attempt to challenge those power structures that attempt to silence them (Aronowitz and Giroux, 1991: 101).

However, based on the evidence of some of my respondents, the research perspectives and interests of some particular movements are at times not quite what popular educators would like or expect. Research as *praxis* clearly entails a negotiation in which different interests have to be reconciled. Evidence from my respondents indicates that their research ambitions and agendas as popular educators do not always coincide with those of social movements. For example, the rhetorical position that popular education is overtly political and critical of the *status quo* can be difficult to square in practice with the 'realities' of research bids to funders where acknowledgement of, and accommodation with, established interests may be seen to be both pragmatic and in the interests of social movements. This is not to say that academics need to sacrifice or compromise their own values but rather that, as part of the research process, they need to move beyond rhetoric and engage in in-depth dialogue with participants about ideology and about means and ends within different contexts of popular education research.

In terms of direct *teaching* input, only four respondents, those from South America, South Africa and Australia, were involved in a formally-recognised training or tutoring role. This is perhaps surprising when we consider the close historical connection of popular education work with the teaching and development of literacy programmes and trade union education. In the specific context of *training*, tensions were apparent in the movements' relationship with the state in the field of employment training. All of the four respondents working with trade unions expressed different degrees of disquiet with their involvement in state-led and funded vocational education programmes which the educators tended to see as essentially reproductive and counter to the historical interests of the trade union and its members. It was interesting here that three of these four respondents specifically identified one of their roles as upholding the historical values and purposes of the trade union and, in the context of national training strategies, trying to hold their trade union colleagues to their traditions of political independence from the state.

This dilemma for educators reflects a central concept in the discourse of popular education, that of 'really useful knowledge' (Johnson, 1988). This implies both a political and democratic approach to knowledge and learning, essentially different from both traditional 'value free' academic knowledge and the more adaptive vocational knowledge which is often part of employment training. This is perhaps another area where the rhetoric of 'really useful knowledge' may need to be examined, developed and contextualised further in relation to the increasingly prevalent and powerful global discourse of human resource development. Clearly, part of this process must involve popular educators in fostering a greater, counter-hegemonic understanding and discussion of political economy (Jackson, 1995; Foley, 1999) as well as developing the whole idea of the active citizen who is both informed and critical (Martin, 2001). Kane's recent work on popular education methodology is instructive:

> The starting point of any educational endeavour should be an attempt to understand the 'social reality', in all its complexity and contradictions, of those (organisations) seeking to bring about change and that a key part of this process is to promote a 'dialogue of knowledges' in which collectively, everyone participates in discussion, analyses problems and considers options for action (Kane, 2001: 17).

In contrast to their surprisingly limited involvement in direct teaching or training, all but one of my respondents identified some kind of *strategic/political input* into the movement/organisation. This input varied from being an active, campaigning member of a social movement in Scotland, to supporting and mentoring key staff in Australia, advising on campaigning tactics in England, curriculum in South Africa, research and publications in Brazil and Belgium, being a spokesperson in Ireland, being a key negotiator between the movement, the city government and the university in Poland. Once again, in several instances this political/strategic role proved to be a difficult and frustrating involvement for some educators, with clear tensions identified between the political/popular education aspirations and directions identified by the educator and the 'real life contexts' and political accommodations sought by the movements. This was demonstrated in the growing unease of a Scottish educator in a situation where traditional academic considerations began to take greater priority over the interests of participants in the development and increasing professionalisation of a research project, which he saw, in many ways, as the antithesis of the values and purposes of popular education. Other examples included an unsuccessful attempt by a North American educator to have a social movement recognise the inherently sexist nature of its organisational culture, and a South African educator's struggle to keep alive the valuing of informal learning in the face of a growing institutionalisation and formalisation of a trade union movement's education programme.

So there may once again be a tension here for popular educators in keeping true to their own political principles, yet also needing to listen to the diversity of voices emerging from social movements and community groups, some of which may not necessarily share the educator's political analysis. This might point to a need for popular educators to think critically about Dekeyser's distinction between social activation and education within social movements, and his contention that educator engagement with social movements is moving from a more formal problem-solving to a more informal problem-posing role (Dekeyser, 2001). In this specific context, it may be necessary to encourage popular educators to try to adopt a more structured approach to their engagement with social movements such as in the practice of 'systematisation' which has been developed in Latin America and which involves a more systematic and reflective engagement with the experience of learners in social movements and a more dialectical understanding of the relationship between theory and practice (see Fischer in this volume; Kane, 2001; Cadena, 1991).

Influencing outcomes

Another key aspect of popular educators' *praxis* is the impact on outcomes for their social movement partners. The evidence from my sample is variable. Relatively traditional education and research outcomes were reported in the broad area of dissemination, with four respondents contributing to formal publications, one developing and editing a movement newsletter and one planning an extensive interchange with corporate leaders on ethical and spiritual issues related to fair trade, responsible trading and environmental care. Further to this, eight out of eleven respondents claimed to have influenced the strategic approach of their partners. This involved in three cases, structured training sessions geared to develop group analysis and reflection, and in other cases more collective involvement as part of the group in policy development and campaigning. While three of these eight were explicit about their involvement having helped to bring a sharper cutting-edge to a movement's action, two further respondents, also involved in an organisational role, were much more sceptical about the impact of their involvement, with one having written an organisational review which was largely ignored and one unsure about the impact of his attempts to keep the voice of social movement participants heard in a multi-agency project. These last two cases highlight again the gap between the aspirations of popular educators and the actual outcomes of their engagement. Indeed, doubts and questions in this area were expressed by five of the sample.

Final reflections

The final reflections of the respondents tended to be brief but were nevertheless significant and illuminative in terms of their views on their own *praxis*. Six of the sample saw their work with social movements as being primarily unpaid or voluntary work with little formal connection with their ascribed role in universities. It may have been that they stressed this as a way of distancing themselves both personally and ideologically from the academy. However, in practice, it was also clear that in each of these cases, their status and experience as an academic contributed both to their attractiveness and usefulness to their partners and to the educational nature of their engagement. This personal/political/institutional tension is something that popular educators need to reflect on and somehow resolve. Further evidence from engaged social movement partners might help in this process.

Another key aspect is the close link with popular educators' ideas of 'self'. Six of the eleven respondents explicitly identified the importance for themselves of their contact with social movements, with two pinpointing positive feed-back loops into their own teaching approach, two showing clear personal pride in the achievements of the groups they were working with and one appreciating the importance of direct personal experience as a social movement member of implicit racism and local state obstructionism and 'spin'. Lastly and significantly, one of the sample specifically stressed her involvement with a young anarchist group as a 'wake-up call', a challenge to our assumptions as educators, demonstrating a 'need to reinvigorate ourselves from time to time and staying in touch with new ideas.' This amounts to persuasive evidence and an active endorsement of Freire's (1972) identification of the roles of teacher/learner and learner/teacher, and is a significant motivating factor for popular educators.

The final question about key issues also allowed respondents an opportunity to reflect more critically and extensively beyond the essentially practice-oriented focus of my questions. A commonly held feeling was the need to move beyond the local in stressing popular education as a global force for social justice and change. However, here an interesting difference of emphasis emerged between European and non-European respondents. The former focused predominantly on local work although linked it to broader considerations. However, all of the non-European respondents, in different ways, used this opportunity to link their own particular responses and contexts much more centrally to wider global issues about the place of popular movements and the role of popular educators in the context of a changing world order. Indeed, a North American respondent went as far as specifically to identify a growing gap between two types of social movements: 'those able to dress as sheep and benefit from government resources' and 'those, standing apart, like globalisation protesters'. Others raised key questions about the relationship of the theoretical to the practical, questioned the (restricted) role of the university in this process, identified the need for popular educators to work with social movements in the 'oppositional spaces that exist' and the importance of facilitating the building of links between different social movements, old and new. It would perhaps be a mistake to make too much of these slight differences of emphasis. However, this may be another good reason for developing further critical and documented explorations of popular education *praxis* in different local/national contexts as a way of fostering greater international understanding and solidarity between popular educators and social movements in the face of the dramatic and differential impact of globalisation on their lives and work.

Re-viewing the responses

So what can be learned from the above responses, granted that they cannot be seen as representative of popular educators across the world? The key themes and issues that appear to emerge most strongly are:

- the balance and tension between these popular educators' personal and institutional links with social movements
- the main educator roles of strategic/policy development, research and teaching *in that order*
- the tensions between some popular educators' aspirations and the 'real-life' interests and processes of some social movements in relation to curricular and policy issues but also, to lesser extent, research
- the significance for the 'self' of popular educators of their engagement with social movements
- the different sorts of links and aspirations made between local and global contexts.

The above findings, tentative and partial as they are, may help to inform, illuminate and problematise the role of academics working with social movements. What they clearly indicate is the diversity of contexts in which popular education is being developed across the world and the range of practices within them. This gives us some insight into popular education *praxis*. While it is still important to identify and maintain some founding principles as outlined at the beginning of this chapter, to avoid these becoming largely rhetorical, there may be a need to have a more extensive mapping and a clearer understanding of different kinds of popular education *praxis* as a first step towards developing it. What this small-scale investigation points to – and this book both illustrates and endorses – is the need to conduct a much more extensive and systematic study of popular education practice as a way both of bridging the gap between rhetoric and reality and of clarifying and promoting its *praxis*.

References

Aronowitz, S. and Giroux, H. (1991), *Postmodern Education*, Minneapolis: University of Minnesota Press.

Cadena, F. (1991), 'Transforming through knowledge: knowledge through transformation', *Convergence,* XXIV(3), pp. 62-70.

Carr, W. and Kemmis, S. (1986), *Becoming Critical: Education, Knowledge and Action Research,* London: Falmer.

Cooper, L. and von Kotze, A. (2000), 'Activists in search of social movements: a critical look at the academy and popular education in South Africa'. Paper presented at International Popular Education Network Conference, Edinburgh, June 2000.

Crossley, N. (2002), *Making Sense of Social Movements,* Buckingham: Open University Press.

Crowther, J., Martin, I. and Shaw, M. (eds.) (1999), *Popular Education and Social Movements in Scotland Today*, Leicester: NIACE.

Dekeyser, L. (2001), 'Citizenship and adult education in social movements' in Bron, M. and Field, J. (eds.) *Adult Education and Democratic Citizenship III*, Wroclaw, Poland: ESREA/Lower Silesian University College of Education, pp. 37-56.

Fieldhouse, R. (1996), *A History of Modern British Adult Education*, Leicester: NIACE.

Foley, G. (1999), *Learning in Social Action*, Leicester: NIACE.

Freire, P. (1972), *Pedagogy of the Oppressed*, Harmondsworth: Penguin.

Gramsci, A. (1986), *Selections from Prison Notebooks*, London: Lawrence & Wishart.

International Participatory Research Network (1982), *An Introduction to Participatory Research*, Toronto: Participatory Research Group.

Jackson, K. (1995), 'Popular education and the state: a new look at the community debate' in Mayo, M. and Thompson, J. (eds.), *Adult Learning, Critical Intelligence and Social Change*, Leicester: NIACE, pp. 182-203.

Jarvis, P. (1997), *Ethics and Education for Adults*, Leicester: NIACE.

Johnson, R. (1988), ' "Really Useful Knowledge" 1790-1850: memories for education in the 1980s' in Lovett, T. (ed.), *Radical Approaches to Adult Education*, London: Routledge, pp. 3-34.

Kane, L. (2001), *Popular Education and Social Change in Latin America*, London: Latin America Bureau.

Kirkwood, G. and Kirkwood, C. (1990), *Living Adult Education*, Buckingham: Open University Press.

Martin, I. (1999), 'Introductory essay: popular education and social movements in Scotland today' in Crowther, J., Martin, I. and Shaw, M. (eds), *Popular Education and Social Movements in Scotland Today*, Leicester: NIACE, pp: 1-28.

Martin, I. (2001), 'Adult education, disability and citizenship: experiencing "inclusive education" – some first impressions . . . and some second thoughts' in Schemmann, M. and Bron, M. (eds.), *Adult Education and Democratic Citizenship IV*, Krakow: ESREA/Impuls, pp. 28-46.

McLennan, D. (1976), *Karl Marx: His Life and Thought*, Frogmore: Paladin.

Merrill, B. (2003), 'Adult education and citizenship: a European perspective' in Coare, P. and Johnston, R. (eds.), *Adult Learning, Citizenship and Community Voices*, Leicester: NIACE, pp. 41-52.

Newman, M. (1995), 'Locating learning in social action' in *Social Action and Emancipatory Learning*, Seminar Papers, School of Adult Education, UTS, Sydney.

Walters, S. (ed.) (1997), *Globalisation, Adult Education and Training: Impacts and Issues*, Leicester: NIACE.

Wildemeersch, D. (1992), 'Transcending the limits of traditional research: Towards an interpretative approach to development communication and education', *Studies in Continuing Education* 14(1), pp. 42-55.

Zacharakis-Jutz, J. and Flora, J. (1997), 'Issues and experiences using participatory research to strengthen social capital in community development' in Armstrong, P., Miller, N. and Zukas, M. (eds.), *Crossing Borders, Breaking Boundaries*, London: SCUTREA/Birkbeck College, pp. 476-80.

Part Two

Generating Knowledge, Radicalising Research

Chapter 7

Workers, their Knowledge and the University

Jonathan Grossman

Drawing on extensive personal experience of workers' education with domestic workers (primarily women) in South Africa, the author argues that university-based popular educators need to work with the previously hidden and suppressed knowledge of those of who are most vulnerable and marginalised in society. This means contesting bourgeois constructions of 'need' and challenging the self-denigration which often accompanies such workers' own assessment of what they know and what is worth knowing.

The movement of resistance in South Africa has secured many changes which not very long ago were considered beyond reach. Specifically in relation to workplace education and training: there is major funding through the Department of Labour; capital is putting resources into workplace education programmes for its own reasons and sometimes as a result of consistent pressure; there is a new education and training levy; a new National Qualifications Framework includes recognition of prior learning and fore-grounds Adult Basic Education and Training; an empire of Sectoral Education Training Authorities has been instituted; people with 'struggle histories' are in key decision-making positions.

All of these trends create possibilities hardly even dreamed of not many years ago. It seems like a situation in which social need can be addressed, whatever the limitations of resources: not simply the need to extend formal training and education to those denied them but also the need to create spaces for the previously wasted and denied knowledge and suppressed potential of millions of the most 'marginalised' and 'vulnerable'. But this notion of need is contested. Subjected to the dictates of the market, need is located and seen as greatest where profit, productivity and international competitiveness can be most immediately enhanced. This notion of need is increasingly evident in what I am going to call the workplace learning industry. It involves education within the framework of tenders, competition, products and clients. The co-ordinators and convenors and collectives of yesterday have given way to the managers, directors, chief executive officers, fund-raisers and career-pathed hierarchies of today (see Samson and Vally 1996a, 1996b; von Kotze, 1998; Cooper, 1998; Cooper et al, 2002). To make the same point in a different way, there is an increasingly dominant bourgeois *ideological* notion of need which is *not* sufficiently contested. The dramatic changes and the new prospects they open up come with a price – a price, I will argue, that is actually denying and closing off those options.

Since 1988 I have been involved in work with domestic workers from unions, political organisations, as a worker educator and as a university-employed academic. From 1988 to 2000 I received generous funding from my university for 'extension work' with domestic workers and from the major state funder for 'research' with domestic workers. My research proposals have been explicit about the participatory, advocacy and action research framework adopted and the fact that I am guided by a Marxist approach. Workers involved in these activities have marched on the trade union federation and the Department of Labour to demand that their needs be taken seriously. Through their self-activity they have unionised. The activities have yielded educational pamphlets and submissions to the Department of Labour, the Employment Conditions Commission and a Constitutional Review Committee advocating changes to the law and Constitution to respond to the needs of domestic (and other) workers. It is likely that funding has been easier to get precisely because I am employed in a university. Without wishing to make claims, I regard this work as better done rather than not done; an instance of using the relative freedom available to me to deploy university resources – primarily myself and some of my time – to the service of those generally denied access to such resources. It would be comforting indeed to leave it there as an example of possibilities opened up by workers' struggle in the old South Africa and extended by developments made possible by the same struggle into the new South Africa. It would be similarly comforting to regard this if not as mainstream in the university, at least as exemplary of the way in which conservative values can be meaningfully challenged in the university. Unfortunately, neither the lived experience of continuing denigration of domestic workers nor the growing experience of retrenchment and wage-cuts by university workers in the new South Africa allow that comfort.

Workplace learning and the knowledge of domestic workers

In South Africa domestic workers form the largest single sector of employed workers, and employers of domestic workers are the biggest single sector of employers. There is also a massive layer of (almost always) women who do domestic work without pay. Much paid domestic work and perhaps much more unpaid domestic work is both socially useful and socially necessary. But it is denigrated and devalued in a patriarchal capitalist society. I have met domestic workers whose work includes acting as secretaries, telephonists, nurses, dressmakers, therapists, linguists, childminders, chefs, cleaners, security guards and many other activities. To do that work, they have been forced to develop skills which very rarely if at all come from formal training programmes. Nor are they 'natural'. They are learned. Most often, they have been developed through ordinary everyday experiential processes of workplace learning – workplace understood in the broader sense. It is doubly meaningless to restrict workplace learning to the site of 'production' in the case of domestic workers; not only do they repeat much of the work as unpaid labour 'at home', many of them are also forced to spend a large part of their lives living in backyards. In that sense, the site of paid employment is also an imposed 'home'.

It would be an extraordinary view of knowledge and its production which sought to argue that there is no socially important knowledge involved in being able to do these various tasks, or that there was no socially important knowledge generated out of the process of doing them. But, in a context dominated by the structured social inequalities of race, class and gender, it has been made unnecessary for the argument ever to be made as an argument. Instead, there is a widespread denigrating social belief that the most appropriate description of domestic work is *just* domestic work, and the most appropriate description of the domestic worker is *only* a domestic worker.

Through processes which will be understood by anyone sensitive to the operation of power in a capitalist patriarchy, domestic workers sometimes repeat the same imposed view of themselves, becoming part of the same pattern of denial. When I have asked the uncertificated nurses and psychologists and educators and child-minders who attend their domestic worker meetings what they would most like to do, very few of them break beyond the perceived boundaries of limited domestic work; fewer still draw on skills which they obviously have in imagining what they could be doing. Why do workers deny their own knowledge? The answers are situationally specific – but general features of the broader context shape what is situationally specific. Workers reflect – through self-denigration – what is the broader pervasive social denigration. But there is a pattern which is significantly different to this. Sometimes, workers perceive an advantage to be gained from the denial of knowledge. In other words, often the denial of knowledge is itself an indicator of specific knowledge and the use of that knowledge. Often that use of knowledge through chosen and assumed denial is expressed through apparent silence.

Well-intentioned observers and even activists talk of the silence of domestic workers, sometimes referring to them as people 'without a voice'. And of course there are problems of lack of organisation, disunity and sometimes subservience. It is part of the daily experience of domestic workers that they should be denied the chance to speak or be listened to. I have also attended many meetings of domestic workers and had numerous discussions. Before, during and after any and all of these, there is the noise of voices. Even when there are actual silences, that is sometimes also the strategically assumed silence of the knowledgeable, not simply the imposed silence of the voiceless. And, too often, the presumption of silence by those who cannot or will not listen is accompanied by a presumption of the ignorance of those they cannot or will not hear when there is noise. They follow a pattern, unable to hear when they don't pick up an echo of their own beliefs and assumptions, unable to recognise knowledge when it is not confirmation of their own, fitting lower down into a hierarchy of knowledge which affirms their own. The dismissal of this knowledge reflects an ignorance in those who cannot or will not see and value workers' knowledge. As testimony from domestic workers repeatedly illustrates, it is not enough for domestic workers to learn and know how to deal with their own lives. They have to be able to understand, predict, know about, and generally cope with the lives of their employers.

Workers, their knowledge, and the university

On the basis of such understanding and skills – only through these – workers are able to manoeuvre for survival and advances within what are extremely constricting limits. It is necessary to highlight the vulnerability of domestic workers in order better to understand the enormity of what they are doing when they survive and rise above the denigration imposed on them.

In everyday life, workers are repeatedly taking information which they have and processing it. They are deciding how to use it in the context in which it has to be used. Similarly – or as part of that – they are deciding when and what to conceal. In other contexts, where information is processed and used for consciously defined outcomes we easily call this knowledge. It is no less knowledge when domestic workers are the actors. But we live in a world where knowledge is either defined in terms of its value for profits, or in an *ad hominem* way. A university course which consists simply of the transmission of information is defined as imparting knowledge – just because it is a university course. A domestic worker, processing the information in ways which take real account of the social context, power relations within it and likely outcomes is defined as being silent and ignorant – just because she is a domestic worker. The problem of those who have the power to impose, benefit from and determine social definitions is turned into the problem of the ignorant domestic worker. We are repeatedly hearing that we live in an economy where information and knowledge are increasingly central. Yet in the case of millions of people forced into poverty even when employed in that same economy, it is not a matter of the content or the social value of what they know – but rather a matter of who they are, who has the power to certify knowledge and the social reality in which knowledge is regarded, above all else, as that which is useful to the generation of profits. The result is surely a waste of human knowledge and potential unprecedented in human history.

Workplace learning and 'skills development' for workers is currently in vogue because it meets the perceived needs of capital. Capital (albeit under some compulsion) and the state are funding it in order to ensure 'skills for international competitiveness'. Universities have become increasingly involved, both as factories for the ideology of competitiveness which underlies this and as functionaries in the actual training processes which embeds this. It would be tempting to believe that the progressive educator is able to exploit the situation to redress some of the waste of knowledge which I have identified. If we are involved in these things, I am sure we carry a commitment to do so in ways which undermine the principles of the market. But good intentions are not enough to constitute challenges to the ideological avalanche imposed on us. University nooks and crannies all too easily become comfort zones, and challenges launched from comfort zones are all too easily overwhelmed by careers, conferences, funding bids and chapters in books.

I want to look at three features which I believe are central to the university-based workplace learning industry, but which undermine the good intentions which may have taken some of us into it: career-pathing and education designed to promote it; the growth of certification and recognition of prior learning; and the growing tendency to focus in on practical work, stripped of the complications of 'totalising vision'.

Career-pathing

There is something immediately and obviously progressive in the notion that people forced into and restricted to domestic work, for example, should be enabled through education to move beyond those restrictions. I am sure that there are domestic workers who could and should be pilots and presidents and paper-writers, just as I am sure that socially useful and necessary domestic work should be valued, affirmed, respected and recognised. Career-pathing seems like an answer. But is it? Career-pathing rests on the apparently benign and incontestable argument that people forced into a situation should be allowed to rise out of it. Where people denied those rights are oppressed in the process on the basis of class, race and gender, career-pathing can be invested with the additional legitimacy of a challenge to those forms of oppression. Tied to workplace learning, it is further invested with the progressive notion of affirming existing knowledge as a basis for individual development.

Recognition of prior learning (RPL)

When we first encountered the injustice of black workers doing work for which they were neither certificated nor paid, we did not talk of recognition of prior learning; but we knew that there was knowledge and potential and capacity amongst all oppressed and exploited people which was denied, suppressed and not recognised. In that sense, RPL was a form of redress and compensation based on recognising already existing knowledge and capacities. In the new climate, it has been turned into something different. It has become the gateway to training for more skilled work. People are not paid more because their experiential learning is recognised. They are not respected and affirmed because of what they already know and the alternatives this can promote. Instead, their already existing knowledge is accepted as valuable only in the sense that it qualifies them to be given 'really useful' knowledge. In practical terms, RPL involves giving them entry points to allow them to study further to fit into things as they are. The most progressive practitioners of RPL in the workplace learning industry argue that it need not be like this (see

Michelson, 1996a, 1996b). That may be true. It is not RPL *per se*, but the ideological underpinnings and context which give it its actual social role. But that is entirely the point. With exceptions which are very hard to find, the workplace learning industry is subjected to the values of the market.

Certification

In terms of those values, further progress has to be confirmed and represented through certification so that it can command a price. Again, it is incontestable that people who have learnt something should have the right to have that certificated. But in a context of competitive individualism where the promise is enhanced employability, the value of certification lies in its exclusivity. It gives you a competitive advantage, in other words, only to the extent that someone else is not certificated. If everyone has the certificate, it is no longer a gateway unless everyone advances. Not so long ago, that could mean something like a living wage for all. In the new context characterised by the ascendancy of the ideology of the market, everyone cannot advance – everyone cannot have a living wage. Career-pathing is 'sold' as offering a route upward to everyone. Certification is seen as the set of steps along that route. To people who have been oppressed, the appeal is obvious. But, to put it simply, there is no room for everyone. What is made possible because of a collective struggle sets individuals against each other in a competitive struggle. Career-pathing is not about advancing everyone. It is about advancing individuals while the basic structure and set of conditions overall remains unchallenged. At most, the struggle is reduced to a struggle over who may compete.

At one stage during the state of emergency, T-shirts of popular mass organisations were banned. There was a time when the T-shirt was, for many workers, the sought after 'certificate'. It announced something that you were part of, proud of and achieving. But it also went with a determined spirit of inclusion. You were more proud when others were wearing the same T-shirt. Your self-worth was nurtured when others were included in the same assertion of identity. What was once a demand for inclusivity – the recognition that we have all learnt and are all using knowledge which you ignore and denigrate – has been manipulated into a process of exclusivity: the value of training lies precisely in the extent to which someone else does not have it. It is the exclusivity which is deemed to make one employable and provide one with the competitive advantage in the job market. Certification becomes the signal of that exclusivity.

Infested with the ideology of competitive individualism, what can career-pathing actually mean for domestic workers? It is a route out of domestic work, necessarily for a tiny minority. Again, that is an incontestable right. But where does it leave the remaining million? Styled as a solution to 'just' domestic work, it serves as a confirmation that whoever is left behind is doing 'just' domestic work. As it is actually envisaged, it ties domestic workers to a form of 'women's work' – the most favoured careers being in catering. Instead of affirming experiential learning and its product of knowledge which allows domestic workers to develop the range of skills involved in 'just' domestic work, it ends up replicating patriarchal thinking which insists that women know how to do such work without learning – naturally. There is no knowledge to affirm and no real learning which takes place – it is something instinctive, truly just 'women's work'.

Experiential learning and the workplace learning industry

Experiential learning is both a method and a philosophy of learning. As philosophy it asserts that learning takes place in the experience of everyday life and that therefore all people have knowledge and expertise. As method, it can be reduced to particular techniques. Of course, education is better done when it extracts some of the thinking and practices of experiential learning. They provide a powerful and effective set of techniques. But they can never be simply a set of techniques. They are always ideologically and politically framed. Those techniques can be and are used in the service of diametrically opposed interests. That in itself tells us that there is nothing essentially nor necessarily progressive or liberatory in the techniques. But how often are we ourselves involved in educational processes in which the techniques have been stripped from the philosophy with which we once justified them? How often, in other words, do we become practical technicians, employing a method whose legitimacy lay in its place within a broader methodology? How often does our scholarship assert the dangers of precisely that situation – and our practice ignore our scholarship? How often is the one reserved for academic conferences and the other used to guide our funding applications?

Experience can be the base of subversive developments, but then it has to move forward as a challenge to conservative obstacles. That process was at the core of the development of the workers' movement – both educationally and more broadly. It was developed as opposition (see Grossman, 1994, 1996, 1999). Even in the height of the struggle, aggressive competitiveness, individualism and instrumentalism were dominant parts of capitalist morality contextually affirmed and corroding collectivism and solidarity inside the workers' movement. If that was the case at the height of the struggle, how much more so is it the case now?

Competitive individualism is not simply an ideological construct. It is reflected in the material experience imposed on workers and others every day. Increasingly, experience can be used to confirm individualism, not challenge it. Production itself is generally being organised on a less collective basis experientially, even if the social nature of it has to remain unchanged. The union is far less the site of collective participation, and increasingly the office which does or doesn't provide what you individually pay for. Where collectives are promoted, they are always competitive collectives – the production team, 'our' company, the 'winning nation'. Educational activity within a progressive methodology has to explore those contradictions and develop challenges to the orthodoxies of the day. A progressive education must surely *explicitly challenge* individualism and the dictates of the market which nurture and insist on it, just as and no less than it challenges sexism and racism. Of course, this can and does invoke the charge of imposition from above or outside: but burying ourselves in techniques, as if these are free of 'agendas', is simply allowing the unchecked imposition of dominant orthodoxies.

I argued earlier that educational work and processes do not just take place: they are imbued with ideological underpinnings and they are always ideologically framed. Part of the core of the development of a progressive workers' education movement was the broader political context in which workers, their knowledge, what they did, their social weight – were all affirmed. Individual workers had places to bring their individual experiences and thoughts and share them. If they contributed and met needs, they were appropriated as the thoughts of hundreds and thousands. This created a different alternative way of seeing who is the prominent individual and another way of defining individual prominence. It created the possibility of individual prominence for the ordinary worker in specific situations – not only the richest, or the best trained, or the best known, or the most powerful. It is an individual prominence which is constructed and exists only within the context of the collective. It depends for its existence on the collective and the individual as part of the collective. Without that context the knowledge of millions of ordinary workers in many different situations would have been wasted. There was a vision of the future based on the alternatives being created in the present. That was a totalising vision and it is impossible to believe that the struggle could have moved so far without it. Its opposite is exemplified in a really horrifying example. After years of struggle, illiteracy was almost completely eradicated in Kerala, India. After further years, it grew again. The technical skill was useless outside of a context which affirmed the possibility and the social value of using it. The different aspects of knowledge and its production cannot be separated from the context in which they are used and affirmed – or wasted and denied.

It is not unusual now to hear calls to revisit earlier worker education and draw on its traditions. But it is also not unusual to meet a desire to avoid 'totalising visions' and just get on with work on the ground. In a sense, it is the cry of the refugee from post-modernism seeking to escape its cynicism and take some refuge from incredulity about everything (see Usher et al, 1997). Much as some of us might like to get on and do things without totalising visions, if we do not choose our own agendas, we are simply fitting into someone else's. If we do not challenge the competitive individualism and hierarchy which dominate, we end up at best conforming and more often endorsing them. We do not need more research, nor can we claim to be unwitting accomplices. There are sufficient conference papers warning of all the dangers, and too many situations when the writers of those papers are involved in the practices which they warn against.

In and against the academy

After initial difficulties in securing funding, my work with domestic workers was handsomely funded for three years. This happened despite the fact that I ignored friendly advice from an authoritative source on the University Research Committee which vets all funding applications to take out the word 'Marxist' from the description of my theoretical approach and replace it with the word 'materialist'. It also happened despite the fact that the successful funding application was initially turned down by another part of the same funding organisation, in part because it was a 'programme of action not a research proposal'. It would be satisfying for several reasons to see this as some sort of victory in challenging the university and some confirmation of the value of pursuing this sort of work within the university context. Unfortunately, it is not nearly that simple. To the extent that outside funders have become willing to fund such work, this is because of factors far removed from the university – to do with the broader political climate. It was not the university or academics who successfully placed women and poverty and struggle and transformation on the South African agenda. Internally for the university, the really important thing about my work is that it can be reflected as research income which is a Good Thing. If it generates research outcomes (meaning publications in peer-reviewed journals), then it is an Even Better Thing because, in the funding formulas being used, it generates further research income for the university. Beyond that, it is essentially irrelevant to the overall role of the university in trivialising and denigrating the knowledge and contribution of ordinary workers, reducing them to the shadows in a world created by great men (and yes, they include women) and most of all, dynamic capitalist entrepreneurs – in other words, in undermining what I seek to affirm and affirming what I seek to undermine.

Universities are often appropriately regarded as sites of much talk and little action. In the final analysis, what the university does is the clearest indication of where it stands in terms of respecting workers and their knowledge. And it is in determining how we respond to what our universities are actually doing that we have the greatest challenge to make something of the papers we write and seminars we hold about respect for workers and their knowledge. Workers in university – like workers anywhere else – have also developed prior learning. In recent years, as the growth of the workplace learning industry and the recognition of prior learning has been developing, the University of Cape Town (UCT) – meaning each effective decision-making body in the executive structures of the University – dismissed this knowledge out of hand. In the University's vision, cleaners and gardeners and maintenance workers had nothing to do with the 'core business'; they cost money and made no contribution to core business productivity. The majority of workers were retrenched, wages were substantially cut in the process of outsourcing and the recognition agreement with the union was terminated on a technicality because the agreement negotiated under apartheid conceded more than the post-apartheid market dictated. If the University saw any place for the recognition of prior learning in this, it was to consider calling in the experts to prepare the workers for retrenchment. All of this was particularly brutally done at UCT but the same pattern is being followed across the country and indeed internationally.

There was, of course, a way of resisting this but it involved pamphlets and pickets and strikes, not debates and carefully crafted research proposals. Respect for workers and their knowledge in this context demanded more than recognition of their prior learning. It was about their jobs, their wages, their conditions and their union. Outside of that, my and similar projects, findings and conference papers might have shared their values, but these did nothing to challenge the university as ideologist, cheerleader and executor (some would say executioner) in the name of market values.

I can now add submissions to important state structures, conference papers, chapters in books and funding to my curriculum vitae. But it's not possible to pretend about what these meant when the university which accommodated them retrenched its workers, trampling on everything I advocate in my work. I faced a challenge then which to me sums up what is in front of us when we seek to be progressive educators within universities which propound and practise market values. I had to ask myself about another curriculum vitae: when last did your worker education mean using university resources to work with rank and file workers? When last was it enough to respond to the wrong thing by saying no and not doing it? When last did you actually heed the warnings that win acclaim at conferences; or draw on the struggle traditions of learning and sharing which allowed you the space to do your work without throwing in something or other about productivity? When last did you venture forth from the comfort zone of nooks and crannies to call what is evil and wrong by their right names, thrust aside your mouse and go and join a picket line? When last did you mention the word socialism? If you believe in socialism, as the necessary alternative to capitalist barbarism, when last did you say so; and when last did you advocate that belief with commitment, not apology?

Acknowledgements

I am grateful to Elana Michelson, Sandra van Niekerk, Linda Cooper, Sally Andrew and the Sea Point, East London and Masiphathisane domestic worker collectives for the shared hours of talking and listening which have helped develop this paper.

References

Cooper, L. (1998), 'From rolling mass action to RPL: the changing discourse of experience and learning in the South African labour movement', *Studies in Continuing Education,* 20(2), pp. 143-57.

Cooper, L., Andrew, S., Grossman, J. and Vally, S. (2002), ' "Schools of labour" and "Labour's schools": worker education under apartheid' in Kallaway, P. (ed.), *The History of Education under Apartheid, 1948-1994: The Doors of Learning and Culture Shall Be Opened*, New York: Peter Lang, pp. 111-33.

Grossman, J. (1994), 'Individualism and collectivism: issues in researching collective working-class experience'. Paper presented to 8th International Oral History Conference, Columbia University, New York, October.

Grossman, J. (1996), 'For our children tomorrow: workers in struggle in South Africa, 1973-1995', *Institute for Critical Research*: Amsterdam.

Grossman, J. (1999), 'Workers and knowledge'. Paper presented to the International Conference on Researching Work and Learning, University of Leeds, September.

Michelson, E. (1996a), 'Beyond Galileo's telescope: situated knowledge and the assessment of prior learning', *Adult Education Quarterly,* 46(4), pp. 185-96.

Michelson, E. (1996b), 'The usual suspects: experience, reflection and the engendering of knowledge', *International Journal of Lifelong Education*, 15(6), pp. 438-54.

Samson, M. and Vally, S. (1996a), 'Snakes and ladders: promises and potential pitfalls of the NQF', *South African Labour Bulletin,* 20(4), pp. 7-14.

Samson, M. and Vally, S. (1996b), 'The NQF: critical questions for labour,' *South African Labour Bulletin,* 20(5), pp. 23-9.

Usher, R., Bryant, I. and Johnston, R. (1997), *Adult Education and the Postmodern Challenge*. Routledge: London.

von Kotze, A. (1998), 'Adult education in the government of national unity's reconstruction and development programme' in Wildermeersch, D., Finger, M. and Jansen, T. (eds.), *Adult Education and Social Responsibility*, Frankfurt: Peter Lang, pp. 151-73.

Chapter 8

Dialogic Learning in Popular Education Movements in Spain

Lídia Puigvert and Rosa Valls

Reflecting recent historical and political developments in Spain, this chapter is based on the educational and political work of the Centre for Research on Theories and Practices that Overcome Inequalities at the University of Barcelona. The authors draw on extensive research and social and pedagogical experience in working with marginalised and oppressed groups to demonstrate the significance and efficacy of dialogical processes of learning as an essential basis for democratic forms of adult education and social action.

Introduction

Popular movements have had a critical impact in Spain in the struggle for radicalising democracy. The growth and impact of these movements today point to their importance and their potential role in the process of social transformation. The voices of people who have traditionally been voiceless in society are beginning to be heard in the public sphere with proposals and actions that arise from their real experiences, and are orienting society towards a more dialogic and egalitarian form.

We see this in the struggles of the 'other women', women with little or no formal education and women from cultural and ethnic minority groups, who have been making their voices heard about issues relevant to their lives, such as democratising education and culture. In popular education women are transforming their lives by reconstructing their own identities through learning and participating in collective struggles for social and educational change (Merrill, 1999). Academic feminists are already recognising the significance of these women's voices, which have an indispensable role in the creation of a more inclusive feminism in the twenty-first century, to promote their proposals for change in public discourse. In a conference on Women and Social Transformation in Barcelona in 2001, women academics and the 'other women' talked together in round tables and panels. Judith Butler, an internationally acclaimed American feminist, was among women like Emilia Clavería, a Romany grandmother. She argued that, 'within her struggle, Emilia is wondering how schools should change so that her culture is included and represented ... She cannot read, but she has a lot to say and to do' (Beck-Gernsheim, Butler and Puigvert, 2003: 141). In education we know that the democratic mobilisation of popular education movements has been an important resource for theoretical development in academia. In the 1960s and

1970s, Freire was theorising about the practice he was directly engaged in with social movements, starting from the transformations that people were making in their life world. The relevance and impact of Freire's work in the field of radical adult education and in popular education movements are a measure of his commitment towards supporting popular movements in their struggle for emancipation through egalitarian, dialogic and democratic education.

In our own experience as university-based teachers and researchers, the only way we can create socially relevant theories that contribute to social transformation is through an engaged collaboration with democratic popular education movements. We have found that our work must be directly linked with social reality in order to avoid developing theories or proposals built in ivory towers. If we want to contribute to improving people's lives we must support their proposals, actions and practices in democratic movements which help to overcome barriers to their full participation in society. We can do this by working with, rather than for, social agents by including their voice in the research we conduct as well as in wider social debates, thus making their struggles visible. Through collaboration and dialogue, we can together develop better practices and better theories. Herein lies the strength of the connection between theory and practice. In this chapter we focus on how popular education movements in Spain are already contributing to social transformation through dialogic learning. Participants in dialogically oriented adult education centres play an essential role within the popular education movement. We draw on the experience of the Centre for Research on the Education of Adults at the University of Barcelona (CREA) in engaging with these movements and the social and educational transformations that participants have been making through the practice of dialogic learning. The creation of shared spaces with these movements has allowed us to come together in an ongoing egalitarian dialogue, to coordinate our actions and to build successful practices and critical theories that can contribute to the process of social transformation. In the last section, we refer to the dialogic and egalitarian activities and projects that have helped us sustain a close relationship with these movements in solidarity with their collective struggles.

The dialogic turn of society and social and educational theories

Today dialogue is spreading through society, changing relational dynamics in the public and private spheres. In this dialogic turn personal relationships, institutions and the political sphere are increasingly guided by processes of dialogue, negotiation and consensus (Flecha, Gómez and Puigvert, 2003). Decisions which used to be taken unilaterally by parents are, increasingly, being taken in dialogue with their children. In relationships between partners, friends and work mates, traditional authority is being questioned and challenged, and substituted by dialogic practices. This dynamic is also being translated into educational practice, in the classroom and in the relationship between teachers and families. In the public sphere, a clear example of this phenomenon is the massive social mobilisation that took place in Spain between the Madrid terrorist attacks in 2004 and the general election when thousands of people took to the streets to claim their right to know the truth. In this process, it was not only the internet but also mobile phones that played a key role in facilitating the collective mobilisation of citizens. All this suggests that social agency has become central, and thus the presence of citizens' voices in decision making processes is becoming more and more essential. Now more than ever, people face varying possibilities and choices, and they are moved to rethink and redefine their lifestyles, family dynamics, identities and social practices. It is people themselves who are now deciding how to live, work and relate to each other, thus building their own biographies (Beck, 1992; Beck, Giddens and Lash, 1994).

Individuals and groups who have traditionally been excluded from making decisions relevant to their lives are now creating their own dialogic spaces. In local organisations, learning centres and citizens' associations, they reflect on their lives, needs and motivations, and agree on concrete actions to address them. This view rejects the elitist claims of a privileged minority in society to decide for everyone else, based on the justification that people are not smart enough or are simply not interested in exercising the right to speak for themselves. Dialogism points towards a radicalisation of democracy that implies the opening up of expert circles to the participation of lay people in the structure and process of decision making through public dialogue and the building of consensus. In this way, individuals can commit themselves to both personal and social projects of transformation.

Critical authors such as Habermas (1984, 1987) developed a theory that recognises people's capacity for language and action, and the significance for democracy of communicative rationality. His theory of communicative action sheds light on the possibility of transformative action between all social subjects through inter-subjective, egalitarian dialogue based on the validity of different knowledge claims and the attempt to reach understanding without the distortions produced by powerful sectional interests. Habermas's theory sets a framework, which inextricably links dialogic processes among different social agents to social action. From a similar perspective, Freire (1970, 1997) defends dialogic education, questioning the traditional banking model and advocating recognition of adult learners' capacities for dialogue, critical consciousness and social action.

Dialogic theories promote dialogic practices in society. In Spain, this is reflected in the gradual shift away from the traditional model of adult education to a social model. The traditional model is based on instruction rather than learning: the teacher monopolises the process of transmitting all the contents that end up being highly academic and not related to the learner's experience. In contrast, the social model is based on democratic principles: it allows for the recognition of both academic and non-academic knowledge as well as the importance of the learner's full participation in the educational process. Popular education practices and movements in Spain have been working to extend democratic processes into the wider system of education in schooling and the academy, and into civil society. In this task, the collaborative nature of the work between university teachers, researchers, practitioners and participants in education and cultural associations promotes the social model of education (i.e. popular adult education) through joint research projects, activities, debates and conferences. This collaboration has resulted in a democratic adult education movement.

Egalitarian and dialogic exchanges have been essential in sustaining solidarity between academics and popular movements, working towards a common goal: to overcome social inequalities and to promote and create critical theories and practices that help sustain this process. This concerted effort has helped to open doors to marginalised groups so that their voices can be heard in new decision making spaces. For example, some important changes were introduced in the university entrance exam, especially for those over twenty-five years of age and without any previous qualifications to access university. As some associations were already collaborating with CREA on this topic, they were able to back up their claims with research findings, proving, for example, the existence of hidden barriers in the entrance exam. It was also through this kind of collaboration that many of the participants' other claims were eventually taken into account by the university authorities – for example, about the need for openness regarding the contents of the exam, the possibility of applying for more than one university, and the necesssity of accommodating the university's organisation and time table to the needs of adult learners.

CREA's work is grounded on this kind of exchange. Through collaboration with social movements we have theorised dialogic learning, a pillar of the democratic popular education movement in Spain. Our aim is to support the daily struggles of people that are grounded in democratic practice and help to overcome social exclusion. From our base in the university, we are also able to make visible progressive theories and good practices in various ways – for instance, by asking participants to become members of our research teams from the very beginning to the very end of the process. In our classes we invite guest speakers from popular education movements who describe their own experience of dialogic learning and other democratic practices which help to foster the creation of spaces for dialogue and exchange between academics and non-academics.

Dialogic learning in popular education in Spain

Social movements have always played a key role in mobilising popular support for education, social participation and a democratic culture. In Spain adult education and cultural associations have taken a lead in the struggle towards these ends, forming networks and alliances to coordinate civil action. Movements that are working from the 'bottom-up' are already making contributions, bringing their reflections and daily life issues to the public forum. Ana, an adult learner member of the Catalan federation of participants' associations, reaffirmed the importance of dialogue in the conference on women already referred to:

> I would like to highlight the importance of dialogue . . . To speak up in public is not an easy thing to do. In fact, it is a really difficult situation. However, those of us who have experienced the practice of dialogue within our experience of literacy have been able to speak up here. Dialogic learning makes possible women's transformation . . . this is the experience of many of us who found a space, a school, where we counted. (Beck-Gernsheim, Butler and Puigvert, 2003: 141)

This woman was able to make public her transformative experience at a conference where women academics and women with little formal education spoke alongside each other on equal terms. Her words express the impact of dialogic learning on people's lives and demonstrate the possibility for those who have been traditionally voiceless to be present not only in their own associations and centres but also to challenge, comment on and contribute persuasively to theoretical and political debates in the wider society. In democratic education and cultural associations adults with no formal academic educational background are deciding how they want to live, work and study and are demanding that both political and academic institutions count them in.

The Spanish Confederation of Associations of Participants in Adult Education (CONFAPEA) has had an important role in fostering dialogic learning through its own participants' network which has been struggling to democratise adult education in Spain. CONFAPEA promotes ways of guaranteeing that participants in adult education are able to decide for themselves what kind of education they want. It is only when the practice is dialogical that participants have a real say. Some of the activities they organise are national meetings to exchange these experiences: the Annual Adult Learners' Conference, Dialogic Literary Circles, and the Summer School. This organisation has been central to the development of the democratic adult education movement in Spain, a platform for collaboration among participants, educators and university teachers and researchers.

The Bill of Rights of Participants in Adult Education (FACEPA, 1999) emerged from the work of this popular education movement. This bill aimed to define the basic rights of participants in adult education. Despite having no statutory effect, the idea is to use it as a framework to claim the support and compliance of government. It was elaborated through a process of dialogue and consensus in different forums of adult education participants. A draft was circulated and discussed throughout Spain, and later the same process was carried out with participants from other European countries such as Belgium, the Netherlands and Hungary. This document now guides many adult education and cultural organisations in our country. Its preamble gives a clear idea of its egalitarian spirit:

Education, an inalienable right of adults, has to serve as an instrument for emancipation, which makes it possible to overcome social inequalities and power relations. Education depends on the recognition and the dialogue between different cultures and lifestyles that coexist in a given community. (FACEPA, 1999: 1)

This process of democratisation within the field of adult education has been possible because there already existed popular education practices grounded in the social, dialogical model, thus opening spaces for egalitarian participation and decision making within learning centres. It is in grassroots democratic schools and centres, like *La Verneda Sant Martí* in Barcelona, that adult learners organise and participate on an equal basis in making decisions about their education.

Dialogic learning is an integral feature of democratic education. Based on a fundamental respect for differences, it ensures that everyone has a voice in the learning process by guaranteeing that it is the force of the argument, not the status of the person who presents it, that makes it valid and persuasive. Every person is considered to have the capacity to learn and to be able to contribute with their knowledge. Egalitarian dialogue does not only take place between teacher and students; it goes beyond that – to create an atmosphere in which all the students interact with each other, increasing learning and promoting solidarity.

Ramon Flecha (2000) proposes seven principles that define dialogic learning: egalitarian dialogue, cultural intelligence, transformation, instrumental dimension, meaning creation, solidarity and equality of differences:

Egalitarian dialogue promotes mutual learning, which takes place in an inter-subjective dialogue based on validity claims aimed at reaching shared understanding and consensus. Egalitarian dialogue thus sets the ground for building what Habermas (1984) calls an 'ideal speech situation' in which all the participants are collectively committed to seeking the truth. This means that there is no place in this process for the pursuit of hidden personal agendas. Through egalitarian dialogue the monopoly of academic knowledge is broken, making visible as well as valuing all other forms of knowledge that have traditionally been disqualified in education as parochial, partial or inconsequential. Freire (1970) advocates the integral role of egalitarian dialogue in the teacher-learner relationship. Habermas (1984) argues that the researcher's subjectivity is not intrinsically superior to that of other social actors. Both must therefore be given equal value. Consequently, in developing rigorous and socially useful theories, we must promote the demonopolisation of expert knowledge through the inclusion of the voices of those whose realities we are studying (Beck, Giddens and Lash, 1994).

Cultural intelligence includes all forms of knowledge that have traditionally been disqualified in the academic sphere, either for having been acquired outside academia or for not emerging from the dominant culture. All people possess the capacity for language and learning at any age (Chomsky, 1988; Scribner, 1988). People without academic skills but with a wealth of practical learning can acquire the former by engaging in a process of dialogic learning. We see this, for example, when the practical mathematical skills women have gained from years of managing household expenditures is used in classes to learn abstract concepts or explain them by using examples from real life situations. The principle of cultural intelligence rejects the deficit theories still deeply ingrained in academia and society in general, and seeks to overcome the barriers these set up against social inclusion. Instead, it fosters a 'pedagogy of maximums' in which educators demonstrate their belief in all learners' intelligence, regardless of age, ethnicity, culture, gender or educational level. This principle opens a new path, where popular knowledge is recognised as an asset in the educational process. Communicative competencies are also taken into account. Between 1995 and 1998 CREA conducted research on the concept of communicative competencies (CREA, 1998). It was found that communicative skills are key components in how people solve daily problems and develop learning strategies, both in academic and life contexts. These learning skills were described and characterised in the research, and one of the main conclusions drawn from it was that these competencies can become the bridge between practical and academic knowledge. Therefore, different forms of knowledge can come together in an egalitarian dialogue to create new ideas and interpretations. A shared understanding of the meaning and significance of cultural intelligence is thus required to make collaborations between academics and non-academics possible in the struggle for social and educational justice.

Transformation occurs in the process of dialogic learning. It is based on the claim in Freire's work about the power of human agency to change the social structures that dominate and constrain people through inter-subjective purposeful interactions. This breaks with the discourse of traditional reproduction theories which assume that there is an unavoidable dynamic embedded in social structures that maintains the *status quo* and therefore the social inequalities that exist within them. These theories are built upon conservative and structural educational traditions and practices that actually contribute to the reproduction of social inequalities. In order to democratise education and society, it is very important to reject these elitist kinds of theory. The changes participants are making in their lives in dialogic popular education are a testament to the impact of this process. These new possibilities, in turn, generate participants' commitment to projects of social transformation.

The *instrumental dimension* of learning is integral to the communicative learning process. Instrumental knowledge is approached jointly through dialogue and reflection, rather than on an individual basis. Communication and cooperation accelerate formal learning as well as building solidarity between people. Both are needed to overcome inequalities (Aubert, Duque, Fisas and Valls, 2004). Dialogic learning supports and enhances the acquisition of all the instrumental knowledge necessary for the information society. At the same time, dialogic learning avoids practices and procedures that favour only a small privileged group, and defends the full participation of all learners in acquiring instrumental knowledge.

In dialogic learning *meaning creation* is a collective and personal process. Meaning emerges in inter-subjective interactions when all participants take an active role in dialogue. Thanks to these interactions, people reshape their personal identity and begin the process of trying out and developing a new social identity. This is evident, for example, in the testimonies of people who have become activists and who are now very involved in their communities. The process of transformation fosters people's agency in the private and public spheres. When participants in popular education shape their educational and personal experiences it infuses their lives with meaning. In democratic learning centres dialogic learning also takes place in the organisation and management of the centres, and participation in associations, committees and other decision making spaces. When someone becomes an activist working for certain rights for their community, this inevitably influences their private lives. Research has shown the process of transformation in the lives of women when they are engaged in a dialogic learning practice. This is when major advances have taken place in transforming gender relations.

Solidarity is an integral part of sustaining dialogic learning practices. In dialogic learning people's motivations emerge from democratic and egalitarian values rather than competition and power claims. Participants, educators, volunteers and community members work together on common goals towards social change. These solidaristic values foster close collaboration between everyone, active participation and the inclusion of those who are normally excluded because of their educational level, age, gender, social class or ethnicity. Solidarity moves beyond the classroom walls to all the learning areas, from the personal sphere and out into the community and public sphere, and eventually ties of solidarity are built in the larger global society. This is manifested, for instance, in the networks that are created with other schools, associations and university-based teachers and researchers who support the democratisation process.

Equality of differences recognises everyone's right to be different and, at the same time, to be equal. But this principle depends on everyone being willing to observe and honour it. It implies respect for people's different cultural and ethnic backgrounds and lifestyles. If, for example, someone holds fascists views, then the establishment of an egalitarian dialogue based on arguments will be needed in order to address the issue. If this person is not willing to engage in such a dialogic process, then he or she will have made a choice: instead of choosing to act according to validity claims, he or she is doing so based on power claims (which have no part in dialogic learning). Dialogic learning includes an intercultural dialogue that opens the door to exchange and therefore mutual enrichment, thanks to the equal respect given to all cultural identities. The concept of equality of differences is distinct from the more frequently used notion of 'diversity', which is adopted in certain educational reforms that do not uphold equality. For example, when being different is used to explain why immigrant children have low levels of academic achievement, it may be inferred that such low levels are part of this difference. The logic of this way of thinking is that these low levels of performance are accepted – rather than being challenged in the interests of achieving equality. The defence of cultural difference must be inseparably linked with equality in order to overcome social exclusion. In education, discourses of diversity that forget about equality have led to watered-down curricula focused on adapting to differences rather than transforming the context in order to promote opportunities for equal outcomes. The principle of equality of differences, on the other hand, lays the ground for an intercultural dialogue in popular education, breaking down barriers of cultural identity or language and allowing us to act together to meet the needs and interests of all participants on equal terms.

Dialogic learning practices that define democratic popular education

The school for adult education *La Verneda Sant-Martí* is a reference point in terms of democratic popular education in Spain, and probably the best example of a dialogically oriented centre. The school emerged in 1978 from the grassroots mobilisation of a working-class neighbourhood in Barcelona, where people decided to come together to fight for their right to education and for other social and cultural services. From its foundation, the school was organised by the participants on the basis of democratic principles, dialogic learning and prioritising the needs and interests of the participants (Sánchez Aroca, 1999). All of this is made possible through the democratic organisation of the school. This means that participants take part in decision making at all levels of school organisation. Participation mechanisms, such as assemblies on a weekly and monthly basis, have been created to take and implement decisions collectively. Participants always have the final say. Power is shared on an equal basis between participants, teachers and volunteers; dialogue, reflection and consensus are the ingredients that lead to proposals for all the actions taken at the school. Activities like dialogic literary gatherings are just one example of the transformations that are fostered through dialogic learning: people with low literacy levels move from never having read a book to reading Dostoyevsky, Kafka and Joyce. In doing so, they demonstrate their capacity for transformation from illiterate to literary.

Personal and social transformation is at the heart of dialogic learning, as the story of Sara illustrates. Sara began by attending literacy courses at *La Verneda Sant-Martí*. She heard about the women's group from her classmates and decided to join them. In the group they addressed many different issues – such as relationships, work, learning and health. Her interactions with other women in this group helped her to make many significant changes in her life. The egalitarian and solidaristic relationships she developed in the group began to touch parts of her life outside the group. She began to change her relationships with family members, for instance, renegotiating the household chores which now became a shared responsibility. In her case, these changes actually deepened and strengthened her relationship with her family – although in some cases they may break them! At the same time, she was able to deepen her commitment to learning and social justice by becoming more involved in grassroots organisations. Her image of herself as well as other people's image of her changed – as a mother, wife and sister as well as an active member of two associations and a student in adult education.

Democratic adult education: engaging the academy

Sara and others in her situation are not waiting around for change to come their way. Through the networks and actions we have described here, they are making changes in their daily lives and in society. They are struggling together in democratic movements to claim what is rightfully theirs: a quality education and access to spaces of decision making. Through dialogue, participation, solidarity and hard work they are creating new and broader horizons for their own lives and everyone else's.

Popular education movements are part of the process of paving the way towards more democratic societies through dialogic learning. By acknowledging this reality, university teachers and researchers who are committed to social justice should seek out ways to align their work with these movements and support their personal and collective projects. As academics, we cannot turn our backs on these groups if we really want to contribute to social transformation. To approach our work with meaning and purpose, we have to develop theories that are based on committed collaboration with democratic movements, which are already finding ways of overcoming social inequalities. Our academic work is to rigorously analyse social processes, trying not only to point out those elements that contribute to the reproduction of social reality but also identifying those elements that contribute to the transformation of social reality. This is what we advocate, and – this is the most important point – we must do it with the very people who are living these realities.

The Democratic Adult Education (DAE) movement in Spain was created with this aim, pooling the energy, differences and dedication of participants, practitioners and university-based academics and researchers. The DAE movement is based on collaboration between three national organisations: the Educators' Network for Democratic Adult Education (REDA), the Spanish Network of University Professors and Researchers in Adult Education (Group 90) and the Confederation of Adult Education Participants' Associations in Adult Education (CONFAPEA). Together, we work for a common goal: to improve and democratise adult education and to include the voices and contributions of all those who have remained voiceless in public discourse. Through the DAE movement we have been able to create new spaces, practices and opportunities that strengthen social participation, intercultural dialogue and democratic principles.

This movement is coordinated and re-created through two main events: the annual CONFAPEA Summer School and the DAE Tri-Conference which takes place every three years as a state-wide forum in which all of these parties come together on an equal basis to discuss the future of democratic popular education. University-based teachers and researchers, adult educators and participants in adult education come together to review their achievements, set out dreams for the future and plan concrete actions to carry them out. This joint process ripples out to many other areas of their work and creates meaning for everyone involved. The first Tri-Conference took place in 2000 and demonstrated that participants in popular education movements have the capacity to guide the future of adult education. At this conference an 'Ethical Code of Democratic Adult Education' was elaborated and agreed by all participants, creating the basis for sustaining their collaboration on an egalitarian basis and always in the interests of the key stakeholders of adult education: the adult learners. The common democratic and egalitarian commitment shared by academia and the popular movements has thus been the basis for the creation of socially useful theories in support of educational and social transformation, and therefore, the promotion of dialogic learning practices that have continued to change people's lives.

References

Aubert, A., Duque, E., Fisa, M. and Valls, R. (2004), *Dialogar y Transformar. Pedagogía Crítica del Siglo XXI*, Barcelona: Graó.

Beck, U. (1992), *The Risk Society: Towards a New Modernity*, Newbury Park: Sage.

Beck, U., Giddens, A. and Lash, S. (1994), *Reflexive Modernization: Politics, Tradition and Aesthetics in the Modern Social Order*, Cambridge: Polity Press.

Beck-Gernsheim, E., Butler, J. and Puigvert, L. (2003), *Women and Social Transformation*, New York: Peter Lang.

Chomksy, N. (1988), *Language and Politics*, New York: Black Rose Books.

CREA, (1998), *Communicative Skills and Social Development*, Dirección General de Investigación Científica y Técnica, Ministry of Education and Science: Madrid.

FACEPA, (1999). *Declaration of Rights of Adults in Education*, European Commission. DGXII, Socrates Programme.

Flecha, R. (2000), *Sharing Words: Theory and Practice of Dialogic Learning*, Lanham, MD: Rowman & Littlefield.

Flecha, R., Gómez, J. and Puigvert, L. (2003), *Contemporary Sociological Theory*, New York: Peter Lang.

Freire, P. (1970), *Pedagogy of the Oppressed*, New York: Continuum.

Freire, P. (1997), *Pedagogy of the Heart*, New York: Continuum.

Habermas, J. (1984), *The Theory of Communicative Action. Vol I: Reason and the Rationalization of Society*, Boston: Beacon Press.

Habermas, J. (1987), *The Theory of Commucative Action. Vol. II: Lifeworld and System: A Critique of Functionalist Reason*, Cambridge: Polity Press.

Merrill, B. (1999), *Gender, Change and Identity: Mature Women Students in Universities*, Aldershot: Ashgate.

Sánchez Aroca, M. (1999), 'La Verneda-Sant Martí: a school where people dare to dream', *Harvard Educational Review*, 69(3), pp. 20-35.

Scribner, S. (1988), *Head and Hand: An Action Approach to Thinking*, Teachers College, Columbia University. National Center On Education and Employment. (ERIC Document Reproduction Service No. CE 049 897), p. 16.

Chapter 9

'The Workers' University': Australia's Marx Schools

Bob Boughton

This chapter offers a unique insight into the largely unwritten history of radical adult education in Australia by examining the educational work of the Australian Communist Party. University adult educators who wish to develop their links with contemporary social movements have much to learn from this invisible and suppressed tradition of connecting learning with struggle. The Australian case is presented as a microcosm of more universal problems and possibilties in reconnecting education with social and political action.

Despite recent efforts to revise the history of adult education, contemporary popular educators rarely locate their work within the long tradition of radical left wing adult education which dates back at least to the eighteenth century (Merlyn, 2001). From a vantage point inside this alternative tradition, attempts by universities in the English-speaking world to engage with popular movements for social change have a contradictory and highly problematic history. This chapter is about a particular strand in this alternative tradition. Tracing its origins back to the independent working-class education advocated by nineteenth century Chartism, a highly sophisticated formal but underground education system for activists emerged in the first half of the twentieth century, the network of 'Party Schools' established by the international communist movement. Some of these schools have been the subject of academic research, but this has mainly been in labour and social history, rather than in adult education, with little overlap or cross-fertilisation. Recalling some of this history helps us to reflect on why universities wrote out of education history one of its most significant stories, about how an organised and militant revolutionary movement sought to teach its members and supporters how to build a more just world.

Hal's story[1]

Hal Alexander lives in a pensioners' public housing unit in an inner suburb of Australia's 'global city', Sydney. No longer very mobile, he recently acquired a computer through which he maintains a prolific email correspondence with people all over Australia, and, indeed, the world. Since 11 September 2001, many of his emails have been about building an anti-war movement. On this topic, as on many others, Hal displays an acute sense of history, which comes as no surprise once you discover his age and something of his life story. In

1939, Hal left school at 15 to join the New South Wales Department of Transport, as an apprentice electrician in the railway workshops in inner-Sydney. Australia was then engaged in a different kind of war – a 'phoney' war, the left called it. The governments of Britain and her allies, having spent the previous decade appeasing fascism at home and abroad, had finally declared war on German Nazism, but nothing much was happening. The Communist Party of Australia (CPA), taking its lead from their Soviet counterparts, as did all the world's communist parties at the time, opposed this 'phoney' war, fearing it a prelude to an Anglo-German attack on the home of socialism. Consequently, not for the first time in their party's twenty year existence, Australia's tiny band of communists faced the threat of illegality. Hal, whose father was a shell-shocked victim of the first 'Great War', was attracted to their anti-war line, and was recruited to the party by workmates. As a new recruit, he was only marginal to preparations to go 'underground', but he watched more experienced comrades move documents into 'safe houses', hide printing presses, and organise for party leaders to disappear before the internal security police came to round them up. His own contribution was confined to clandestine on the job activity, distributing copies of the banned communist newspaper. When the Soviets joined the war on the side of the Allies, and the bans and threats were replaced by a 'United Front Against Fascism', the young Sydney communist had already begun an education which would last a lifetime. Today, he is still passing on the lessons he learned to later generations of activists, who somehow find their way to his door, or his email portal, in search of understanding about how to change the world.

Stories like Hal's are not unusual. They were repeated in the lives, not of thousands, but of millions of twentieth-century communists and socialists around the world. While their political education almost invariably began with experiences like this, of activism in the face of harsh repression, it was not simply informal, or learnt 'on the job.' From the late nineteenth to the mid-twentieth century, and in some countries until much more recently, the world was witness to a popular socialist education movement of huge proportions, a story now all but buried in the West under the weight of Cold War historiography. From the 1920s onwards, the major vehicles for this education movement were socialist and communist party schools, one of which the young Hal attended in evenings after work. In Sydney, as in Melbourne and other centres all over Australia in the 1940s, the CPA opened an adult education centre, called the Marx School. For an annual fee, members and supporters enrolled to study historical materialism, scientific socialism, Marxism-Leninism – in a word, communism:

> Marx School was founded as a memorial to the great leader and organiser of the working class, Karl Marx (1818-1883), to provide facilities for an advanced study of scientific socialism and to supplement the educational activities of the Political, Trade Union, Workshop and other organisations of the working class. It is the Workers' University. (*Melbourne Marx School Programme* 1947, quoted in Boughton, 1997b)

Few adult educators today, even those committed to popular education, know that mainstream adult education in the English-speaking world built its support and credibility with government in the years following the Second World War chiefly by presenting itself as a more palatable alternative to this kind of adult education.

An international movement

The communist schools were an international movement, in the best socialist tradition of which they were a product. In Australia these overseas links were part of their strength, but also what their enemies most feared. Half a world away from Sydney, a similar institution, the New York Workers School, was offering a very similar range of courses (Gettleman, 1993). The defeat of Mussolini's fascists in Italy was followed by the opening of schools by the *Partido Communiste Italia* (PCI) throughout that country (Bellassai, 1999). In Indonesia, as the Dutch left, the local Communist Party established its own version (McVey, 1990). In fact, in every country which had a communist party – and very few did not – thousands upon thousands of young and not so young activists, cadres as their movement called them, undertook adult study designed to give them the intellectual and practical tools they needed to play leading roles in all the popular struggles of their times.

Despite the claims of its academic detractors, of whom there were many, communist education was no fly-by-night operation, no quick injection of propaganda and the party line to brainwash mindless worker militants into becoming canon fodder in the class war. On the contrary, communist adult education was based on a long and demanding curriculum, taught over many levels spanning a whole lifetime. From the archives of the CPA, only recently made available for public study, and supplemented with material from the files of Australia's political police, the Australian Security Intelligence Organisation (ASIO) and its predecessors, it is possible to construct a detailed account of the curriculum of communist education. While adapted to local conditions and supplemented with local material, this was nevertheless part of an international process of cadre training, overseen and regularly reviewed from the Moscow headquarters of the movement, the Communist International, or Comintern.

In Australia, the most basic form of communist education – what today we might call 'entry-level' – was a small study circle, conducted for all new and intending members within a factory or locality branch, led by a more experienced branch member using a tutor's handbook. The Australian version was developed from an earlier one produced by the Communist Party of Great Britain. From here the new recruit progressed to more advanced classes, held at the Central School in the nearest capital city, and taught either in residential blocks or, for those living nearby like Hal, in evening classes after work. Subjects ranged across political economy, labour history, philosophy, public speaking, literature, women's issues, trade union law and bargaining, and journalism. For more advanced topics, the residential school was the norm, sometimes held at the Central School, but as the CPA grew, conducted in more secluded settings outside the city, usually, as records now reveal, under the watchful eye of the political police. In the 1940s and 1950s, such schools regularly lasted for as long as three or even six months, though shorter residentials, from one week to a month, were held in specialist areas – for example, trade union work in a specific industry, or 'work among women'. Longer residentials were primarily for those in full-time industrial (i.e. trade union) or Party work, and were taught only by the most experienced cadres, who themselves had reached the highest level of qualification, gained through attendance at an international school, held in the CPA's case in either Moscow or, later, Beijing. The international schools regularly took from one to three years.

Lifelong learning, we would call this today, and perhaps Etore Gelpi, who helped popularise this term, was drawing on his experience with the Italian communist movement and its equivalent institutions. It is definitely no coincidence that theorists struggling today to understand the relationship between adult education and social change turn first to the writings of Antonio Gramsci, the Italian communist leader whose ideas informed the work of these communist schools long before his 'discovery' by the academic new left in the 1970s. Hal Alexander, coming from one of the smallest of the world's communist parties, was both beneficiary and bearer of this extraordinary tradition, gaining access through it to the best education the international movement had to offer. After nearly two decades of preparation in Australia, he joined a group smuggled out of Australia at the height of the Cold War to undertake twelve months' study in 1957 at the Beijing Institute for Marxism-Leninism. On his return, the fully-qualified leader worked as a full-time functionary, taking his own turn in teaching Party classes, writing leaflets and articles for the communist press, and organising militant workers into factory 'cells' in the industrial area of Sydney known in those days as the 'Red Belt' (Alexander and Griffiths, 2003).

The new left and the old

In the 1960s and 1970s, a 'New Left' opposed to the US-led war in Vietnam emerged on university campuses throughout the developed world, and new forms of education began to replace the old approaches. With his years of training and experience as a full-time communist organiser, Hal threw himself into that movement with more gusto than many of his contemporaries. This is how I met him, and how I too came to join the CPA, through the anti-war movement of the time. Our generation had grown up in economic boom times, and universities were becoming mass institutions, no longer simply havens of the privileged few. Academics themselves began taking a lead in popular education, organising teach-ins on campuses to help build the movement. Soon after I joined the CPA, I discovered that some of the more outspoken academics themselves had previous 'form', having also spent time in the communist movement of the 1940s and 1950s, going through the same education processes that working-class activists like Hal had attended. A brave few had even written about this, wry or ironic pieces reflecting on their youth and naiveté, but acknowledging how formative such experiences had been (Turner, 1974).

Rex Mortimer, a Sydney University political scientist, had a particular influence on students like myself who were active in the anti-war movement, thanks to his extensive knowledge of the politics of imperialism in South East Asia. Many years later, I learned via an obscure personal memoir, ironically entitled *The Benefits of a Liberal Education*, that Rex, like Hal, and at the same time, had studied in Beijing, where members of the Vietnamese party in exile taught them of their struggles with the French. In the 1950s, the newly victorious Communist Party of China took over the overseas 'postgraduate' education of Asia Pacific region communists, a role previously performed by the Soviet party, and the Moscow road was gradually supplanted with the new 'Chinese method' of education. The Australian students had to be smuggled out of the country through Eastern Europe; travel to China was banned, with Australia fighting wars against communism in Korea and Malaya. Many of their counterparts from more oppressive regimes lived in exile for longer periods (Aarons, 1993; Mortimer, 1976; Boughton, 2003).

Until the Cold War, socialist and communist adult education enjoyed an often conflictual but nevertheless acknowledged relationship with the mainstream adult education promoted by University Departments of Adult Education and Extension. The Eureka Youth League, the communist youth organisation in Australia, even had an entry in a 1940s edition of the Australian Directory of Adult Education. Before the war, especially in the period of broad anti-fascist alliances in the 1930s, university adult educators, some (but not many) of whom were communists, assisted in working-class education programmes run by trade unions such as the Australian Railways Union and organisations of the anti-war movement in which the communists had extensive influence. One of the great and still largely untold stories of Australian adult education is the way the Australian Army Adult Education Service during the Second World War was staffed by many educators who had learnt their trade in a Communist Party school. By the end of the 1940s, however, the combination of the US-led Cold War and historical splits within the labour movement created a situation where leading Australian adult educators – and similar developments occurred in the UK and US – branded communist and other socialist education efforts as propaganda, not real education at all, and assisted in driving a wedge between the independent or socialist education tradition and what we now know as modern adult education (Boughton, 1999).

The long view

While mainstream Cold War historiography was burying the communist schools, the Stalinist historiography of the communists underplayed some of their own links to the longer, broader and more diverse tradition of independent working-class education. Throughout the nineteenth century, as bourgeois revolutions swept landless labourers into the maelstrom of industrial capitalism, European socialists of every persuasion struggled to educate themselves and others to understand and take control of the social forces overwhelming them. Similar self-education movements emerged in the colonial world by the end of the nineteenth century, as part of national anti-colonial movements which also built links to the socialist movement. Once you begin to look, you find these popular education movements everywhere by the early twentieth century, many of them tracing their own lineage back to the Chartists and before that to the Correspondence Societies of the French and American revolutions. Some, like the socialist-feminist cooperative movement which was a backbone of the peace movement in the First World War in Australia, or the Christian Socialists inspired by Hilaire Belloc who likewise advocated cooperative forms of agricultural production, dropped out of the communist pantheon, but others such as the independent Labour Colleges and the Plebs League movement in Britain and Australia were claimed, quite correctly, as the forerunners of the communist schools. In Australia, a good number of the founders of the Communist Party in 1920 had previously been members of these earlier socialist education organisations, and the first party schools and study circles they established simply continued this older tradition, to which they added the prestige of the Russian Bolsheviks and the backing of the Comintern established by Lenin in 1919 (Boughton, 1997a). The pre-1917 tradition of socialist schools also continued through organisations not associated with the highly-organised and centralised Comintern-affiliated parties, such as the American Labour College movement (Altenbaugh, 1990).

Researching the links between the communists and earlier generations of Australian socialist educators associated with the First International eventually took me back to Friedrich Engels recollections of his time with Marx in mid-nineteenth century London. There they met, for the first time, he says, 'genuinely revolutionary workers', members of an émigré organisation known as the League of the Just, later renamed the Communist League. Publicly known by their 'front' name, the Communist Workers Educational Association, the group included Germans, Swiss, Scandinavians, Dutch, Hungarians, Czechs, Slavs, Russians and Alsatians, and maintained contacts with similar organisations in France, in Poland and in Germany itself (Engels, 1970). This 'red WEA', formed several decades before its more widely recognised namesake, worked with English socialists like Ernest Jones, one of the Chartist leaders whose advocacy for independent working-class education under the slogan 'A People's education is safe only in a people's hands', is still remembered in histories of radical adult education (Armstrong, 1988; Johnson, 1988). In 1847, as Marx School textbooks quoting these recollections would teach a century later, the Communist Workers Educational Association commissioned Marx and Engels to write their political programme, published the following year as the *Communist Manifesto*. Had

English-speaking adult education constructed a history to define its field in a period other than the Cold War, this pamphlet might now rate as its most famous text. For most of the twentieth century, and still in some parts of the world over a century and a half after it was written, it has been used by millions of adult educators and adult learners as a basic introduction to world history, economics and politics – and as a vision of the 'society of equals' which we can aspire to achieve.

Contemporary lessons

This collection of essays is examining ways that university-based teachers and researchers might engage the academy in supporting popular struggles for equality and social justice. Academic adult education has recently witnessed a revival of interest in its history, driven by a similar concern to re-establish the link between education and movements for social change (Gettleman, 1993; Welton, 1993a, 1993b). The result is a growing body of 'revisionist' historical writing, which casts serious doubts on liberal adult education's mantle of benevolence, assumed early on by the London Working Men's College, and handed on down via a century and a half's tradition in the English-speaking world through university extension, Oxford's Ruskin College, the Workers Educational Association movement, the progressivism of Dewey and Linde-man in the United States, and the community development tradition of the Colombo Plan. Despite this new critique, the liberal (but non-socialist) tradition would still, if it could, merge itself seamlessly with Freirian-style education for empowerment, failing to acknowledge the serious historical fault lines and discontinuities separating first world university adult education from culture circles teaching revolutionary Marxist politics to the urban poor.

University adult educators wanting to strengthen links with movements for social change must first locate their work in relation to this alternative historical tradition. In Australia, labour historians Tim Rowse and Lucy Taksa have helped reveal some of the contradictions in the alliances forged between liberal university-based educators and the Workers Educational Association (Rowse, 1981; Taksa, 1996), while left wing historians of adult education in Britain and Canada have been pursuing similar interests. Adult educators in the US, given that country's history of anti-communist and anti-socialist activity in universities (Schrecker, 1986), may find it even harder to assert any affinity with this old left tradition. Some historical work does point in those directions, and there is growing recognition of the value of education conducted within contemporary revolutionary movements of the south, as documented in Hammond's work on Salvadorean guerillas and political prisoners (Hammond, 1998). The most ambitious development to date has come from New York labour historian, Marvin Gettleman, who has launched an international project to provide comparative historical analyses of communist and socialist party education.[2]

What university adult education stands to learn from these ongoing historical efforts is why communist and socialist adult education programmes, predating Freire by decades, made university-based adult educators a principal target of their critique, and fought such battles with them over the control and content of working-class education. Far from ignoring the radical socialist education movement, university adult education departments from the 1930s onwards rightly saw it as their main enemy (or 'competitor', as we might rephrase this in today's marketised world). In Australia, as elsewhere, this led some prominent university adult educators into an unholy alliance with the anti-communist intelligence services, who had something less polite than liberal academic debate on their agendas. These alliances, still in place when the Vietnam War spawned a new generation of student activism in the 1960s and 1970s, had so successfully silenced most intellectual 'fellow travellers' on the campuses, that even the most radical wing of university adult education minimised the affinities and history it shared with the older socialist and communist tradition. Even today, we call what we do 'popular' education, not socialist education, though many of us know full well that populism as easily becomes a vehicle for the political right as for the left.

In re-engaging with popular movements, academic adult education needs to re-examine the education work of those nineteenth and twentieth century social movements on whose shoulders today's activists unconsciously stand. Of these the most important is the international socialist, and – yes, we dare now say it – communist movement.[3] One cannot, after all, be post-communist or post-socialist, without knowing better what we are trying to be 'post'. What we think we know of these movements has so far been refracted through a Cold War lens. Detailed historical research will reveal that for much of the last one hundred years, a significant proportion of the world's most active and successful campaigners for social justice, people like Hal Alexander, lived and learned their politics within social movements which inscribed socialism and communism on their banners. To think that we can understand how to link education and social change without closer study of those socialist and communist education traditions would be a serious mistake. The path of study will lead through Stalin's Gulags, but just as surely it will lead through some of the noblest stories of our times. As Mahatma Ghandi put it: 'The road to the future lies over the bones of the past, on which we dare to tread'.

Notes

1. Hal's story, and much of the information which follows, was originally collected as part of research for my doctoral thesis (Boughton, 1997b). My thanks to Hal, for permission to retell his story for this collection. My thanks also to many other unnamed members of the Communist Party of Australia, who shared with me their recollections, their own writings and archives, and the heavily censored extracts they are gradually

retrieving from the personal files kept on them over many decades by ASIO, Australia's internal security police, and its forebears.

2. The Comparative International History of Left Education Project was launched in 1995 via H-Labor, an international labour historians email discussion list, by Marvin Gettleman, then at the Polytechnic University in New York. Since that time it has proceeded largely by way of panels convened at international conferences on labour and social history, which have stimulated a small but growing body of published work.

3. This paper was originally written in 1999. In revising it for publication, I want to acknowledge the recent work of John D. Holst, who is exploring similar themes in his research on adult education within contemporary socialist and Marxist political organisations in the United States.

References

Aarons, E. (1993), *What's Left? Memoirs of an Australian Communist*, Ringwood: Penguin.

Alexander, H. and Griffiths, P. (2003), *A Few Rough Reds: Stories of Rank and File Organising*, Canberra: Australian Society for the Study of Labour History, Canberra Region Branch.

Altenbaugh, R. (1990), *Education for Struggle: The American Labor Colleges of the 1920s and 1930s*, Philadelphia: Temple University Press.

Armstrong, P.F. (1988), 'The long search for the working class: socialism and the education of adults, 1850-1930' in Lovett, T. (ed.), *Radical Approaches to Adult Education: A Reader*, London and New York: Routledge, pp. 35-58.

Bellassai, S. (1999), 'The party as school and the schools of party: the *Partito Communista Italiano* 1947-1956', *Pedagogica Historica: International Journal of the History of Education*, XXXV(1), pp. 87-107.

Boughton, B. (1997a), 'Does popular education have a past?' in Boughton, B., Brown, T. and Foley, G. (eds), *New Directions in Australian Adult Education*, Sydney: University of Technology Sydney (UTS) Centre for Popular Education, pp. 1-27.

Boughton, B. (1997b), *Educating the Educators: The Communist Party of Australia and its Influence on Australian Adult Education*. Unpublished PhD thesis, La Trobe University, Bundoora, Victoria.

Boughton, B. (1999), 'Just as impelled as ever to try the liberal racket: the influence of communism and anti-communism on Australian adult education history, as seen through the life of Esmonde Higgins' in Reid-Smith, E. (ed.), *Some Topics on Adult Education in Australia: Papers Presented at a Seminar on the History of Adult Education*, Canberra: Adult Learning Australia Research Network and Centre for Learning and Work Research, Griffith University.

Boughton, B. (2003), ' "Advanced Chinese methods": transformative pedagogy and the Communist Party of Australia in the 1950s'. Paper presented at the Eighth National Labour History Conference 'Transforming Labour: Work, Workers, Struggle and Change', Griffith University Brisbane.

Engels, F. (1970), 'On the history of the Communist League', *Karl Marx and Frederick Engels. Selected Works in Three Volumes (MESW)* Vol 3, Moscow: Progress Publishers, pp. 171-90.

Gettleman, M. (1993), 'The New York Workers School, 1923-1944: communist education in American Society' in Brown, M., Martin, R., Rosengarten, F. and Snedeker, G. (eds), *New Studies in the Politics and Culture of US Communism*, New York: Monthly Review Press, pp. 261-80.

Hammond, J.L. (1998), *Fighting to Learn: Popular Education and Guerrilla War in El Salvador*, New Brunswick, New Jersey and London: Rutgers University Press.

Johnson, R. (1988), 'Really useful knowledge' 1790-1850: memories for education in the 1980s' in Lovett, T. (ed.), *Radical Approaches to Adult Education: A Reader*, London and New York: Routledge, pp. 3-34.

McVey, R. (1990), 'Teaching modernity: the PKI as an educational institution, *Indonesia*, 50, pp. 5-27.

Merlyn, T. (2001), 'The longest war: the two traditions of adult education', *Australian Journal of Adult Learning*, 41(3), pp. 297-313.

Mortimer, R. (1976), 'The benefits of a liberal education', *Meanjin*, 35(2), pp. 115-26.

Rowse, T. (1981), 'Pedagogy of the detached? Lloyd Ross's challenge to the WEA', *Radical Education Dossier* (Winter), pp. 21-5.

Schrecker, E. (1986), *No Ivory Tower: McCarthyism and the Universities*. New York: Oxford University Press.

Taksa, L. (1996), 'Imperial influences, national imperatives and class struggles: the early years of the Workers Education Association in Australia'. Paper presented to the International Institute of Social History Conference, Labour and Empire, Amsterdam, May.

Turner, I. (1974), 'My Long March', *Overland,* 59, pp. 23-40.

Welton, M.R. (1993a), 'In search of the object: historiography and adult education', *Studies in Continuing Education,* 15(2), pp. 133-48.

Welton, M.R. (1993b), 'Memories in time of troubles: the Liberatory Moments History Project', *Convergence,* XXVI (4), pp. 3-7.

Chapter 10

Researching Women's Auto/ Biography as Emancipatory Practice

Sue Mansfield

This chapter reflects the author's extensive experience as a feminist educator and researcher. It focuses on the significance of women's distinctive, and often idiosyncratic, biographical experience as a resource for learning and, in particular, for connecting the personal with the political. What do these distinctive voices bring to the debate about popular and community-based education? How can this kind of 'feminist action research' act back upon the academy?

Background and context

At first glance the casual observer would probably be hard-pressed to identify a coherent theme running through my research over the years. Yes, it has all been within the broad domain of 'community education', but that is an ambiguous domain, one that will always take its meaning from the context in which it is used. Yes, most of it has been about women, but anybody writing about community education is going to find it hard to do otherwise given the composition and nature of the profession in both Scotland and the rest of the United Kingdom. Yes, most of it has been conducted within a feminist research perspective, but some of it was undertaken before I fully understood that that was what I was doing. Yes, much of it has had a historical focus, but that research has now served its purpose of enabling me to connect the present with the past I suspected was there to be found and I have moved on. So has there been a single unifying theme? I would argue that there has, but it is only recently that I have been able to identify it.

The nature of my present research into the discourses to be found in community education practice in Scotland demands a high level of critical reflexivity on my part and I have come to realise how inextricably it, as well as my previous work, has been linked to my own developing autobiography. What I have researched has always been prompted as much by my personal as professional or academic concerns. Furthermore, I have come to appreciate that the very essence of my research and my educational practice has always been the focus on the biographies, mine and others'. At its core is the notion that our biographies are fluid and self-created, that we create them by the lives we lead and the sense we make of our experiences, the meanings we take from them and the way we conceptualise those meanings. Actively creating one's biography by exercising agency on it can be an emancipatory and liberating process in that it makes each of us the subject and not the object of our lives (Alheit, 1995; Stroobants and Wildemeersch, 2000). We become those that act, not those acted upon.

Within the context of my own experiences of second wave feminism and the women's movement of the 1970s and the early 1980s, these were pretty heady ideas and I can trace the genesis of the life I live now back to the life course decisions I took then. I spent the 1980s trying to translate those insights into my professional practice and then into my work with students in the 1990s. However, it is only recently that I have been able to achieve congruence between who I am as a feminist, the pedagogical approach that informs my teaching and what I do as a researcher. This paper attempts to share with the reader the latter part of that journey and hence has a strong element of the autobiographical to it, for which I make no apology. It is thus less an account of my research and teaching and more a history of the development of my thinking. In particular, it discusses some of the issues that have arisen in trying to pursue my research, whilst also attempting to ensure that the process is an emancipatory one for those who choose to participate in it.

In my previous research into the historical antecedents of community-based adult education practice in the United Kingdom and the position and role assigned to women in it, my objective had been not just to critique the accepted histories but also to see if it was possible to construct alternatives. I thus needed to turn to other texts that lie outside of the accepted historical canon of the profession. Auto/biographies of feminist and suffrage activists proved to be useful and major sources as well as transcribed oral histories. Exploring these sources was an important way station on this journey for they were in essence accounts of how these women's lives had changed as a result of their actions and how they made sense of this. But attempting to reconstruct a collective women's history from these individual accounts also raised questions for me about reconstructing the present. If it is possible to reconstruct alternative women's histories, might there not also be alternative women's presents and presences that are both unrecorded and unexamined? I thus set out to see if I could begin to record the present day experiences of women community educators, albeit in a small way, so that their presence was recorded and available for future reference.

Emerging discourses

Initial dialogues with a small group of former students (of the professional qualifying courses for Community Education practitioners at the University of Dundee in Scotland) enabled the development of fresh and challenging insights into the way I originally framed the research and reframe it as it continues. All the initial participants had become involved in the broad field of community education as adults and their accounts of the process by which they had each travelled the road from volunteer activist to practitioner were diverse. However, common to all of them was the theme that essentially this process had been driven by the fact that they were mothers, all looking for financial independence and all making the connection that what they were doing for free as volunteers could be the basis for a paid career. Given that they had all become involved as adults (rather than this being an immediate post-school career choice), the *fact* of their motherhood was not surprising. However, the extent of the biographical *agency* of their experience of mothering (as both daughters and mothers) had not been anticipated, especially by me, a childless woman of broadly the same generation (Mansfield and Erskine, 1998). More crucially, in each case they had only become volunteers because of their children, starting with the playgroup and moving on to work with an older age group each time their children did.

This challenged my thinking because it suggested that these women had primarily become practitioners because they were mothers and not because they were necessarily the social or community activists that I had presumed them to be. It prompted me to reflect on the reasons that candidates being interviewed for a place on the courses articulated for wanting a career in community education. I concluded that I had listened to these biographies and other similar ones before, but that I had clearly not fully 'heard' them at the time. This was followed by the realisation that though I could recall that I had heard many variations of a biography that in essence began 'I am a mother' and concluded 'therefore I want a professional qualification in community education', I could not recall a single instance of one that began 'I am a father'. Instead, I could recall male accounts of political activity, for example in the work place or local government. I started to consider whether these were emerging discourses of maternality, and what: non-maternality, paternality? I also began to wonder what, if any, discernible effect this had on the way they conceptualised their practice. Finally, it prompted questions about the discourse that was shaping my own discourse and which I was beginning to suspect had far more in common with that of their male peers. Why was this important to me? As Zeegers (2000: 1) points out:

> Discourse is social practice, not just verbal or written texts, that constitutes and is constituting of a social self. Human beings thus do not create unified social theories or observe an objective reality, but through discourses construct and constitute social reality. Discourses constrain the possibilities of thought, keeping the 'unthinkable' at bay so that certain discourses are privileged over others by virtue of their unquestioned application. This opens up to us the concepts of marginalised and dominant discourses, and the network of conditions that maintain their position within fields of knowledge.

As an educator and as a feminist, my self-identity is as someone who is primarily engaged in emancipatory activity. How could I not be concerned with the need to uncover and analyse the discourses that were present?

I revisited the historical accounts of community education, both my own and those of others. It struck me forcibly that those writers (e.g. Johnson, 1988; Kirkwood, 1990) who were setting out to lay claim to a radical past were, to borrow from Bauman's (1999) account of the Greek *polis* (cited in Martin, 2000) constructing those histories around men's political activity within the *ecclesia* (the public world of the state). However, the accounts of women's activities that were featured in the histories focused on their role in the development of welfare and social services, accounts that tended to locate women's activity within the private world of the household or *oikos*. It occurred to me that perhaps the discourses I thought I was starting to identify were not discourses of motherhood and fatherhood but those of the *oikos* and the *ecclesia*. My historical work, coming from an avowedly critical, feminist perspective on those histories, was based on reclaiming an activist past that was located within the *ecclesia* for women too. I think those criticisms are still valid in that this division between the *ecclesia* and the *oikos* in the histories was gendered. Loath as I was to acknowledge it, by implicitly valuing the arena of the *ecclesia* over that of the *oikos,* I was implicitly devaluing not just the work undertaken within the more domestic arena of welfare-orientated practice but also the women who were doing it.

I began to be exercised by the notion that this tension between the *ecclesia* and the *oikos* was at the heart of my discomfort at what I was hearing from these ex-students. Was I concerned that despite everything I had been trying to accomplish, a discourse located in the *oikos* was now dominating their practice rather than one arising from the *ecclesia*? However, I became convinced that continuing to perceive these issues as dichotomies was not helpful. Martin (2000) has argued that adult educators should work towards reconstituting the *agora*, the 'dialectical space of civil society . . . between the private world of the household *(oikos)* and the public world of the state *(ecclesia)*'. It seemed to me that the crucial question facing me was 'What was I doing in my teaching and my research to reconstitute the *agora*?' However, if I was to try and bring them together into a personally reconstituted *agora* I needed first to critically reflect on my own pedagogical and research practices and the curriculum and knowledge they were delivering.

Cornerstone principles

Identifying as a feminist is at the core of my being. It is the source of both my motivation and commitment to promoting and adopting emancipatory approaches to adult education and it has been equally important to me that I work within a research paradigm that embodies the same principles. Hence, my research can never be just an exercise in detached data gathering and critical interpretation of it. I seek instead to adopt a feminist epistemology that has also been influenced by Freirean consciousness raising pedagogical approaches, and recent developments in critically reflexive action research and collaborative inquiry (see Reason and Bradbury, 2000). Within such a research paradigm, people are not 'data'; instead, the purpose of my research is to legitimately enable them not only to give voice to their experience but also to critically reflect on it. There are thus four cornerstone principles around which I am seeking to build the inquiry process.

First, I am committed to conducting my research within a feminist framework. However, feminism is not just a theoretical construct but a lived experience and it cannot be divorced from the way I and other feminist researchers live our lives (Mies, 1983; Stanley, 1990). The characteristic that more than any other distinguishes feminist research and researchers is the idea that it should enable women to make greater sense of their condition and position in society. There is no single, agreed feminist methodology (Williams, 1993; Maguire, 2001) but central to all of them is the recognition that research is not, and never can be, value free; on the contrary, the aim of all feminist research should be not just to study the world but to change it. Ramazanoglu (1989) emphasises that what truly distinguishes feminist research is not that it is *on* women but that it is *for* women, in which case female, feminist researchers can never be disinterested inquirers. The critiques of feminist research which are based on rational scientific paradigms (Hammersly, 1992) make the assumption that the research process can stand apart from the uses to which the results of it are put. This position denies that the act of knowing is an intrinsically political act and appears not to recognise that maintaining the status quo is as much of a political act as seeking to change it (Griffiths, 1998).

A second important consideration for me is that whereas traditional positivist social and educational research has generally not conceptualised the relationship between the researcher and the researched as being a power relationship between people, feminist researchers have done so. Ramazanoglu (1992) points out that it is their commitment to ways of knowing that avoid subordination which unites feminist researchers despite the diversity of thought amongst them on other matters. I am in sympathy with Oakley (1990) who not only rejected traditional interview techniques because they treated interviewees as objectified sources of data but also because interviews have no personal meaning in terms of social interaction. Like her, I reject the notion of needing to keep research 'hygienic' in favour of one which acknowledges self-disclosure on the part of the researcher as one way of maintaining the feminist integrity of the relationship between myself and the participants. One consequence of this is that I seek to establish a relationship between researcher and participants based on reciprocity and the dismantling of barriers rather than the maintenance of them. Research is therefore a process of collaborative inquiry. As a result, I share my own experiences as both a woman and a practitioner where relevant, and I acknowledge that I am not a disinterested observer and openly share this with participants.

This gives rise to the third cornerstone – the need to maintain a critically reflexive perspective:

> ... a heightened awareness of the self in the process of knowledge creation, a clarification of how one's beliefs have been socially con-

structed (self-revelation) and how these values are impacting on interaction and data collection in the research setting (Grbich, 2004: 28-9).

The function of reflexivity in this context is to 'expose the underlying assumptions on which arguments and stances are built' (Holland, 1999) and to recognise that we are often enmeshed in the very structures we are researching (Weil, 1997). I am, thus, continually examining both my own experiences and what the research tells me about myself as a practitioner, as a researcher and as a woman – not just what it tells me about the participants. In such a context, ethical and quality concerns cannot be separated from epistemology (Lincoln and Goober, 1987), but this is all the more reason for being ready continuously to critically examine how this affects the way the research is framed as well as the way the data is interpreted.

Fourth, it is important to me that the inquiry process should validate the experience of participants and that it should also enable them to critically reflect on it. The consciousness raising process was central to the women's movement of the 1970s and also to those approaches to adult education which claim to be emancipatory: that process of *praxis* whereby the bringing of a critical analysis to bear on one's experience enables the deconstruction and reconstruction of experience out of which grows the creation of new knowledge. However, my experience of trying to reconstruct the historical record has made me acutely aware that such new knowledge, whilst undoubtedly of continued significance to the individuals involved, can so easily turn out to be transitory or ephemeral in the wider arena if it is not also recorded in some way. I decided, therefore, to focus my research on the co-creation and recording of the autobiographies of women practitioners. As Cotterill and Letherby (1993) point out, the development of such narratives is a significant way of giving voice to otherwise silenced women and enabling them to critically reflect as part of the creation process. It also allows them to choose how they tell their stories, validate their individual and collective experiences and enable these to be shared with a wider audience with a view to bringing about change. I am also seeking to explore how the research process can itself be an emancipatory process, one that generates a radical feminist pedagogy and curriculum (Chovanec and Scott, 1993; Walters and Manicom, 1996). It is a practical exploration of how the *oikos* and *ecclesia* can be brought into dialectical relationship and how women can be enabled to move between these two worlds, as symbolised by the discourses to be found in the historical accounts.

Research as feminist pedagogy

I have been much influenced in my own practice by the work of Paulo Freire (1972) and would share Foley's (1999) view that 'the unlearning of dominant, oppressive ideologies and discourses and the learning of insurgent, resistant ones are central to processes of emancipatory change'. Foley acknowledges that this is not straightforward and suggests that it is most likely to be authentically achieved when the learning processes embody the five conditions:

- the learning group must be representative of an oppressed or marginalised group
- the experience, assumptions and social position of members of the learning group must be relatively similar
- the learning group must develop a 'structure of equality'
- members of the learning group must have the motivation and the time to reflect critically on their subjective experience
- members of the learning group must gain a 'theoretical distance to personal experience'. (Foley, 1999: 50)

Incorporating these conditions into my prior professional practice and current academic teaching has at times been problematic but not incongruent. The tensions that arise from trying to incorporate these principles into research practice become apparent immediately one substitutes the word 'sample' for 'learning group'. Questions of bias, validity and rigour are inevitable, especially from colleagues working within a more traditional scientific social research paradigm. Such questions are not to be lightly dismissed but are based on the premise that there are universal truths and rules to be discovered within a unitary reality. However, social research is located in knowledge-producing communities and cannot be divorced from them (McKenzie et al, 1997). Rather than denying this, I have instead sought not only to acknowledge it but to make that social practice the focus of my research. The members of the co-inquiry learning groups that are at its core are clearly engaged in a social practice that through a process of critical reflexivity is deconstructing and reconstructing their personal and professional world.

My starting point can, therefore, be summarised as being the explicit acknowledgement that the personal is political. This is not just a nostalgic harking back to the slogan of the women's movement of my youth but a key feature of the development of a methodology that seeks to forge a synthesis between feminist research and feminist pedagogy. As Maguire (2001: 65) points out:

Feminist action research seeks to connect the articulated, contextualised personal with the often hidden or invisible structural and social institutions that define and shape our lives. How *do* things work? How do we contribute to the workings? How can we collectively change them?

Similarly, Mills (1970) contends that 'social science deals with problems of biography, of history, and of their intersections within social structures'. The statement is equally true of emancipatory curricula. Mills also attempts to draw a distinction between 'the personal troubles of milieu' and 'the public issues of social structure' whereas Martin (2000) argues that the role of the popular educator is to draw attention to how the former is often the direct consequence of the latter; to promote the sort of critical reflection that enables learners to identify the collective, structural dimensions of their personal experiences and to act accordingly on the basis of that knowledge. Thus, though the starting point for the research process is the building of, followed by critical reflection on, the autobiographies of the participants, it is only a starting point. Stroobants and Wildemeersch (2000) make the distinction between such biographical reflectivity and biographical agency and suggest that engaging exclusively in the former will result in an emphasis on 'thinking about and comparing her possible selves' whereas extending the process to include the latter enables the finding of 'a balance between the reconstruction of past choices and events and the construction of a project for the future. She has realised one of her dormant unlived lives'. This distinction is especially important in this context and it echoes the point that Stanley (1990) makes that feminism is concerned with both the epistemological (ways of knowing) and also the ontological (ways of being). I thus wanted to ensure that the research process encompassed both reflexivity and conscious biographical agency.

The epistemology and methodology of this research has thus provided me with what has at times felt like the very risky but exciting opportunity to redefine emancipatory pedagogical activities as data gathering instruments. I began by reviewing the techniques and methods I employed as a practitioner and lecturer to deliver an emancipatory curriculum. All of them are designed to enable critical reflection on past experience but as Brookfield (2000) points out, criticality is a contested idea. He identifies three extant traditions which I could detect to a greater or lesser extent in my own practice. First, there is the *ideology critique* where the focus is on:

> . . . the ways in which people learn to recognise how uncritically accepted and dominant ideologies are embedded in everyday situations and practices. As an educational activity ideology critique focuses on helping people come to an awareness of how capitalism shapes social relations and imposes – often without our knowledge – belief systems and assumptions (i.e. ideologies) that justify and maintain economic and political inequity. (Brookfield, 2000: 51)

This might initially appear to be of great relevance to my present work, especially as it has informed my professional practice in the past, conducted as it was within the consciousness raising tradition of the women's movement. The second tradition is that of *psychoanalysis and psychotherapy* which 'emphasises criticality in adulthood as the identification and reappraisal of inhibitions acquired in childhood as a result of various traumas' (Brookfield, 2000: 52).

The latter is clearly not a tradition that I am drawing on for I am uncomfortable with the notion that to be a woman is to be traumatised, and, whilst the former initially might appear relevant, it is one that I have also rejected as inadequate in this context. Both of these traditions are rooted in an objectivist epistemology and the notion 'that there are truths "out there" waiting to be revealed and that if people study them long enough they will stumble on these' (Brookfield, 2000). But my experience of working for over twenty-five years with women who bring a diverse range of experiences with them has led me to the conclusion that there are no universal truths out there because there is no single oppressor of women to be identified. Ideology critique as an educational approach essentially developed out of Marxist/ socialist critiques of capitalism and is too narrow for my purposes because it can only accommodate with great difficulty the notion that the oppressed can also be the oppressor and that this depends on context. My own experience tells me that a broader approach that recognises the complexity of women's oppression is required. My primary identity as a woman means that I can readily identify myself as someone oppressed by a patriarchal, capitalist hegemony but I remember acutely, with pain and embarrassment, the moment when I was first confronted with the notion that as a *white* woman I was party to the oppression that black women and women of colour experienced. My own mixed race heritage counted for nought in a context where I had been brought up as white, was regarded as white by nearly everyone I met and had never knowingly experienced racial prejudice. Reflecting on this over the years, I have come to understand that as a woman I am a member of one of the communities of the oppressed but that as a white, able-bodied, academically and professionally qualified woman I am also a member of a number of communities of the preferred (King, 1989). I cannot easily resign my membership of them. The recognition that oppression is contextual means that I tend to bring a subjectivist rather than objectivist conception of knowledge to my research. As such, my approach falls within the third tradition identified by Brookfield as *pragmatic constructivism*, where the emphasis is on:

> ... the way people learn how to construct, and deconstruct, their own experiences and meanings. Constructivism rejects universals and generalizable truths, and focuses instead on the variability of how people make interpretations of their experience. This strand of thought maintains that events happen to us but that experiences are constructed by us. (Brookfield, 2000: 52)

I am aware of the tensions and contradictions that are thus brought into being as a result of wishing to engage in an emancipatory action research process that is epistemologically based on a specific ideological critique: one that recognises the power of discourses to create an unquestioned hegemony, whilst at the same time wishing to remain true to a feminist ontology that is committed to validating women's experiences and enabling them to discover and use their own authentic voices to make them visible. If those voices sometimes say things that I would rather not hear, that is my problem not theirs. For the moment, I see no easy way of reconciling these contradictions and, indeed, think that they are partly responsible for the richness of the ongoing research process.

Achieving congruence

I began by inviting the reader to share with me this part of my journey on which I am seeking to achieve congruence between who I am as a feminist, the pedagogical approach that informs my teaching and what I do as a researcher. Have I reached my journey's end? No, even though the first stage of it was relatively easy. Ensuring that my current teaching practice within the academy was congruent with both my feminist ideals and my previous professional practice as an emancipatory educator has been achieved. It is entirely congruent that in the context of preparing students for professional practice I should model in my work with them one of the approaches that they might wish later to adopt themselves. I might now call this 'critical reflexivity' and do it within the context of my social science and research teaching. However, working with students to become critically reflexive, enabling them to identify and question the discourses which shape the way they view and interpret their world, is indistinguishable from the work I did previously outside the academy. Academic freedom gives me control of my seminar room and the opportunity to pursue within it an emancipatory curriculum that might well be denied to me outside it in the current policy context in Scotland. I think that my seminar room is a twenty-first century version of the *agora* where my students are actively engaged in examining the dynamic relationship between the *oikos* as typified by their personal and home lives and the *ecclesia* as the context for their professional practice.

Similarly, I have achieved a degree of congruence between being a feminist and the underlying principles I seek to build my research practice and teaching on. I am, after all, standing on the shoulders of giantesses and can look to a respected body of feminist researchers and emergent methodologies. My students tend to respond positively to my research teaching, mainly I suspect because they warm to me as an iconoclast who might set them exercises as part of their research training that they find strange, unexpected or uncomfortable but who also sets them free from the language of samples, data sets and tables and many of the constraints of positivist, empirical research. Convincing colleagues who locate their research within those more traditional paradigms that the research that I do is as valid as theirs has proved to be a little harder, especially with regard to my use of co-inquiry learning groups as both the source and the method for data collection. For myself, however, I find no incongruence here because I am generating data that is rooted in the authentic experiences of the participants and they are party to the way that data is interpreted, and it is this which gives it its validity.

So why do I think that I have not reached my journey's end? Mainly, because I have yet to find a way of resolving a particular ethical dilemma to my own satisfaction. The methodology I have developed is firmly based on redefining the power relationship between researcher and researched, but I can never totally eradicate the inbuilt power relationship that exists between myself and my students as long as the university requires me to mark, assess and grade their own research. Thus for the present, though my research feeds and nourishes my teaching and vice versa, and the students I work with are, I think, equipped to engage in emancipatory practice and action research themselves, the participants in my research are practitioners, some of them ex-students, because I am reluctant to run the risk of exploiting the student/tutor relationship. But the current solution to this dilemma is also an opportunity because it enables me to engage in a continuing and dynamic relationship between the academy and professional practitioners in the field of community-based adult education.

In this paper I have travelled over some very mixed terrain, including the auto/biographical, the practical and the theoretical. I hope that I have at the very least provided an insight into the development of my thinking and the emergent methodology for my research and provoked some self-reflection on the part of the reader. I would stress, however, that this journey is a continuing one, and I expect the need to maintain a high degree of personal critical reflexivity on my own part will be the one thing I can be sure of as it proceeds.

References

Alheit, P. (1995), 'The "biographical question" as a challenge to adult education', *Adult and Continuing Education*, 12(1), pp. 75-92.

Bauman, Z. (1999), *In Search of Politics*, Cambridge: Polity.

Brookfield, S. (2000), 'Contesting criticality: epistemological and practical contradictions in critical reflection'. Paper presented at the Adult Education Research Conference, Vancouver, Canada.

Chovanec, D.M. and Scott, S.M. (1993), 'Critical philosophy-in-action: power and *praxis*'. Conference paper presented to the Canadian Association for the Study of Adult Education.

Cotterill, P. and Letherby, G. (1993), 'Weaving stories: personal auto/biographies in feminist research', *Sociology*, 27(1), pp. 67-79.

Foley, G. (1999), *Learning in Social Action*, Leicester: NIACE.

Freire, P. (1972), *Pedagogy of the Oppressed*, Harmondsworth: Penguin.

Grbich, C. (2004), *New Approaches in Social Research*, London: Sage.

Griffiths, M. (1998), *Educational Research for Social Justice: Getting off the Fence*, Milton Keynes: Open University Press.

Hammersley, M. (1992), 'On feminist methodology', *Sociology*, 26(2), pp. 187-206.

Holland, R. (1999), 'Reflexivity', *Human Relations*, 52(4), pp. 519-50.

Johnson, R. (1988), ' "Really useful knowledge" 1790-1850: memories for education in the 1980s' in Lovett, T. (ed.), *Radical Approaches to Adult Education*, London: Routledge, pp. 3-34.

King, M. (1989), 'On transformation: from a conversation with Mel King', *Harvard Educational Review*, 59(4), pp. 504-19.

Kirkwood, C. (1990), *Vulgar Eloquence*, Edinburgh: Polygon.

Lather, P. (1991), *Getting Smart: Feminist Pedagogy and Research With/In the Postmodern*, London: Routledge.

Lincoln, Y. and Goober, E. (1987), 'Ethics: the failure of positivist science'. Paper presented to the American Educational Research Association.

Maguire, P. (2001), 'Uneven ground: feminisms and action research' in Reason, P. and Bradbury, H. (eds), *Handbook of Action Research and Participatory Inquiry and Practice*, London: Sage, pp. 59-69.

Mansfield, S. and Erskine, S. (1998), 'The lass o'pairts: women returners in community education', *Canadian and International Education*, 27(1), pp. 1-11.

Martin, I. (2000), 'Reconstituting the *agora*: towards an alternative politics of lifelong learning'. Paper presented at the Adult Education Research Conference, Vancouver, Canada.

McKenzie, G., Usher, R. and Powell, J. (eds), (1997), *Understanding Social Research: Perspectives on Methodology and Practice*, London: Routledge.

Mies, M. (1983), 'Towards a methodology for feminist research' in Bowles, G. and Duelli Klein, R. (eds), *Theories of Women's Studies*, London: Routledge and Kegan Paul.

Mills, C. Wright (1970), *The Sociological Imagination*, Harmondsworth: Penguin.

Oakley, A. (1990), 'Interviewing women: a contradiction in terms' in Roberts, H. (ed.), *Doing Feminist Research*, London: Routledge and Kegan Paul, pp. 30-61.

Ramazanoglu, S. (1989), 'Improving on sociology: the problems of taking a feminist standpoint', *Sociology*, 23(3), pp. 427-42.

Reason, P. and Bradbury, H. (eds), (2000), *Handbook of Action Research: Participative Inquiry and Practice*, London: Sage.

Stanley, L. (ed.), (1990), *Feminist Praxis: Research, Theory and Epistomology in Feminist Sociology*, London: Routledge and Kegan Paul.

Stroobants, V. and Wildemeersch, D. (2000), 'Work? I have learned to live with it: a biographical persepective on work, learning and living . . . more than just a story'. Conference paper presented to the Canadian Adult Education Research Conference.

Walters, S. and Manicom, L. (eds), (1996), *Gender in Popular Education: Methods for Empowerment*, London: Zed Books.

Weil, S. (1997), 'Postgraduate education and lifelong learning as collaborative enquiry: an emergent model' in Burgess, R. (ed.), *Beyond the First Degree*, Buckingham: RHE/Open University, pp. 119-39.

Williams, A. (1993), 'Diversity and agreement in feminist ethnography', *Sociology* 27(4), pp. 578-89.

Zeegers, M. (2000), 'Accessing Foucault: an introduction for the social researcher'. Paper presented at the University of Ballarat Research Conference, Ballarat, Australia.

Chapter 11

The Methodology of 'Systemisation' and its Relevance to the Academy

Maria Clara Buena Fischer

This chapter argues that in both the production and socialisation of knowledge, popular educators employed in universities should strive to work for and in conjunction with others, not on their own. The distinctively Latin American process of 'systematisation' offers one example of how popular social movements have attempted to link learning theories with practice, something that is also important in higher education. Drawing on her experience of working with 'movements' in Brazil, the author describes and analyses her attempts to apply the process of systematisation to her own work as an academic and as an integral part of her wider commitment to solidarity and social change.

Universities have an important role to play in building any future society which would be based on the principles of justice and would put people, not profit or the market, at its centre. Towards that end they require to constantly rethink the ways in which they produce knowledge. Those of us working in universities need to try and *socialise* knowledge *for* others; to *produce* knowledge *with* others and break with political-epistemological frameworks which strengthen the culture of *banking education* (Freire, 1975), something still deeply rooted in all of us, both in and outside the university.

It is not a new challenge, of course. Freire's *Pedagogy of the Oppressed*, for example, was written at the end of the 1960s! But it has currently been given new life through the gradual demystification of the dominant, neoliberal ideology, with popular progressive forces everywhere opening up spaces for exchanging experiences and building joint projects. The various World Social Forums in Porto Alegre, Brazil are a prime example. The Forums recognise the urgent need to produce new knowledge which could influence policies in a range of areas such as economics, politics and education. Universities are thus being called on to engage in effective dialogue with different social actors, to reclaim their social role – autonomously and with commitment – in confronting the levels of exclusion and discrimination experienced every-where throughout the world.

In this context, as a methodological tool rooted in the experience of popular education, 'systematisation' has a role to play both in social move-ments and in universities. This paper presents an exploration of the nature and purpose of systematisation followed by my analysis of one ongoing attempt, within a university, to use systematisation in the production of knowledge.

Systematisation: a tool for enabling collective reflection on practice

In a recent article, Elza Falkembach (2000) describes and reflects on the process of systematisation carried out within a programme called *Training the Trainers in Professional Education* run by the Brazilian Central Workers Union (CUT) in 1998 and 1999, an experience in which I myself was an active participant.

Kane suggests that ' "systematisation", usually takes the form of a written document, it is the attempt to bring order to, reflect on, interpret and make sense of a practice which intervenes in this constantly changing reality' (2001: 20). It can be characterised as a tool enabling people to think and act as subjects of *praxis* because it allows people to 'recuperate' and reflect on an experience they have shared (the text being an important resource, though not the only one, in presenting the results of the systematisation). It is a systematic, collective process in the production and socialisation of knowledge about practice; it presupposes a commitment of those involved to the transformation of oppressive relations; the results of a systematisation should intervene in practice – while the process is still going on – and should help socialise the experience for the benefit of other groups. Systematisation implies, then, a description and analysis of practice by those who experience it. Those who are involved say what they know about the experience, the bare facts of what happened, and the narrative which links events together and their own intentions throughout. The different interpretations of these facts and events are then brought together. The analysis carried out seeks to explain how particular facts and events are interconnected but also, at the same time, to challenge such an explanation. Other elements for analysis are the problems, tensions and potential opportunities, which present themselves as events develop. The whole process of systematisation is an instrument for understanding a group's shared experience, with a view to improving, changing or transforming its practice or, indeed, that of others.

In the process of systematisation an exchange of knowledge (philosophical, scientific and technical) takes place between the participants. Collectively, pulling together their differing perspectives, they seek to find out as much as possible about the research topic. Attitudes and values come into play: you are challenged to be open-minded towards others and also towards yourself, to be open to changing your way of thinking and acting.

As a tool for collective reflection on practice, the roots of systematisation lie in the 1980s, with the involvement of professional social scientists in the practices of Adult Education, Participatory Planning and Participatory Research – all carried out in a spirit of working for emancipation. In the 1990s, systematisation began to take on an important role in addressing the countless questions and uncertainties springing up around that particular historical moment. Its purpose related to (a) questioning and developing the knowledge produced by and with popular social movements and (b) publicising what these liberatory practices can teach us, thus contributing to the struggle for hegemony in society. With this understanding, the Latin American Council for Adult Education (CEAAL) created a Support Programme for Systematisation in 1993.

Falkembach (2000) also comments on the question of paradigms and systematisation. Drawing together the views of various authors, she says there is clearly no single paradigm underpinning the process of systematisation. Regarding the case in question – the training programme for the Trade Union movement – the process of description, systematic reflection and transformation of practice was inspired by a historical-dialectical (but non-deterministic) perspective which included the dimensions of culture and intentionality as well as an appreciation of the different meanings participants attribute to the topic (or the experience) being researched: its uniqueness is guaranteed. 'Perfection (in systematisation) is not measured by external parameters but by the possibilities of the individuals who experience the processes. Systematisation, therefore, is a word which can be invested and disinvested with meanings; a word which can be dressed up in images which are a reflection of life' (Falkembach, 2000: 30).

Implicit in systematisation, then, is an ongoing dialogue for emancipation. For Freire, the radical transformation of the relationship between educator and learner means 'to conceive of teaching and learning as two dialectically related processes within each person' (Allman, 1989: 180). In this radically different view of the relationship between teachers and learners in relation to knowledge, the educator becomes a teacher-learner and the learner a learner-teacher. Only through dialogue can such an educational practice be developed. 'Dialogue becomes a confirmation of the epistemological relations between those involved in the act of knowing' (Freire, 1974: 21). Thus, we have to insist that Freire's understanding of dialogue is not that it is a technique for encouraging participation in 'discussion'. Dialogue is a revolutionary form of communication which enables those involved in the educational process to search for an increasingly authentic and deeper knowledge of reality. Dialogue, then, is a critical *praxis* because it represents a struggle to unite, dialectically, reflection and action. At the same time, it is the result of changed relationships between teachers and learners in relation to knowledge – as well as a medium for transforming these relations. Problematisation is an essential element of dialogue. Through dialogue, participants are encouraged to problematise established knowledge and their own empirical experience; both are to be researched (Fischer, 1997: 41-2).

A case study

The experience under discussion took place over two consecutive modules of a Masters course in education in my own university. One module was entitled 'Problems and Research in Education II' and the other, a follow-up to the first, on the initiative of the students, was 'The Construction of Knowledge: A Multifaceted Process'.

The first module focused on deepening students' understanding of the theoretical and methodological processes involved in research-related activity. The main contents were (a) the relationship between theoretical and empirical dimensions at different stages of research and (b) the relationship between paradigms, methodology and the act of writing in conducting research. Students attending the modules varied widely in terms of their chosen topic of research, their theoretical orientation, the maturity of their writing, their political tendencies, their gender and race and their levels of awareness of – and involvement in – the world of education.

Following an initial group analysis to identify potential problems or special needs, the module began. From the start, students were encouraged to consider everything occurring in class as a topic for reflection, to write down a record of each meeting's discussion and to produce other texts geared more specifically towards their research projects. When produced, these texts acquired an ongoing mediating function between stimulating creative thinking, on the one hand, and crystallising our thoughts, on the other.

From the beginning I tried to encourage a positive atmosphere in the group, a basic requirement for fruitful discussion. The process of producing the text became an important way of mediating our reflections and, at the same time, of collectively developing the group. In the written texts we registered the 'content' of these reflections, both the subjects under discussion and our reactions and attitudes towards them. Through the development of the group as well as its mediating text, the 'collective' dimension received a lot of positive stimulation which in turn engendered a feeling of solidarity with each individual's project; it also meant that the world of education, the wider theme relating to all participants, could become the common object of study, though looked at from a variety of perspectives.

One of our presuppositions was that a favourable learning climate exists among those who share equality of status and similar interests. Conducting a piece of research and communicating this through a text which would be acceptable to the university was (and remains) both a source of tension – given that the institution is so permeated with individualism and competition – and a great opportunity for the advanced development of a group which was already keen to engage in discussion, such an important step for the serious production of knowledge.

As a theoretical and practical basis for my own contribution, I relied heavily on my personal experience of systematisation from my previous work as a popular educator in social movements. And I had particular views with regard to dialogue as *praxis*. I also drew from studies on the importance of the act of writing in educational research (Marques, 1998) and the complex relationship between work and education (Arroyo, 1982). All this convinced me of the need to experiment with a pedagogical research practice directed by: a practical articulation, a dialectic between theory and practice; the promotion of individual and collective pieces of writing; dialogue and vigilance on the material aspects influencing human personal development. And to experiment also with systematisation within the university, the locus of my current professional practice.

I was convinced of the need to capture, methodically, the essence of what was being said in each meeting: I did not want to lose any 'new' insights which came out of these discussions. But in accompanying this process of knowledge production, I did not want to engage in the bureaucratisation of thought either (neither that of the students nor my own). As an educator devoted to freedom, Paulo Freire always treated with great care this necessary dialectical relationship between knowledge which comes from experience and knowledge which has been acquired academically or otherwise. For me, inspired by the idea of systematisation, the process of engaging in, thinking about and communicating classroom dialogue would make a real and profound contribution to everyone's learning.

Both the content and the method of producing knowledge, as well as the people taking part, would constitute the topic of research. With the advantage of being both the 'object' and the 'subjects' of research – present at all times to construct, reconstruct and deconstruct representations, concepts and categories – the students identified what needed to be described and analysed as they went along. We became aware, in doing so, that the process of knowledge construction experienced in the classes contained many similarities with the dynamics of teaching and research. To highlight one specific element, much is discussed, on the one hand, about the non-neutrality of the researcher but also, on the other, the question of the teacher's directiveness and, likewise, the difficult and deliberate task of showing respect to those people being researched. To turn the common experience shared in the classroom into a topic for research was a very significant exercise for learning more about the complexities of this question in so far as we took the collective experience, which was sometimes written up, as the focus of our attention.

So, as a group, everyone – or at least a significant number of the participants – took ownership of this process and we began. It was on one special moment that everything started to really take off. One day, in the module on Research and Educational Problems II, I was unable to attend and the students became aware of the need to write up their discussions in order to communicate what had been said. It was the first 'collective' text and naturally took the title 'Writing Collectively'. This is part of systematisation: it 'patches' things up, adds on extra dimensions and develops people's autonomy.

From that moment on, in every class we had a text before us which had recorded the discussions of the previous class, enriched by the particular interpretation and theoretical strengths of whoever happened to be that week's author. There was variety in the way final texts articulated the different contributions of the group members. Generally, one person was responsible for writing up the version which would be read in class; the others sent their contributions, usually by email. The text undoubtedly became an essential mediator and companion to our reflections, helping identify new questions to be explored and, in the process, further encouraging our collective involvement in the module.

Five texts in total were produced in this way, each one passing through the whole process. The titles varied: 'Writing Collectively'; 'Reflections on

Conducting Research'; 'Research: A Continuous Development'; 'Reflections from the Defence of a Dissertation'; 'Ways of Writing'. These all came under collective authorship, expressed by acknowledging the names of all those involved in the task of contributing to the development of the texts. This was a tense but gratifying practice which, from my point of view, contributed to breaking down the strong competitive and individualistic culture of academia.

At the end of the module the students requested a continuation of this experience. Six students organised themselves to ask the course co-ordinating team to put on a module entitled 'A Popular Approach to Constructing Knowledge'. When the request came in with this title it made me think about the contribution popular education had to make to the academy. So, from the desire to continue with discussions and dialogues mediated by group-authored texts and with a vague notion of doing this through a 'popular approach', after much discussion we decided to call the new module 'The Construction of Knowledge: A Multifaceted Process'.

We defined our objectives as: to enhance our understanding of dimensions of the process of knowledge construction; to continue systematising the reflections made by participants inside and outside the class, including relevant bibliographical references; to enable the module to contribute even to dissertations. Among the chosen contents we opted for an in-depth study of the construction of the 'object' and 'subject' in both research and teaching; methodological procedures for knowledge construction, as used in epistemo-logical approaches such as action and participatory research; the question of interdisciplinarity; we even decided to look critically at how we ourselves constructed knowledge in our own relationships as members of the group. We effectively problematised the course content in our discussions and, naturally, we agreed to document these discussions as a way of both deepening our thinking and as an exercise in collectively producing a text.

After defining what we wanted, the group confronted some unforeseen issues. The group was no longer the same as before. This proved difficult to address because 'being a group' had become a central element in facilitating reflection and the production of texts. Only six members of the original group remained, and they were now joined by two newcomers who were not aware of the importance of the collective production of knowledge, expressed in written documents, as a key mediator in the work of the class. This situation influenced the way in which the module was conducted, its potential for development and the tensions experienced within it. Of many possible comments, I just highlight the fact that there was tension between the development of the group, on the one hand, and the collective production of knowledge, on the other.

A whole process of negotiation had to be carried out in this group because it had now become more autonomous from the structure of the postgraduate programme as a whole. The module was by and large the students' own initiative, and it was breaking new ground. The participation of new members meant the group had to explain more clearly what it was that it 'wanted to continue with' and check to see if there really was a consensus. Tensions rose to the surface between the individual and collective dimensions of the process of knowledge construction and in the constitution of the group itself. These had not been properly noticed in the previous module. The group had to revisit the original task and ask itself: What exactly was our proposal again? What was it we were writing? A record of discussions? Stories? Collective texts? Which authorities were effectively involved? More 'theoretical' interests concerning 'the collective' and 'groups' intermingled with more existential and political desires to build effective collectives and groups both inside and outside of the academy.

The tension generated showed that there was a clear need to make a political-pedagogical decision with regard to the authorship and production method of these texts. In the end the text was more than a text: it was a challenge to the academy's way of working. The group chose to continue documenting the discussions carried out in class although this time from the particular research interest of each person, with a 'more individual' author-ship. The idea was to try this method, which some experienced as a backwards step, and then later come back to a properly collective authorship and process of knowledge construction. A difficult task! Of the eight, three of the 'records of discussions' took as their focus the process of collective construction of knowledge. In the end, four people from the group even produced a small text, already a form of collective production itself, which they presented for discussion by all the students on the post-graduate programme, with a view to evaluating the experience of 'the collective construction of knowledge and texts' carried out in the two modules. One person even produced a more theoretical, individual text on the process of working in groups; he did not directly deal with the *experience* of the module, however. All the group members considered the process to have been positive in terms of their individual growth and development. With regard to specifically collective issues, many questions remained for those more interested in delving deeper into this political and pedagogical apprenticeship. In this group the will to work together remained after completion of the module.

Gradually there materialised a desire to produce a deeper analysis of what had been experienced and to present this analysis in the form of a text. We decided to start from the main questions which came up: to what extent is it possible to build a collective? How do the questions of 'imposition' and 'proposal' fit into this process? How do we deal with the expectations of the participants? To what extent do the tensions help build or obstruct the process of building a collective? What is the political dimension to the process of collective construction of knowledge (and of the text)? In connection with that, what is the role of personal commitment and group pressure on the individual to be part of the process? Beginning with these questions, those who decided to keep going are once again analysing their experience. Many are finishing their dissertations, seeing them as part of the same process; others are looking for theoretical tools to deepen their analysis. One important phase in this systematisation occurred in the small group which stayed on 'right to the end'. We met up to analyse all the material written up on the modules and to check on what it already contained regarding representations, concepts and arguments on the various themes associated with the issues emanating from the evaluations. The documentation and the recording of discussions was analysed. Each person wrote something, taking one of the key questions as his or her focus. The process is not yet complete and it may not be possible to finish it as a group exercise. If we manage to keep going we will 'synthesise' our discussions in a collective construction of knowledge of our experience.[1] We do not yet know the format of this text: it could be one single text in which we all participate or different individual comments or 'windows' within an agreed, common structure. Again, in the very act of re-creating the text, some creative tensions will remain. We have learned that we are problematising our experience, with a collective commitment to 'unveil' the mysteries of the group and, in doing so problematise our theory.

Reflections on the process

Part of what is learned can only be gleaned from the experiential nature of this process. Systematisation goes as far as a group is able to go, another lesson from popular education. This understanding of systematisation leads us to reflect more deeply on the pedagogical practice and unique experience of the modules under discussion.

One of our many queries is the extent to which educational practice was problematised by the participants when they were carrying out their research. If it was, this suggests that the process highlighted the reproductive interests of formal education, in our case of the university and its individuals. Systematisation and dialogue would have maintained their political and epistemological radicalism. If it was not, the reproductive interests of the academy would have domesticated the methodology of systematisation in popular education.

For some time now, challenges have been made to the culture of banking education within universities. Miguel Arroyo, for example, insists on the need to pay close attention to the many material processes affecting human training and education. Reflecting on one of his experiences of working in a university he makes important points which force me to think more deeply about my own experience:

> But among the students who work in schools or popular education, there is still a perception that after attempting to find a link between theory and practice in the real work of the Masters Programme, they then *know* how to integrate theory and practice in their pedagogical work in schools or in popular education projects. Practice then becomes the central focus of programmes, of teaching history, geography or language. The group working on the Masters assimilated a new method through their own practice. What the group learned came about through the type of work jointly developed by the students and their teachers.

> The student's social practice outside and inside the Masters course becomes a learning experience when it is reflected on collectively . . . The working group would be the space where students and teachers re-educate themselves to listen to, read and learn about the theoretical dimensions underpinning practice . . . Remember that we start from the supposition that in all educational activity in school or in society there are inherent theoretical expressions which ought to be acknowledged and theoretically structured. (Arroyo, 1982: 125)

Further on the author tells us that in his experience what was happening was an attempt 'to introduce within the university structure itself, in isolation from the world of production, the pedagogical force which derives from social practice and work-experience' (1982: 127).

Note that we are talking about the social aspects of their work or the specific way in which group members participated in the process of the production of new knowledge and a new educational practice. This is the basic link giving identity and strength to the group. When this participation is weak or formal, the group doesn't meet and tends to take refuge in traditional, individualistic academic practices. The collective production of intellectual work is only possible in formal education when it engages with the social process of knowledge production, which happens in the struggle to create new social relations (Arroyo, 1982).

This is not the place to describe the specific experience referred to by the author but I will outline some of the deeper questions he highlights with regard to academic structures, education materials and training and education. Arroyo (1982) claims that 'no workplace is neutral, far less a workplace concerned with education':

> The divisions between departments and areas of specialisation appear artificial when confronted with the interdependence and totality of the real focus of a group's work. The teacher, joining the group, is obliged to redefine his previous role as a specialist in a particular area of knowledge. On the other hand, knowledge of the real world through social practice gives a certain unpredictability to the group, a characteristic which is inherent to history's own dynamics and which enters into conflict with the static character of the organisation of our programmes (of education). How can we unite the official curriculum with the demands of the real world? (115)

This question can only be answered with a flexible structure. In this sense self-organisation and real, historical, integrated knowledge are inseparable in the working group. To seek the latter without the former is utopic.

Miguel Arroyo's reflections problematise things even further by arguing strongly for a process of knowledge production which will challenge the 'method of appropriation-expropriation of knowledge and thinking' (in capitalist society) (114). All of this helps us to understand our experience better and to explore the potential of so-called systematisation in the production of emancipatory knowledge. There is an undoubted need for us to continue experimenting with new forms and contents within our overriding, guiding principles.

Conclusion: systematisation and the academy

Does the experience outlined here mean that systematisation was used as a 'pedagogical technique', divorced from its political commitment and emancipatory philosophical reference or, by contrast, was it resignified within the academic space, maintaining the essential elements of its emancipatory vigour? At this point I'll return to my initial statement, to the need to continue struggling with the task of socialising knowledge and producing knowledge *with* others, breaking with the culture of banking education in whichever context we find ourselves engaged.

Provisionally, within the context of academia, I believe that this experience offers lessons for thinking about courses of an 'emancipatory' nature, courses promoting the self-development of committed intellectuals who intend to work as educators or researchers with popular social movements or in other types of emancipatory activity. One of the key points to highlight is the constant, angst-ridden search for both the collective construction of knowledge and, simultaneously, a positive experience in group development, with the text as the fundamental object of mediation. A related point is that the classroom experience of constructing knowledge also becomes, in itself, a focus for collective research, bringing alive the concepts of dialogue and practice. The basic elements of all the relevant processes of knowledge construction were also present: listening, observing, recording, selecting information, articulating representations and concepts and categories, engaging in dialogue, achieving interdisciplinarity, permanently reflecting on the dynamic relationship between subject and object and even expressing all of these aspects together in the form of a text. This experience shows the potential to challenge the way knowledge is produced in the context of a contemporary capitalism permeated by fragmentation, competition, individualism, knowledge valued as exchange rather than use and, even, the control of knowledge by teachers and researchers to the detriment of the knowledge of students and the people who are the focus of research.

As far as the limitations of the exercise are concerned, it became clear that there was insufficient analysis of broader educational practices and how these related to the themes researched by the students. And how far would such an analysis be possible in a discipline focusing mainly on issues of methodology? In problematising the content of practice, real success depends on the impact of the whole curriculum and on the political-epistemological place of social practice – in its multiple dimensions – as a complete programme (including the curriculum, teachers, methodology etc.).

One hopeful sign is that I continue to be involved in similar experiences with classes for researchers. The results are quite interesting. The students become involved and the groups develop solidarity while producing their work, and the tensions between the individual and the collective are expressed when issues of educational practice are brought to the class and discussed. I believe this is a promising way forward. I am trying, in the meantime, to carry out a longitudinal study and to consider the process in greater depth, both from a theoretical and a practical point of view.

Acknowledgements

Seminars on Paulo Freire, which I shared with Paula Allman at the University of Nottingham, England in the early 1990s, contributed greatly to my understanding of the meaning of 'dialogue' in Freire's work and its relationship to *praxis*. Many thanks to Liam Kane for his help with the translation of this chapter.

Note

1. I borrow the term 'window' from another experience. It was used as a metaphor in a national systematisation project in the training of trainers carried out by the Brazilian Workers Central Union (CUT) in 1998 – 1999 (see CUT, 2000).

References

Arroyo, M. (1982), 'A reforma na prática (a experiência pedagógica do mestrado, FAE – UFMG)', *Educação & Sociedade*, 11, pp. 106-32.

CUT (2000), 'Sistematização . . . de qual falamos?' in *Formação de Formadores Para Educação Profissional: A Experiência da CUT 1998/1999,* Florianópolis: Rocha Gráfica Editora.

Falkembach, E. (2000), 'Sistematização . . . de qual falamos?', Equipe Tecnica National/SNF/CUT *Formação de Formadores para Educação Profissional: A Experiência da CUT 1998/1999.* Florianópolis: Rocha Gráfica Editora.

Fischer, M.C.B. (1997), *Radical Trade Union Education in Practice? A Study of CUT's Education Programme on Collective Bargaining.* Unpublished PhD thesis, University of Nottingham.

Freire, P. (1975), *Pedagogia do Oprimido*, Rio de Janeiro: Paz e Terra.

Kane, L. (2001), *Popular Education in Latin America*, London: Latin American Bureau.

Marques, M.O. (1998), *Escrever é Preciso: O Princípio da Pesquisa*, Ijuí: Unijuí.

Chapter 12

Biographical Research: Reasserting Collective Experience

Barbara Merrill

There is now a great deal of interest in biographical research in adult education and life-long learning. The general tendency, however, is for learner identity and experience to be presented and analysed in highly individualistic and decontextualised terms. This chapter, which draws on evidence from a major European comparative research project, sets out to challenge this individualisation of biographical research and to relocate it within the collective dimensions of people's experience. Particular reference is made to the significance of gender in constructing collective experience.

In discussing the 'sociological imagination', C. Wright Mills (1970: 12) argued that it

> ... enables us to grasp history and biography and the relations between the two within society ... No social study that does not come back to the problems of biography, of history and of their intersections within a society has completed its intellectual journey.

Biographical research, in recent years, has increased in popularity amongst social scientists, including European adult educators, as a means of understanding adult learning experiences within the context of educational biographies. So much so that its current resurgence has been referred to as 'the biographical turn' (Chamberlayne et al, 2000). Many researchers in adult education favour biographical methods because they reflect a tradition within adult education of placing adult learners at the centre of the process by giving them a voice through which they are able to construct and give subjective meaning to their life experiences. Life history or biographical research, however, is largely associated with understanding lives and the social world from an individual perspective. This chapter aims to critique this emphasis on the individual and argue for the use of biographical methods as a means of highlighting and understanding the collective experiences of people's lives by locating biographies within their socio-economic and political context. Such an approach identifies with the everyday struggles of ordinary people, reveals the nature of inequality in society and thus has the potential to promote transformative action within communities. Biographies, importantly, illustrate the dialectics of agency and structure. Viewed from this perspective, biographical research has the potential to offer a radical and emancipatory approach to research within popular education.

Transforming biographical research from an individualised research process into a collective one that engages with communities requires change within the academy itself. Although not an easy task, the current research function of the academy has to be challenged and stretched if it is to promote a popular education process through research. Academics undertaking social science research need constantly to ask themselves, in Becker's (1967) words, 'Whose side are we on?' In arguing for the reassertion of collective experience through biographical research, three key issues will be explored: first, how to make collective experience more explicit in researching the social world by moving away from the individualising tendencies espoused by the kind of postmodernism that is currently favoured by many academics; second, how to challenge the emphasis of much current policy-led research which treats participants as objects rather than subjects of the research process; third, how to clarify the values of researchers and their research role. Within this framework a crucial question concerns how biographical approaches can move research in the academy in more radical directions. This chapter explores this key issue by arguing that the ideology and values underpinning popular adult education and biographical research are linked, and that these need to be harmonised and developed in terms of practice. However, it is important to recognise that this is also problematical. The task is to identify ways of moving towards a popular education biographical research *praxis*.

Looking at the academy

Universities are changing institutions. It is argued that the model of universities being the preserve of knowledge no longer holds in late modernity. Globalisation and the emergence of the knowledge society have permeated and undermined the university as an ivory tower (Delanty, 2001), forcing it to engage with the wider society. Barnett (2003: 2) elaborates:

> On the one hand, its key concepts of knowledge, truth and reason are in difficulty in the contemporary age (the epistemological undermining) and, on the other hand, the autonomies that the university has enjoyed for 800 years are being reduced as it becomes interconnected with the wider society both nationally and globally (the sociological undermining).

Market forces are now deeply entrenched within the academy, impacting upon research and forcing institutions to establish partnerships with outside stakeholders, many of whom are also making their own claims on knowledge and research. The value of research now lies in both its monetary worth and, in the UK context, standing in the competitive Research Assessment Exercise (RAE) determines the distribution of government-funded research monies. The marketisation of the academy is breaking down the collegial structure of the university as academics pursue their own individual agendas. Whilst this process and its underpinning values need to be challenged, the emergence of new forms of knowledge (as opposed to supposedly elite knowledge) offers a potential and a space for promoting 'really useful knowledge', radical research and popular education. Delanty is optimistic that 'a new role is emerging around the democratisation of knowledge', engaging the university in the politics of citizenship: 'The university must recover the public space of discourse that has been lost in the decline of the public sphere. In Habermas's epistemological terms, it must relink knowledge and human interests' (2001: 7). Similarly, Barnett asserts that within the changing university a more humanistic value system can be constructed despite the growth of individualism and market values: 'The spaces that are opening for the university to take on new values are also opening spaces for a leadership that deliberately attends to communicative and community values and for values in which individuals matter' (2003: 129-30).

Researching through biographies

The 'biographical turn' has now permeated European adult education research. It is less popular, however, amongst radical adult educators with the exception of colleagues working for the Centre for Research in the Education of Adults (CREA) at the University of Barcelona. Biographies/life histories yield a wealth of powerful data, but they are analysed largely in a personal and individualised way. Alheit and Dausien (1999), for example, use the concept 'biographicity', that an individual's biography provides a knowledge resource for dealing with life in late modernity. However, although the stories people tell illustrate common life experiences in relation to, for example, class, gender and ethnicity, researchers rarely make the connection between the individual and the collective. Biographies offer a tool for critiquing structural inequalities and the inadequacies and contradictions of lifelong learning and social inclusion policies.

Biographical research is rooted in a humanistic tradition, developed by the Chicago School of sociology in opposition to the supposed objectivity of the then dominant paradigm of positivism and its neglect of agency in human interaction. Thomas and Znaniecki's (1958) classic study of the Polish peasant and migration is cited as an early example of the biographical tradition, marking new ground in sociology. As Plummer (2001) points out, it was one of the first studies to engage with the objective and the subjective, the social and the individual. Biographical research in the UK has largely followed the tradition of the Chicago School and that of feminism rather than the more individualised approach of the German tradition as developed by Schutz (1932) and more recently Rosenthal (1993).

In the 1970s and 1980s biographical methods were radicalised by feminists like Oakley (1992) and Reinharz (1992) as a means of bringing women out of obscurity and into historical and sociological research, giving them a voice. Women's stories illustrated the relationship between the personal and the political. Reinharz maintains that feminist life histories 'assist in a fundamental sociological task – illuminating the connections between biography, history and social structure' (1992: 131). Symbolic interactionists also made the connection between the private and public world through life histories to reveal 'an inner world of thought and experience and an outer world of events and experiences' (Denzin, 1986: 66).

Symbolic interactionists like Denzin (1989), Becker (1967) and Schutz (1932) used biographical methods to look at how 'subjects give subjective meaning to their life experiences' (Schutz, 1932). Biographies not only highlight the subjectivity of the self but also locate people within a historical and structural context. They reveal the dialectical relationship between self, groups and society. As the Personal Narratives Group states, life histories, '. . . are particularly rich sources because, attentively interpreted, they illuminate both the logic of individual courses of action and the effects of system-level constraints within which those courses evolve' (1989: 6).

Experience is essential as a means of making sense narratively and symbolically of the life struggle over material conditions (Brah, 1992). What many biographical researchers fail to do, however, is to move beyond the individual to the collective. The French tradition makes some attempt to do this – for example, in the work of Bertaux, for whom, 'The intent of the biographical project is to uncover the social, economic, cultural, structural and historical forces that shape, distort and otherwise alter problematic lived experiences' (1981: 4).

In the UK in the early 1970s, the Centre for Contemporary Cultural Studies at the University of Birmingham linked biography and society in their work. Clarke et al's (1976: 57) study stressed that:

> Biographies cut paths in and through the determined spaces of the structures and cultures in which individuals are located. Though we have not been able, here, to deal at all adequately with the level of biography, we insist that biographies only make sense in terms of the structures and cultures through which the individual constructs himself or herself.

According to Chamberlayne et al (2000: 7-8), the last decade has witnessed a concern with historical and cultural forces in relation to biography:

> Biographical social researchers in the 1990s are increasingly attempting to describe people as historically formed actors whose biographies are necessary to render fully intelligible their historical action in context – its conditions, meanings and outcomes, whether such conditions, meanings and outcomes be conscious or unconscious.

Historically, therefore, biographical methods have been used in radical ways by particular groups of researchers. We now need to reclaim and reassert a radical approach to biographical research which stresses the collectivity rather than the individuality of social life.

Biographical approaches within a popular education framework

Research in education, and in the social sciences more generally, has become policy-oriented in recent years, with funding bodies such as the European Commission (EC) and the Economic and Social and Research Council (ESRC) in the UK stipulating the need to identify policy issues and make policy recommendations. Research is also being driven by economic factors (Barnett, 2003) and the need to obtain funding in a climate of increasing competitiveness with research institutes outside of the academy. As researchers and popular educators within the academy, we need to counter the objectivity and obsession with such research which is also often uncritical of policy. The biographies of adult students highlight the problems that they experience as a result of government policy. Specifically, biographies powerfully reveal the contradictions within narrow, vocationally driven lifelong learning policies: those without economic power continue to be excluded from access to learning, perpetuating class inequalities. One woman explained her dilemma:

> I went the first day . . . I thoroughly enjoyed it [college] and I came home and my fiancé wasn't working at the time and he said 'there's absolutely no way we can afford this'. I've been to the welfare rights officer and I've been down to the Social Security and there's no way. Because we are two single people living together we basically have to pay full rent . . . It was just a nightmare. We were going to end up worse off than we were and I spent the whole night crying my eyes out. I really did and I was very disappointed. (Merrill and McKie, 1998: 5)

Another woman (a single parent) had to leave a course because her benefits were cut upon receiving a college bursary. Working-class students in higher education also struggle financially, and this can affect academic achievement:

> I feel that the financial assistance offered to mature students is appalling and the only way I have been able to continue my degree has been to work throughout term-time and the vacation period, usually to pay off an overdraft. Working in paid employment in the third year, I am sure, has a negative effect on my academic achievement. (Merrill and McKie, 1998: 6)

The contradictions of lifelong learning policies can be challenged both within institutions and at national level by using the voices of adult students, working with them to take action. We need constantly to ask ourselves who the research is for and what its purpose is.

A key question is how the values and processes underpinning biographical approaches can move research into a popular education perspective and practice. In comparing the pedagogical principles and ideology underlying popular education and biographical research, links can be identified. First, participants involved in the research process are the subjects, not the objects, of research – in a similar way as learners within a popular education tradition are viewed as the subjects, not the objects, of the learning process. Subjectivity is, therefore, central to both. Second, and following on from this, the researcher and the researched are perceived as being equals in the research process – there is no distance between the two. A biographical interview is conducted as a conversation rather than the interviewer asking a set of structured questions as characterised by a more traditional interview approach whereby the researcher is in a position of power over the researched. Many biographical interviewers also disclose information about themselves – it is not just a one-way process. Oakley (1992), for example, talked about her interviewees as being friends. Third, popular education recognises that learners are equal to educators in the learning process as all contribute to knowledge production: the learner learns from the teacher and the teacher learns from the learner (Freire, 1972). Through the sharing of biographies, interviewers and interviewees also contribute to the production of research knowledge. Both biographical research and popular education therefore demand an equal dialogue between those involved in the academy and those outside it. The difficult task is to transform this ideological common ground into practice.

Revealing collective lives

In researching the biographies of adults in further education (participants and non-participants) and 'non-traditional' adult students in higher education, the stories I heard highlighted collective experiences. For them gender, class and, in some cases, race played a significant role in shaping their lives and, in particular, their experiences of initial education, family and employment/ unemployment. Their stories also illuminate how past biographies have impacted upon the decision to return to learn as an adult. Often this was the result of a critical incident such as unemployment or divorce. For others, learning is something they had always wanted to do but were constrained by class and gender factors. Biographical research about adult students helps to inform educators where their students are coming from. As popular educators, starting from learners' experience and using it in the curriculum are fundamental in order to enable them to challenge the structural inequalities they face, both individually and collectively, in their communities and in society at large, 'The objective of learning is to liberate the participants from the social pressures and internalised ideas that hold them passive in conditions of oppression – to make them capable of changing their reality, their lives, and the society they live in' (Castano Ferreira and Castano Ferreira, 1997: 19).

Biographical research, I would argue, can be developed and used in transformative ways through three different approaches within a popular education framework. First, researchers/lecturers can use their research in their teaching (particularly in the social sciences and education) to raise awareness about power inequalities in society. Second, this requires research-ers to challenge traditional notions of the role of the researcher, the purpose of research and the funding of research projects, both within and outside the academy. Rather than leaving the groups and sites of research once a project has been completed, researchers should build into the process the opportunity to share their findings with the subjects of the research, using the biographies to work with participants in a community-based learning or a community development context. This means going well beyond the common practice of sharing the interview transcripts with individuals. Engaging participants in dialogue about their collective biographies provides a powerful tool both for understanding social, economic and political inequalities at a local and national level and as a mechanism for potentially changing their social reality. Although funding constraints make this difficult, spaces need to be found and used. Some academics manage to do this – for example, CREA at the University of Barcelona. Using Habermas's idea of communicative action, life histories and dialogue, their work involves transforming working-class and Gitano (gypsy) neighbourhoods in Catalunya. Biographical research can also be used politically to raise awareness of inequalities in people's lives, as illustrated in the work of Skeggs (1998). She considered the political purpose of her ethnographic study of working-class women engaging in further education. The biographical interviews enabled the women, through reflect-ing upon their lives, to realise that their individual problems were collective ones:

> Providing explanations which linked the individual to structures not of their making helped dislodge feelings of personal inadequacy. They had already been classified as academic failures when I met them. Along with unemployment this was experienced at an immediate intimate level. They blamed themselves for the lack of jobs and their lack of interest in schooling. The ability to put this into a wider perspective blocked their tendency to victim-blame and take on responsibility for social structural problems ... The political consequences of epistemological battles hopefully should mean that they may be pathologized less through representation; that they may be taken more seriously. (Skeggs, 1998: 37-8)

Finally, biographies can be used as a learning approach within the 'classroom' both in the university or in community-based learning. This idea draws on the work of Pierre Dominicé, as outlined in his study *Learning From Our Lives* (2000). For Dominicé: a 'person's life history is an educational process' because it links the personal and social aspects of learning. Adult learners narrate, orally and in writing, their biographies as a means of understanding their way of learning. He argues that:

> The educational biography approach offers the adult an interpretation of his or her never-ending struggle for identity. The difficult process of

becoming oneself implies confronting one's life project and learning experiences, the values and models acquired from family, school and social life. (Dominice, 2000: 73)

Similarly, this approach could be adapted and developed by popular educators working with marginalised groups in a community context or with non-traditional adult students in higher education. In these situations biographies could be used as a learning tool for understanding and challenging inequalities in schooling, family, workplace and the wider society. People may share similar backgrounds and face similar problems (related, for example, to poverty, unemployment or gender inequality), and yet many of them may view these as individual difficulties and dilemmas. Their biographical experiences could provide the starting point for a curriculum based on 'really useful knowledge' expressed through egalitarian dialogical learning in a similar way to the approaches of Freire. Community-based learning can offer such spaces. Importantly, as Flecha (2000: 20) argues, 'egalitarian educational practices must be grounded in conceptions of solidarity'. Biographies enable adult learners to reflect critically not only about themselves as individuals but also as members of a community. This is illustrated by the following female adult learner who began her learning career on a return-to-learn course in further education, and ended up taking a degree:

See it also matters for the community. We are classed as a deprived area. I think when you say that you come from here everyone thinks you are a waster. But this (learning) gives people the chance to show, yes there might be problems here but we have brains and don't write us off cos we come from here. (Merrill and McKie, 1998: 7)

Developing a popular education approach

Emancipatory and transformative research is not new as witnessed by its application in the context of participatory action research, particularly in the South. As Usher, Bryant and Johnston (1997: 193) remind us: 'Emancipatory research seeks to address directly issues of power within an unequal world'. Synthesising biographical research and popular adult education approaches, however, is relatively new. Although the idea of a popular education biographical approach to research may appear idealistic, and, some would argue, unrealistic, it is important constantly to question the culture of the academy and work towards changing its practice. While it is possible to show ideological links between popular education and biographical research and outline the implications of this for practice, as this chapter has attempted to do, the next task is to find ways of implementing these ideas. Finding a space to research in a radical way is more difficult in some institutions than others. Research in the academy remains largely distant and removed from the subjects of research. Even academic feminists, who once sought to empower working-class women through their research, have now retreated into the ivory tower favouring instead the abstract language and ideas of postmodernism. A popular education approach to biographical research would engage universities with their local communities in a democratic way.

Utilising biographical methods within a popular education framework offers an alternative paradigm that empowers the subjects of research. As Deshler and Selener (1991) argue, research should address issues of human rights and social justice. Biographies are also a powerful tool for illustrating the dialectical processes in people's lives and thus, through reflection and empowerment, have the potential to enable people to take collective action against the structures that oppress them. The challenge is to develop a research of possibility and hope.

References

Alheit, P. and Dausien, B. (1999), 'Biographicity as a basic resource of lifelong learning' in Alheit, P., Beck, J., Kammler, E., Taylor, R. and Olesen, H.S. (eds), *Lifelong Learning Inside and Outside Schools* Vol 2, Roskilde, Denmark: Universities of Roskilde, Bremen and Leeds, pp. 400-23.

Barnett, R. (2003), *Beyond All Reason: Living with Ideology in the University,* Buckingham: SRHE/ Open University Press.

Becker, H. (1967), 'Whose side are we on?', *Social Problems*, 14, pp. 239-47.

Bertaux, D. (ed.), (1981), *Biography and Society: The Life History Approach in the Social Sciences,* Beverly Hills: Sage.

Brah, A. (1992), 'Difference, diversity and differentiation' in Donald, J. and Rattansi A. (eds), *Race, Culture and Difference*, London: Sage, pp. 126-45.

Castano Ferreira, E. and Castano Ferreira, J. (1997), *Making Sense of the Media: A Handbook of Popular Education Techniques*, New York: Monthly Review Press.

Chamberlayne, P., Bornat, J. and Wengraf, T. (eds), (2000), *The Turn to Biographical Methods in the Social Sciences*, London: Routledge.

Clarke, J., Hall, S., Jefferson, T. and Roberts, B. (1976), 'Subcultures, cultures and class' in Hall, S. and Jefferson, T. (eds), *Resistance Through Rituals*, London: Hutchinson/Centre for Contemporary Cultural Studies, pp. 9-74.

Delanty, G. (2001), *Challenging Knowledge: The University in the Knowledge Society*, Buckingham: SRHE/Open University Press.

Denzin, N.K. (1989), *Interpretative Biography*, Newbury Park: Sage.

Deshler, D. and Selener, D. (1991), 'Transformative research: in search of a definition', *Convergence*, XX1V(3), pp. 9-21.

Dominicé, P. (2000), *Learning from our Lives*, San Francisco: Jossey-Bass.

Flecha, R. (2000), *Sharing Words*, Lanham, Maryland: Rowman & Littlefield.

Freire, P. (1972), *Pedagogy of the Oppressed*, Harmondsworth, Penguin.

Merrill, B. and McKie, J. (1998), 'Money and the mature student', *Adults Learning*, 9(6), pp. 6-7.

Oakley, A. (1992), 'Interviewing women: a contradiction in terms' in Roberts, H. (eds), *Doing Feminist Research*, London: Routledge, pp. 30-61.

Personal Narratives Group (eds.), (1989), *Interpreting Women's Lives: Feminist Theory and Personal Narratives*, Bloomington: Indiana University Press.

Plummer, K. (2001), *Documents of Life (2)*, London: Sage Publications.

Reinharz, S. (1992), *Feminist Methods in Social Research*, New York: Oxford University Press.

Rosenthal, G. (1993), 'Reconstruction of life stories: principles of selection in generating stories for narrative biographical interviews' in Josselson, R. and Lieblich, A. (eds), *The Narrative Study of Lives*, Newbury Park: Sage.

Schutz, A. (1932), *The Phenomenology of the Social World,* Evanston: Northwestern University Press.

Skeggs, B. (1997), *Formations of Class and Gender*, London: Sage.

Thomas, W.I. and Znaniecki, F. (1958), *The Polish Peasant in Europe and America*, New York: Dover Publications.

Usher, R., Bryant, I. and Johnston, R. (1997), *Adult Education and the Postmodern Challenge*, London: Routledge.

Wright Mills, C. (1970), *The Sociological Imagination*, Harmondsworth: Penquin.

Part Three

Engaging in Educational Practice

Chapter 13

Justice for Pensioners! Some Reflections on Popular Education Practice

John Payne

This chapter is based on the author's personal experience and involvement in the struggles by British old-age pensioners for dignity and social justice. The focus of interest is on informal learning processes and the educative force of collective social action. Case material from pensioners' campaigns in both London and Somerset is used to develop and support an argument which significantly extends and enriches the debate about what life-long learning means, who it is for and why it matters.

London in the 1980s: the context

During the 1980s London enjoyed a progressive form of local government. Based on a relatively high level of local taxation, the Greater London Council (GLC) and the Inner London Education Authority (ILEA) attempted to shift public resources within London from richer communities to poorer communities, and to recognise explicitly the many ways in which community might be understood with respect to ethnicity, gender, age, ability/disability and sexuality, as well as social class. This placed it on a collision course with national government, committed to neoliberal economic policies, tax and benefit cuts and a restructuring of the UK economy which produced unemployment levels of over three million in the mid-1980s, widening gaps between rich and poor, and the collapse of many traditional manufacturing industries. The GLC was abolished in 1986 and the ILEA in 1990. I worked for the ILEA, was made redundant in 1990, and since 1990 I have earned my living as a lifelong learning consultant, a writer on broader social issues, and a university researcher.

From adult education to popular education: working alongside community groups during the 1980s

It did not feel like adult education. As a professional adult educator, I had been socialised into thinking about adult learning from a provider perspective, in terms of identifying and meeting needs, making provision in dedicated buildings (adult education centres), and employing specialist tutors. During this period, I came to recognise that changing participation in formal adult education was less important than developing forms of adult learning which were more closely identified with the priorities of people living in deprived communities and working alongside those communities to define what they wanted to learn in order to achieve their own personal and collective aims. This is what I now understand the role of the professional educator to be in the context of popular education as defined in this book.

The Putney and Roehampton Organisation of Pensioners (PROP) was a voluntary group I had come to know in the 1980s when I was Head of Centre in an ILEA Adult Education Institute in South West London. A good number of PROP members also came to the adult education centre as 'students'. Knowing them as friends and community activists helped me to look at the very narrow curriculum on offer there, to listen more carefully to their views, and to begin to make changes in the way the curriculum was structured. It was an important relationship in a part of London where older people tended to live quite local lives in rented accommodation, unlike the younger ones who tended to be either very transient or had bought private houses or flats in 'posh Putney' and travelled into Central London to work each day.

At the same time, my involvement with PROP was part of a wider effort by the statutory authorities to provide support for voluntary and community organisations in London. This was not led by education. The main driving force was the GLC which financed a network of community resource centres and gave grants to a wide range of voluntary organisations. As I have described elsewhere (Payne, 1995), the Putney Resource Centre (1983 – 1986) had premises in Putney High Street, employed staff, worked with 130 local organisations, and was controlled by a voluntary management committee. Despite the wide variety of organisations using the centre, the key political players in the resource centre and its management committee were the tenants associations. I showed how this struggle to assert the use value of the city and to acquire an element of control over the spatial dimensions of the city was also part of a global fight against the forces of neoliberal capitalism. I used the term 'global economy' at that point rather than globalisation, but it is significant that the intellectual grounding of my view of 'what was going on' both in South London and in other parts of the world was the work of Manuel Castells (1983). He documented key struggles over control of urban space, such as the citizens movement in Spain in the final years of the Franco regime and the transition to democracy (1970 – 1980) and the gay rights campaigns in San Francisco.

At the same time, the close personal relationships developed during the 'GLC period' led to a number of unintended outcomes. The first two can be described as oral history projects, a field in which I learned skills 'on-the-job', itself a useful lesson for popular educators. First, *We Survived* (1988), an oral history project with PROP which documented important experiences of community, trade union and political activism over a period from approxi-mately 1930 to 1970.[1] Second, I helped a small tenants association in Roehampton to write the history of their tower block (*Rising Above It*, 1989) in terms of their early memories of slum conditions in Central London and elsewhere, the development of the Roehampton estates in the 1950s with model housing but no social facilities, the social problems that had emerged, and the efforts of the various tenants groups to resolve those problems.

A more substantial and innovative outcome was the series of workshops planned with the tenants associations in response to the 1987 Housing Bill, which later became the 1988 Housing Act. As I have previously described (Payne, 1995), this was a cross-ILEA initiative in relation to national enabling legislation which held a particular threat in Wandsworth, one of the few London boroughs where the national Conservative government was operating alongside a Conservative local administration. As adult educators, we did not see it as our business to drive the political agenda, but to support tenants organisations in working out how to respond. In the workshops I helped to organise, the meeting format was used. In the first half I presented a summary of the government proposals, and in the second half a tenant activist chaired a discussion on how to respond. The format challenged a number of notions about 'informal' community education: on one occasion I found myself standing on a platform with a microphone, an audience of nearly 100 tenants, and the club bar doing a steady trade at the back of the hall. Sessions with 30-40 tenants and without the distraction of a bar were probably more successful in developing considered responses! Three of the workshops were held in adult education buildings and the remainder in tenants halls and community centres. Sue Gardener, who also worked for ILEA at that time, emphasised in a letter to the author that the politics were 'their' politics, not 'ours':

> I think the good practice embodied in the Housing Bill work was trying to attend to political agendas outside and not drive them from the relatively weak and detached position of Adult Education – trying to work out how to be genuinely instrumental and informative. (Payne, 1995: 265)

This point seems to me to go to the heart of the concept of 'popular education' as used in this book. If adult education is 'detached' from people's lives, then popular education is 'attached' to the individual and collective lives of local communities.

London in the 1990s

It is not my intention to give a potted history of London politics or my own life, but to sketch in the main events which provide the background to the practice reported here. In 1990 ILEA followed the GLC into defeat. The intentions of the government to reduce expenditure on adult education in Inner London to the 'national average', thereby ensuring in turn that that 'national average' would fall even further, were achieved. I took redundancy, bought a VW campervan from a visiting Australian adult educator, and went off to Catalonia to write a book. On my return I gradually developed a successful research consultancy which also allowed me sufficient time for part-time writing, parenting and equally part-time community activism, supplemented by a couple of spells as a university researcher. As a 'flexible' worker, I both raged at the insecurity and welcomed the relative freedom of my new position!

So when in 1996 Laurie Green, a leading member of PROP, phoned me up and asked me if I'd like to write a history of the organisation, I was in a position to respond positively. There was no question of payment, of course. I agreed to PROP's request but on one condition: I would write the book with them rather than for them. And that is what I tried to do. There is considerable use of interview material and each draft was read and commented on carefully and at length by the informal group which came to be known as 'the Book Committee'. Laurie himself wrote a Foreword, his daughter Stephanie wrote an Afterword on the theme of solidarity between the generations, there are poems, extracts from Minutes Books, Letters to the Editor, and so on.

Justice for Pensioners! (the title of the book) was a nice community effort but scarcely in itself 'adult education'. However, as I interviewed members, and worked through the large box of press cuttings, reports, leaflets and photos that constituted the raw material for the book, some of those insistent questions about the relationship between formal and informal adult learning began to surface. Here was an organisation, dedicated to improving the status of older people, which month after month over a 15-year period (they meet on the first and third Monday of each month) had set out to enhance the knowledge and understanding of a sizeable group of people (50-60 is an average attendance) on subjects which directly affect pensioners: health; pensions; care in the community; personal security; European, parliamentary and borough council elections. This knowledge was in turn being spread more widely by the regular reports of meetings prepared by Laurie Green and printed in the local paper, the *Wandsworth Borough News*. And the Really Important Knowledge they were gleaning from external speakers and their own discussions was giving rise to action – in particular, campaigns to bring home to other people and to government the extent of poverty and hardship among older people, and the differential impact on older people of changes in social services and the Health Service. Again, this comes close to the notion of learning in popular education as both ordinary and related to people's everyday concerns.

Within the book, there is a rumbling critique from the older people themselves of some of the trends in our society which run in directions contrary to the liberating purposes of popular education:

- A critique of formal school education. Laurie Green writes in the foreword: 'Many people in their sixties and seventies had a poor education, interrupted by the war and often irrelevant or hostile to working-class values and ideas.'

- A critique of cuts in the learning opportunities available to older people through the local authority adult education service in London, as centres closed, fees rose, concessions dwindled, and the range of opportunities available shrank.
- A critique of the notion of 'authority' in a society run by experts (doctors, social workers, politicians, civil servants, educators) who 'know best'. Pensioners leader and former General Secretary of the Transport and General Workers Union, Jack Jones, is quoted in the book as saying 'Don't tell us, ask us!' The book is aimed not just at pensioners but at professionals who work with older people, politicians and opinion-formers.

Alongside criticism of the way things are, there is a cheerful optimism about the way things might be in the future.[2] Here are people arriving in the later stages of their lives with an unquenchable belief in the future. Not for them the deep pessimism of post-modernism and the 'end of history' but an assertion that the collective efforts of ordinary people can change things for the better. It is not a selfish or sectarian feeling, either, but a feeling that reaches out in solidarity across the generations and across barriers of gender, disability, ethnicity and nation. It is also, and this takes us back to Castells' (1983) pioneering work on 'urban social movements', a feeling that stretches across divisions of social class and voting patterns. Finally, it is a feeling that has yet to take form as international civil society.

Reflecting on the past and looking to the future: 'adult learning' or 'popular education'?

At the launch of *Justice for Pensioners!* in Putney on 7 December 1998, a number of speakers referred to the community work tradition from which PROP had emerged 15 years before, and in particular the principle that the objective of social policy is to enable individuals and groups to both define and achieve their own objectives, their own solutions to the problems which face them in their daily lives. Yet there is a question of resources here. The range of community support mechanisms which existed in London in the mid-1980s – community workers, adult education workers, community artists – were an invaluable tool in helping to build strong and vibrant local communities which are (for me at least) the essential 'other face' of the processes of economic and cultural globalisation. There is a further question about how far such workers were attending to their own professional agendas rather than community needs. Conceptually, popular education does not require such professional input, but can benefit from it, providing power remains in the hands of civil society rather than of professionals. I am by no means convinced that the National Lottery and the European Social Fund, or other short-term funding initiatives can guarantee the same kind of open-ended commitment to what people actually want for themselves and their communities. Indeed short-term project funding is a major constraint on development. It creates dependency on public funding, while ensuring that individual and community learning are 'framed' within a professionalised view of education and learning. This is done through complex bidding procedures, and through the use of evaluation and audit techniques controlled by government or government-based agencies. But fortunately people and organisations will not always sit around waiting for government agencies, community workers and adult educators to show on the horizon.

Four questions for popular educators

The present conceptualisation of adult learning provokes four sets of relevant questions, which are dealt with in turn below:

- questions about whether the present identification of 'adult learning' with 'economic prosperity' is an adequate understanding of the term, and of the many purposes that people bring to learning
- questions about curriculum, and to what extent the twin tracks of accreditation, on the one hand, and 'leisure learning', on the other, are an adequate conceptualisation of the field
- questions about the meaning of informal learning and its connection with informal education
- questions about the role and status of professional educators ('the academy' for the purpose of this book) in either supporting or constraining popular education.

Learning and the economy

From 1997, the newly elected Labour government increased firstly the public profile of adult learning and, secondly, the amount of public resource devoted to it. There has been criticism, however – much of it centred on the relationship between 'lifelong learning' (the phrase most used in policy texts) and the economy (e.g. Cole, 2000). Trowler (1998) has demonstrated that the link between lifelong learning and economic prosperity is, at best, overstated. Paid employment is, after all, a minority activity, compared with all the other kinds of work that go on in our society, especially domestic work, voluntary work and the organisation of a wide range of activities in 'civil society'. I referred to this as 'social work' in the first draft of an academic article (Payne, 1996), though the final published version used Michael Welton's term 'development work' (Welton, 1995). By using that term 'social work', I implied that the unpaid work of people in their own communities is of rather more political significance than the 'social work' performed by government agencies to cover the failure of neoliberal economics to deal with real social needs.[3]

Learning and the curriculum

Within lifelong learning debates in England, there has been relatively little attention paid to the curriculum, despite the petrification of a traditional schooling curriculum in the National Curriculum. The main thrusts of the adult learning curriculum have been towards accreditation across a large, but nevertheless rather narrow range of fields, including basic skills, trade union education, academic qualifications and national vocational qualifications (NVQs). While Open College Networks continue to thrive, their potential to accredit any kind of learning which is of interest or importance to adults has never been entirely fulfilled. On the other hand, the curriculum of 'leisure', recreational and cultural activities continues to flourish, but with usually relatively high levels of fees and relatively poor concessions, so that this sort of learning has reinforced its socially exclusive identity. Overall, participation in adult learning remains static (Aldridge and Tuckett, 2002). The development of an adult education curriculum which builds on the interests and experience of people, and can relate 'personal troubles' to 'public issues' (Mills, 1959) remains what it has always been – a task for the future. In my opinion, it can only be done by popular educators who owe their first allegiance to social movements rather than to professional bodies or academic institutions. In that sense, the existence of an 'academy' which claims prior rights to the definition of knowledge seems to me a problem that the popular education movement has not yet addressed convincingly.

Informal learning and informal education

There still seems to be confusion, even at a high level, about the meaning of these terms. I take 'informal learning' to refer to any purposeful learning undertaken by individuals or groups (as opposed to learning that is incidental or even accidental) *with or without professional support*. Informal education, however, is often used to refer to state-funded adult education happening 'in the community' (e.g. village halls, pubs, tenants rooms, and so on). It is all part of the conceptual sogginess of 'community' from which popular education has attempted to disentangle itself. This type of informal education may simply replicate the adult education curriculum from more formal settings and the power relationship of teacher-student. Like the emphasis on 'community' rather than 'academic', or the emphasis on 'learning' rather than 'education', the use of 'informal' may simply be a rhetorical move to increase surveillance over what, where and how people learn.

Further, this 'informal learning in community settings' may be seen not as a valuable activity in its own right and in terms of individuals and community organisations participating, but as a professionalised form of 'outreach', drawing people away from their own interests and priorities and into more work-orientated, accredited courses in a formal setting. In that sense, it is the antithesis of popular education, in which everyday concerns are the focus of learning. Informal and community-based adult education is not just of value because learners may progress to formal adult education. This is a useful point at which to underline that what I am interested in is how, if at all, state resources can be used to support informal learning where the priorities of the learners are an important influence on the curriculum.

Development activities still go on, not least resourced by the UK government's Adult Community Learning Fund in England. It would be good to hear more about such projects in the pages of adult education journals, and to know how easy community groups find it to get support from colleges and local authorities. It would also be interesting to see an objective evaluation of the Adult Community Learning Fund, and to know how many projects have made a lasting difference to local communities, and how many have disappeared without trace once time-limited funding finishes. Of course, it is important that adult learning should underpin the economic activities on which national prosperity in a globalised economy depends; but it is also important for adult learning to support a wider range of essential social and community activities. Since the globalised economy is inherently unstable and environmentally unsustainable, we need to think about adult learning for a post-globalisation world. We need more public debate on this, and we need more research and writing about what is actually going on at the interface of formal and informal adult learning, and at the interface between the artificial global economy and the 'real world' economies of communities in both the North and the South.

Adult learning: the role of the professional

In this chapter, I have attempted to plot in semi-autobiographical form the changing relationship between an individual adult educator and community organisations, and my own changing understanding of the concept of 'popular education'. I owe a lot to the academy: my own training with Nell Keddie at the University of London Extra-Mural Department (now Birkbeck College) and Stephen Ball at King's College taught me the overriding importance of identifying who benefits, and how they benefit, from all the resources and effort that go into publicly funded adult learning.

At the same time, I also have a strong sense of the academy as having 'failed' the communities they claim to serve.[4] There has been a significant decline in the kind of 'social purpose' adult education in English universities which once gave meaning and shape to the work of extra-mural departments. 'Widening participation' is seen primarily as a way of recruiting more students to formal higher education courses dominated by abstract academic knowledge, rather than a way of making the resources of the academy available to civil society. Research in the continuing education field has become dominated by, on the one hand, technical considerations of educational technology and methodology, and, on the other hand, by a pessimistic post-modernism which denies agency to social actors.

Future prospects for adult educators wanting to engage in forms of popular education as defined in this book may have to depend on committed individuals who are prepared, like me, to occupy a position mid-way between the academy and civil society. Equally, it would be pessimistic to discount the possibility of either radical change within the academy or (and this seems to me more likely) civil society itself producing leaders who recognise the importance and significance of learning to their organisation and its members.

Notes

1. 'Community publishing' is surprisingly successful commercially, and all the community texts referred to in this chapter sold out years ago. However, I am always happy to provide photocopies at cost price for interested parties.
2. My own claim that 'In social terms, optimism remains the most rational of all philosophical positions, because without it the future will be as dark as our darkest fears' (Payne, 2000: 77) owes much to working with organisations like PROP.
3. Readers wishing to pursue this point might refer to the publications of the New Economics Foundation: www.neweconomics.org.
4. In some ways it seems easier to deal conceptually with higher education institutions in which 'continuing education' is seen as a market mechanism to link university knowledge with the needs of the economy through post-experience courses at market rates for relatively well qualified workers than with institutions which make rhetorical claims to 'serve the community' in ways which may or may not stand up to close scrutiny.

References

Aldridge, F. and Tuckett, A. (2002), *Two Steps Forward, One Step Back*, Leicester: NIACE.

Castells, M. (1983), *The City and the Grassroots*, London: Edward Arnold.

Cole, M. (2000), 'The issue of age in The Learning Age: a critical review of lifelong learning in the United Kingdom under New Labour', *Education and Ageing*, 15(3), pp. 437-53.

Mills, C. Wright (1959), *The Sociological Imagination*, New York: Oxford University Press.

Payne, J. (1995), 'Adult learning in the context of global, neoliberal economic policies' in Mayo, M. and Thompson, J. (eds), *Adult Learning, Critical Intelligence and Social Change*, Leicester: NIACE, pp. 262-74.

Payne, J. (1996), 'Adult education and "the economic": paid work and "development work" in the late modern world', *Scottish Journal of Adult and Continuing Education*, 3(2), pp. 67-80.

Payne, J. (2000), *Journey up the Thames: William Morris and Modern England*, Nottingham: Five Leaves Press.

Trowler, P. (1998), *Education Policy: A Policy Sociology Approach*, Eastbourne: The Gildredge Press.

Welton, M. (ed.), (1995), *In Defence of the Lifeworld: Critical Perspectives on Lifelong Learning*, Albany: State University of New York Press.

Chapter 14

A Hard Road: Learning from Failed Social Action

James Whelan

Even when social action fails something positive can emerge in terms of what a popular movement learns. This chapter draws on the author's personal experience as both partici-pant and researcher in an Australian environmental group's campaign to oppose the building of a new motorway by Brisbane City Council. Whilst the main practical objec-tives of the protesters were not achieved, the campaign helped to develop a potent range of knowledge and skills amongst a new learning community of committed environmental activists.

Environmental activists: a neglected species

Non-governmental organisations (NGOs) oriented towards advocacy play an important role in contemporary politics. Despite activists' remarkable contri-butions to social and environmental health, there is minimal Australian research exploring how these individuals learn to effect change. Environmen-tal literature tends to describe and decry contemporary environmental problems (see Porritt, 1990, 1991; Brown, 1998) rather than offer a critical analysis of the role played by activists in achieving environmental objectives such as the declaration of national parks or increased funding for public transport. In fact, Foley (1999: 134) laments that there has been 'almost no extended analysis of social movements or examples of social action.' In particular, he observes the lack of analysis from participants' perspectives. Activists' disinclination to theorise their strategies for change is attributed by Heaney (2000) to their preoccupation with organising and their sense of alienation from the 'ivory tower' of academia. This case study is a response to these observations as it explores an innovative community campaign from the perspective of an activist-researcher in order to identify the means and ends of learning for advocacy.

The romantic popular image of environmental crusaders successfully conceals the learning associated with effective advocacy and militates against deliberate educational efforts that might enhance environmentalists' efforts. During my own development as an activist, I have learnt to work with volunteers and the media, raise and manage campaign funds, communicate and educate, research, develop policy and utilise democratic processes to bring about positive social and environmental change. Activists' learning is often unplanned, incidental and incremental, and it is generally acquired through struggle. Interviews with participants in the 1974 – 1979 Terania Creek rainforest conservation campaign, for instance, enabled Foley (1999: 29) to identify a range of new skills and understandings acquired by rainforest activists. Campaigners 'learned a lot about the dynamics of campaigning, about the need for accurate knowledge and persistence, about the importance of identifying the real decision-makers [and became] clearer about their own and their opponents' values and strategies.' These dimensions of activist learning resonate with those identified through more recent interviews with environmental advocates (Whelan, 2000).

Campaigns also present opportunities for intentional learning. For example, the Highlander Centre in Tennessee, USA provides retreats and other educational activities for activists while the Mid-West Academy and the Doris Marshall Institute have trained North American community and campus organisers for decades. Intentional activist training was a significant element in the Franklin River campaign during the late 1970s and early 1980s, arguably Australia's best-known environmental dispute. Environmentalists participated in non-violence training before travelling up-river to participate in direct action intended to obstruct the damming of the wild river. This training was influenced by Gandhian and Quaker non-violence philosophy and Coover et al's (1978) *Resource Manual for a Living Revolution*. More recently, activists preparing to participate in direct action against the proposed uranium mine and processing plant at Jabiluka in northern Australia were trained in non-violence and environmental campaign strategy.

However encouraging, these examples are the exception rather than the rule in environmental campaigning. The author's experience as an environmental advocate and researcher suggests that activists are likely to speak of being 'thrown in the deep end' when they joined organisations and campaigns, receiving only minimal training or support. Engaging in political campaigns, however, provides excellent opportunities to learn social change skills and knowledge. By recognising and harnessing these opportunities, activist organisations can enhance this kind of learning. This case study aims to illustrate both the potent learning opportunities presented in a community campaign and strategies through which such opportunities may be harnessed.

A city in decline: a community ready for change

Brisbane, the state capital of Queensland, is a city of approximately one million people. Like many Australian cities, Brisbane is increasingly car-dependent. In recent years, the city has experienced sharply increasing population, car ownership levels and per capita vehicle use. Since the 1960s, public transport has declined from 40 per cent to less than 10 per cent of all trips (Queensland Government, 1995). This trend has been compounded by other factors such as the closure of the city tram service in 1969, poorly integrated bus, train and ferry services, fare hikes and state subsidies that deliver the nation's cheapest petrol. As city engineers have gradually implemented their 1960s transport plan, new and widened freeways have increasingly dominated the city landscape.

Brisbane City Council (BCC) is Australia's largest municipal government. All twenty-six BCC councillors are aligned with either the (left wing) Australian Labour Party or the (right wing) Liberal Party. The city's preferential electoral system effectively militates against the election of independents or minor parties that might be more responsive to community concerns. At the time of this campaign, the Labour council was in its third term and had a strong environmental policy, especially in the area of nature conservation and waste management. Despite the council having a pro-public transport policy, road-building programmes still enjoyed unprecedented funding.

LULUs mobilise NIMBYs

Local community activists in Brisbane have mobilised around sustainable transport issues on a number of occasions. For instance, the Route 20 proposal in the 1980s that entailed widening and connecting several arterial roads to create concentric ring roads triggered widespread community opposition and prompted major concessions. The influence of community activists was also evident when three members of State Parliament were voted out of office in 1995 following their support for a proposed second motorway from Brisbane to the Gold Coast. The motorway would have cut across significant koala habitat and was effectively opposed.

In the early 1990s community campaigners targeted another unpopular transport infrastructure project. This project involved widening a major arterial road and the consequent removal of several stately trees. Residents groups diplomatically expressed their concerns to the city council but made little progress. By the time bulldozers arrived, activists had resorted to more confrontational tactics such as occupying a giant fig tree destined for removal and driving spikes into tree trunks so that chainsaws could not be safely deployed. Despite these actions, the council's plans were implemented with little apparent regard for residential or environmental concerns. This campaign was demoralising and exhausting for many of Brisbane's transport activists. Debates over campaign strategies and political orientations also created tensions within and between community groups.

Then in 1997 the council announced plans for a six-lane freeway, to be called the City Valley Bypass. The road was promoted as the solution to inner city congestion. However, local residents and environmentalists were concerned by the proposal and began meeting at the home of a prominent community organiser. An informal network was born.

People had a variety of motivations for participating in this campaign. Many fitted the NIMBY (Not In My Back Yard) stereotype. NIMBYism hinges on local and immediate organising to oppose Locally Unwanted Land Uses (LULUs). NIMBY groups also had broader concerns such as the loss of parkland and cultural heritage, increased traffic, noise and air pollution and related impacts on urban amenity. Of particular concern was the fact that the proposed freeway would dissect Victoria Park, Brisbane's oldest reserve, which provided sweeping lawns, attractive trees and gardens, and habitat for water birds.

Victoria Park also has significance as a site of cultural value. The park follows the course of an ancient string of lagoons, where the region's original inhabitants camped at the time of Brisbane's early European settlement. Indeed, the Turrbal people had maintained relationships with the Victoria Park area for thousands of years. Only one small pond remained, York's Hollow, which was named after the Duke of York, a prominent Aboriginal elder at the time of European settlement.

These potential impacts galvanised and mobilised groups from across the inner-northern suburbs, many of whom had been involved in successful campaigns against the same road proposal during the preceding decade. Members of the network helped each other learn more about the proposal. Representatives met with council engineers, transport planners and local representatives. Delegates debriefed after these meetings to share their emerging understandings. Their discussions focused on emerging opportunities to infiltrate council's tight power arrangements and how best to articulate the anti-bypass position and mobilise the community.

One of the key areas of informal learning concerned campaign tactics. Anti-freeway alliance activists held diverse dispositions toward power-holders. The two 'natural leaders' in the alliance represented extremes of this continuum. While the network operated as a collective, without designated office bearers, Richard and Anne emerged as leaders, perhaps due to their high level of commitment. Both were spokespeople for residents' groups opposed to the freeway. Richard's group expected him to represent their organisation with a high degree of diplomacy and tact. Accordingly, Richard enjoyed a close working relationship with city councillors proposing the freeway. Anne, by contrast, had a long history of community leadership and influence, often entailing confrontational tactics. As a result, she had become a key target of council's aggressive public relations strategies and was labelled a radical extremist. Her group gave her free rein regarding public statements and endorsed her 'head-kicking' style.

Novices joining the campaign were exposed to both extremes. Meeting time was allocated to exploring and assessing the relative merits of adversarial and diplomatic tactics. Network meetings often closed with an evaluation session (see Ritchie, 1999) during which participants briefly shared their feelings about how the campaign was proceeding and how meetings could be improved. This evaluation process also helped define and value participant learning, and identified the activist skills and understandings related to both the sustainable transport and social change processes that campaigners felt they were developing.

It's not easy being green: overcoming ignorance and structurelessness

The draft road proposal contained thousands of pages of technical information. Activists familiar with such documents helped others interpret the proposal, identify potential impacts and critique council's justification for the road. The group also recruited transport and land-use planning experts to help interpret the documents and identify weaknesses susceptible to criticism or legal challenge. Flaws in reasoning, data gaps and under-stated impacts were identified and simplified into fact sheets and sound bites for media spokespeople.

Campaigners learned about different options for funding transport infrastructure. A strategic leak to opposition councillors and the media on this point contributed to the council dismissing the 'build-own-operate-transfer' option that would have been a very costly funding arrangement. In addition to gaining specific knowledge about transport infrastructure funding, novice campaigners were exposed to an apparently effective strategy. The funding exposé unfolded exactly as planned by the campaign network and was highly embarrassing to council. Activists who had previously doubted the network's capacity to exert influence reported renewed confidence.

Campaigners needed an inside view of council's decision-making processes. Legal advice on this point gave them the confidence to utilise Freedom of Information legislation. Novice activists were encouraged to help secure and interpret the voluminous documentation of the council's deliberations. Documents obtained through this search included a risk management strategy that identified the legal and political obstacles the council believed it faced in proposing, assessing and constructing the freeway. Discovering this strategy was a significant milestone in the group's evolution. Most campaigners espoused a strong commitment to open and accountable democratic procedures and uncritically believed that majority opposition to the road would naturally lead to a council decision to revise their transport plans. In the event, the council's apparent willingness to refute, attack, marginalise and divide anti-freeway elements of the community forced members to reconsider their naive political analysis. Ironically, campaigners who had utilised a legal instrument associated with openness and freedom of information had to learn the importance of cunning. It was evident they needed to develop a mature and coherent strategy to match that of their opponents. Effective engagement in the democratic process demanded a high level of acumen and creativity.

Discovery of the risk management strategy provided an important affirmation for group's members as many political risks identified as high impact had already been realised through sustained community opposition. The sense of achievement that followed this and similar discoveries helped build a belief that change was possible. This resonated with Alinsky's (1970) advice that organisers should steer groups toward initial campaign tactics likely to meet with success. Novice activists whose initial tactics accomplish their intended objectives are likely to develop confidence in their ability to effect change and to learn required activist skills – particularly if they perceive a pattern of success in progressively achieving more challenging campaign objectives.

During the initial stages of the anti-bypass campaign, the community groups aligned in opposition to the freeway were referred to collectively as the Northern Brisbane Residents and Owners Coalition. Ten to twenty community activists met on an *ad hoc* basis in members' homes and offices. The focus of energy shifted rapidly from fact-finding to strategic opposition to the freeway proposal. But lack of structure and routine became an obstacle to active recruitment. It appeared newcomers were also overwhelmed by the apparent expertise of seasoned campaigners and reluctant to take on responsibility. Despite positive media coverage and evident community support, the campaign did not appear to gain momentum. Council showed no signs of prevarication.

An opportunity to learn, an opportunity to teach

At the time of the campaign, I was coordinating a community education programme with a major non-governmental environmental organisation, the Queensland Conservation Council (QCC). The programme promoted sustainable transport through both education and advocacy. For several years, I had been researching education and training for effective environmental advocacy, at the same time as being a full-time advocate and activist educator.

QCC fitted Bill Moyer's (1990) stereotype of a 'Professional Opposition Organisation'. Most of its staff held degrees in environmental science and received funding and support for professional development. Anti-bypass campaigners, by contrast, participated voluntarily and represented variety of backgrounds: business people, professionals, tradespeople, students and unemployed people. Their participation in the campaign was oriented primarily toward achieving one short-term outcome: stopping the road. Members often commented that they had no interest in activism as an ongoing pursuit and would much prefer to be home watering the garden than attending endless meetings.

QCC was slow to join the campaign. As an 'umbrella' organisation that supported and coordinated conservation groups across the state, QCC generally prioritised long-term and regional concerns. QCC did not believe the transition to more sustainable transport patterns would be achieved by campaigning against specific road proposals. The organisation's strategies were generally consistent with Dryzek's notion (1997: 92) of *democratic pragmatism*: advocating environmentally oriented policies through research, government committees, lobbying and submissions. Transport campaigners at QCC also developed and trial-led systematic behaviour change programmes to engage specific neighbourhoods, schools, universities and workplaces and to promote cycling, walking and public transport. QCC worked on social, cultural and institutional change rather than short-term battles with politicians and planners. By participating in this campaign, QCC hoped to assist activist learning in three ways: by promoting a broader view of sustainable transport; by imparting specific campaign planning tools such as power-mapping and media strategy; and by fostering organisational learning within this community coalition.

As an established campaigning organisation, QCC offered potential benefits as well as *dis*benefits to the nascent anti-freeway network. On the one hand, QCC's organisational capacity offered a smaller community group resources, expertise and procedures. Seasoned QCC staff and volunteers were generally willing to share their experience and skills. On the other hand, QCC was, to some extent, inflexible in its campaigning approach and politics.

The organisation's administrative support led to more regular network meetings that were minuted and generally more purposeful. For instance, tasks were carefully tracked from one meeting to the next and agendas were negotiated and followed. Exposure to this professional face of community organising was a new and significant learning opportunity for many alliance members. Participants were encouraged to facilitate meetings, take minutes, propose tactics for consideration, and observe and evaluate campaign activities. Experienced activists encouraged and affirmed novices' tentative contributions, thus providing mentorship and modelling and contributing to the development of a learning culture. Several budding activists participated with the express objective of enhancing their advocacy abilities. The campaign was no longer primarily reactive. Rather, the campaign focus came to encompass a longer-term view. Activists began to speak of the anti-freeway battle as one chapter in a long-term social change movement away from car-dependency. Campaign outcomes unrelated to this specific freeway proposal began to be valued.

Getting angry, getting even

While initial campaign activities had emerged spontaneously, QCC encouraged the alliance to plan more strategically. One useful planning tool was 'power-mapping', a structured and participatory process I had developed in facilitating activist workshops. Campaigners brainstormed lists of individuals and organisations that could potentially influence the freeway decision and those who would be affected. Cards bearing these people's names were organised and re-organised on a desk or on the floor, graphically exploring power relations, affiliations and networks. A consensus configuration emerged depicting individual and organisational dispositions. Stakeholders were categorised as freeway champions or supporters, those without strong views, potential freeway opponents and active opponents. Stakeholders' motivations were also analysed. What factors explained their dispositions, and how could they be influenced?

This dynamic power map became a useful frame of reference when contemplating potential strategies and appeared to lead constructively to the broadening of the alliance and to help identify campaign opportunities. The map suggested that campaign support in conservative suburbs would enhance the campaign's political leverage and prompt conservative local and state government representatives to take up the issue. Although most participating groups had left-wing tendencies, there was no reason why the alliance should exclude conservatives. This led alliance members to help establish two new residents' groups and stage the campaign's most successful public meetings.

Disgruntled residents packed public halls to exert pressure on council and attract media coverage. Seasoned alliance spokespeople resisted the temptation to dominate these media opportunities. Instead, emerging groups were encouraged to learn and practise advocacy skills and increase their autonomy. Core alliance members provided political advice, helped to draft media releases, contributed to newsletters and leaflets, and mentored emergent local leaders. As a result, there was a dramatic increase in local media coverage, community awareness and anti-freeway political pressure in these suburbs. Local groups planning media releases regularly liaised with QCC's professional advocates to draft statements and rehearse interview responses.

The network became increasingly formalised, taking on the attributes of established non-governmental advocacy groups. With a name change, website and logo, the Inner Northern Coalition (INC) frequently dominated local media. The coalition met regularly and initiated a newsletter for distribution to households in target suburbs to communicate campaign momentum and success. Electronic communication effectively broadened the circle. Designated spokespeople issued media statements consistent with the agreed campaign strategy. Member groups were encouraged to maintain parallel media and community strategies so long as these were consistent with INC's statements.

Group members' expectations concerning coordination, consensus and the campaign's prospects of success increased dramatically. Nonetheless, group cohesion was regularly tested. Times of conflict involving difficult decisions often presented potent learning opportunities. For instance, the group's second attempt to gain access to council documentation under Freedom of Information legislation uncovered potentially explosive material. Leaders of alliance groups met to study the material and agree upon strategy. Despite consensus at this meeting, one activist leaked material to the media within hours. Although the resultant media coverage generated sought-after controversy, the impact was much less effective than anticipated. Despite failing to achieve their desired outcomes, campaigners discussed how the incident had highlighted the importance of media strategy.

Just as activists' own learning was valued, community education was also considered crucial to the campaign. INC tactics were based on two assumptions: that the city council's plans would be shelved in the face of sufficiently vocal dissent, and that the most certain trigger for such dissent was systematic awareness raising. Council inundated the community with pro-bypass messages through leaflets, media campaigns and other public relations strategies. With minimal funding, the INC sought to balance the scales. Leaflets were designed and printed *en masse*. By helping to draft, edit and distribute these materials, novice activists gained skills in community education.

Fortuitously, an international circus troupe erected their tents in the path of the intended freeway. INC volunteers gave leaflets to patrons each evening for a month. Although people were shocked to hear about the freeway, this failed to mobilise the community and dissent remained at levels readily managed by council's media strategists. The anti-bypass sentiment and activity reported in suburban newspapers could generally be traced directly to the core group. Councillors increasingly stereotyped INC spokespeople as unrepresentative and as 'greenies up trees', a reference to tactics emerging from an earlier anti-freeway campaign.

In an attempt to popularise anti-bypass sentiment, the alliance orchestrated a series of demonstrations, media stunts, community arts projects and other public events. These helped create a sense of identity for the campaign and gain new supporters as well as funding for the production of attractive banners and placards. During rallies in the park, the intended route was marked with lime and appeared on the evening news. Bands and performers drew a small crowd to a rally followed by an all-night vigil. INC organisers invited the region's Aboriginal groups including Turrbal spokesperson, Maroochy Barramba, and her family to join them in the park. Maroochy recounted ancestral stories to the group during a fireside vigil. The coalition's legal advice was that council had extensive powers to prosecute protestors who slept in the park, but the demonstration proceeded.

Your City, *Our* Say

The INC developed innovative communication strategies. Seasoned environmental communicators in the group seized on the idea of subverting the city council's expensive *Your City, Your Say* public relations strategy, a well-orchestrated programme entailing glossy materials distributed city-wide and targeted mail-outs soliciting citizen comment. Activists attended community events to solicit anti-bypass comments on the council's *Have Your Say* feedback forms which were then faxed to the Mayor's office.

A community education grant was secured to publish and print a tabloid for distribution to 80,000 households. *Our City, Our Say* contained contributions from anti-freeway community leaders, business people, local historians and others. This publication appropriated the colours and fonts of council's public relations literature, utilised simple yet powerful graphics to convey the road's potential impacts and provided sample letters to politicians and media outlets. Volunteer teams coordinated by resident groups across inner northern suburbs distributed it.

During the community coalition's eighteen month campaign, participating activists had given as much time and money as they could afford. Council was due to make a decision.

One last-ditch strategy the INC considered was a legal challenge. With expert advice, the groups had successfully broadened the terms of reference for the road's impact management plan. The resultant study had not fulfilled these demanding requirements. INC members speculated whether a judicial review could be mounted on this procedural neglect. Lack of expertise, lack of funds and, perhaps, a failure to recognise the value of legal action and outside expertise meant this strategy was not adopted.

The people united will sometimes win, and sometimes lose!

The day of judgement arrived. Council papers leaked to the group foreshadowed a vote on the road's funding. In a desperate attempt to stop the vote, INC members rallied to the council chambers, smuggled placards into the gallery and warned the media to expect a rowdy mob. Anger towards council was palpable. Jacket-and-tie-wearing activists joined the jeering and placard-waving, and several were evicted. Despite impassioned speeches and vigorous interjection by councillors and protestors, the vote was carried. Councillors aligned with the majority Labour party were not permitted a conscience vote. Yellow billboards heralding the freeway's promised benefits reminded campaigners daily of their defeat. Public relations material declared the road would actually improve air quality!

Community campaigns often start too late, after key political decisions have been made. Activists outside the alliance reacted spontaneously to the commencement of construction. Trees were spiked along the freeway route. New groups sprang up to protest against the destruction of heritage buildings and trees.

Alliance meetings were not convened for several months. Several campaigners contested the local government election as independent candidates, successfully making the bypass a lead issue during the election campaign. The core group finally gathered at a cafe to reflect on the campaign. Although they acknowledged defeat, activists valued the campaign's learning outcomes and the networks they had built. Rather than focusing on the shortcomings of the campaign, the group concluded their local communities would resist LULUs with increased vigour and effectiveness in the future.

Learning about learning

Several observations concerning learning for environmental activism may be drawn from this campaign:

- Environmental campaigns offer excellent opportunities for activists to learn social change skills and acquire confidence.

- By recognising the learning opportunities inherent in campaigns, activists and activist educators can maximise and harness this potential.
- While much activist learning is incidental, it need not be unconscious or neglected. Specific opportunities for overtly valuing learning include group discussions to identify learning opportunities and to reflect on and evaluate learning outcomes. A *learning strategy* can become an important element of a *campaign strategy*.
- Mentorship in the context of environmental campaigns offers a potent and appropriate learning opportunity for novice activists.
- Immediate campaign goals such as blocking development or influencing regulatory decisions often obscure equally significant outcomes including activist training and movement building. Reactive NIMBY campaigns are especially likely to focus on immediate objectives at the expense of longer-term movement building.
- The 'siege mentality' arising from rapid environmental degradation and the alienation of community members from decision-making, coupled with acute resource constraints, may lead environmentalists to prioritise immediate over long-term objectives. Learning and movement building tend not to be factored into campaigns to an extent commensurate with their potential.
- Reorienting campaigns to identify, value and harness activist learning opportunities has the potential to contribute to a more inclusive, skilled and effective environment movement.
- Research by and with activists offers rich locations for inquiry with potentially significant social and environmental benefits. Collaboration of this kind requires different parties to resolve their sense of alienation from the 'other'.

Activist organisations can readily enhance activist learning opportunities. Campaign planning, analysis and evaluation processes that are inclusive and continuous provide excellent opportunities for novice activists to develop political acumen and advocacy skills. Novices benefit from opportunities to observe and participate in increasingly complex and challenging campaign activities. Recent recruits can be asked to assist with meeting minutes or the distribution of publications before progressing to drafting correspondence and accompanying lobbyists to political briefings. This progression should provide opportunities for leadership such as coordinating working groups and facilitating meetings. Accomplished activists can offer encouragement and mentorship to novices, making learning an explicit, conscious component of each campaign.

In this community campaign, active citizenship was modelled and prac-tised, leading to experiential and participatory learning. Activists 'cutting their teeth' in the campaign went on to occupy leadership roles in other social change campaigns, sharing their knowledge and experience to build the capacity of grassroots community activism in the region. Learning through social action, as reflected in this community campaign, is a potent strategy to build knowledge, commitment and motivation.

References

Alinsky, S. (1970), *Rules for Radicals*, New York: Vintage Books.

Brown, L. (1998), *State of the World: A Worldwatch Institute Report on Progress towards a Sustainable Society*, London: Earthscan Publications.

Coover, V., Deacon, E., Esser, C. and Moore, C. (1978), *Resource Manual for a Living Revolution*, Philadelphia: New Society Publishers.

Dryzek, J. (1997), *The Politics of the Earth: Environmental Discourses*, Oxford: Oxford University Press.

Inner Northern Coalition. On-line http://www.powerup.com.au/~qccqld/INC/. Accessed 16/10/01.

Foley, G. (1999), *Learning in Social Action,* London: Zed Books.

Heaney, H. (2000), *Adult Education for Social Change: From Center Stage to the Wings and Back Again,* ERIC Monograph. On-line http://nlu.nl.edu/ace/Resources/Docment/ERIC1.html. Accessed 12/1/01.

Moyer, B. (1990), *The Practical Strategist: Movement Action Plan (MAP) Strategic Theories for Evaluating, Planning and Conducting Social Movements*, San Francisco: Social Movement Empowerment Project.

Porrit, J. (1990), *Friends of the Earth Handbook*, London: McDonald & Co.

Porrit, J. (ed.), (1991), *Save the Earth*, London: Harper Collins.

Queensland Government (1995), *Integrated Regional Transport Plan for South East Queensland*, GoPrint.

Ritchie, K. (1999), 'Incorporating group discussion as a critical reflection evaluation tool for learners', *Australian Journal of Adult and Community Education*, 39(3), pp. 154-61.

Whelan, J. (2000), 'Learning to save the world: observations of training for effective advocacy in the Australian Environment Movement', *Convergence*, 33(3), pp. 62-73.

Chapter 15

Popular Education and Popular Schools in Latin America

Claudia Flores-Moreno

The author, who is currently a research student at the Institute of Education, University of London, is interested in the recent reconsideration of how popular adult education can forge connections with schooling and the education of children. She argues that schools must become significant sites for political struggles and social action. Case material, drawn from research conducted in Mexico, demonstrates how this kind of work can be developed to broaden the base of popular education.

Popular schools flourished in Latin America after the 1960s in revolutionary contexts like Nicaragua, El Salvador and Guatemala, or under the influence of socialist ideologies, as in the cases of Peru and Chile. But schools with a popular education orientation also burgeoned in non-revolutionary contexts, as was the case in Brazil and Mexico since the 1970s, in relation to grassroots organisations and social movements. In the latter case, activists have become teachers in popular schools, practising popular education for social change within their communities.

However, the relationship between popular education and schools in Latin America has been a contentious one. On the one hand, academics have argued that popular education can be identified with pedagogical alternatives that have taken place inside and outside education systems and aimed at the transformation of societies (Gómez-Sollano and Puiggrós, 1986). This trend has addressed research on national policies in the region that have endorsed the extension of education services to popular classes as popular education over the past four decades. On the other hand, popular education, inspired by Freirean thinking, considered education in schools as resistant to social change until the end of the 1980s. However, the relevance of schools for social change has been reconsidered through important wide-scale attempts since the 1990s to 'rethink the basics' of popular education, a process known in Spanish as *refundamentación* (Kane, 2000).

The focus of this chapter is on how popular educators have engaged with academia in reconsidering the relevance of pedagogical knowledge and the possibility of popular education to reassess schools as sites of social change has emerged. I argue that popular schools, formed by radical grassroots organisations provide key opportunities to engage popular education and the academy, in ways which have usually been overlooked. With this in view, I will first discuss how schools were excluded as means for social change in the early stage of the popular education movement. Second, this opened up other possible ways in which the academy has engaged with popular learning and teaching practices. Third, I present an overview of the ways in which education systems have been tackled through *refundamentación*, and the main issues that emerge in revaluing popular education in schools. Fourth, I explore some of the relevant issues researched in popular schools. Lastly, I consider the links between *refundamentación*, pedagogy and popular schools, and the challenges they present for research.

Do schools matter for social change?

Based on the Freirean critique of banking education (Freire, 1972), a pivotal assumption during the early stage of the *foundational discourse* of the popular education movement during the 1970s and 1980s was that schools reproduced social, cultural and political inequalities. The main site of engagement for popular education in this discourse was in non-formal educational contexts. There were three main moments in the pedagogical process: starting from the practice of popular organisations, theorising them, and finally 'going back to practice' (NuÕez, 1992). In workshops and other non-formal teaching contexts, participatory methods and 'conscientisation' were enhanced through this approach.

In the 1980s the term 'crisis' was frequently applied to the complex economic, political and cultural changes in Latin America (CEAAL, 1994: 6). As a result of structural adjustment policies imposed on all governments in the region by international financial institutions such as the International Monetary Fund, which subordinated social policy to economic policy in most countries, a wide range of popular sectors, including the waged middle classes, were abandoned by the state and marginalised. Consequently, during the 1980s popular groups of resistance proliferated, producing significant clashes with the state. This crisis was intensified in the 1990s after the collapse of socialist economies and the crisis of Marxism internationally, which led to a vacuum which has been used by neoliberal politics to articulate their discourse as the only viable approach for the construction of modern societies (De Souza, 1996).

In a wide range of national contexts, popular education aimed to be practised by grassroots organisations to promote the interests of not only the working class but also organised *pobladores* (self-promoted peasants), women struggling for gender equity, indigenous peoples fighting for their rights, or urban youth groups were social actors who practised the three moments of *the* methodology of popular education. However, even though public education was a claim of some of those grassroots groups, it was excluded from the agenda of popular educators and their institutional work through Non-Governmental Organisations (NGOs). Some of the main reasons for this were that, on the one hand, schooling was considered by NGO promoters to work against social change, and, on the other, that international cooperation funded popular education through NGO practices in the privileged workshop modality, overlooking the demands of grassroots groups for schooling.

In the 1990s many institutions and agencies advising popular movements expressed the view that they 'did not understand the relationships between organisational process of the working class, social popular movements and popular schooling, maybe due to the lack of appropriate studies looking at these links' (De Souza, 1996: 71). The trend until the end of the 1980s was to consider education in schools as repetitive and resistant to change, with an orthodox understanding of official schooling as an ideological apparatus of the state (Althusser, 1974), or as a process of cultural reproduction (Bourdieu and Passeron, 1990). Although popular education denounced authoritarianism inside schools, there was no further research to analyse how it took place nor any direct attempt to counterbalance hierarchical power. Neither theories of reproduction nor accounts of resistance in schools were analysed (De Souza, 1996).

Popular educators representative from 195 civil organisations based in Latin America and the Caribbean formed CEAAL in 1982, working mostly with young people and adults. It is organised in three thematic networks: 'Popular Education between Women', 'Education and Local Power', and 'Education for Peace and Human Rights'. There is also a group on literacy and basic education, and a systematisation programme (CEAAL, 2001). It is mostly through the debates and documents produced by CEAAL members that *refundamentación* of popular education has been conceptualised. Given the diversity of popular education experiences and organisations, a range of questions and reflections emerged around the concern for a systematic pedagogy, which was lacking in such educational practices (Tábora, 1995).

Pedagogy and *refundamentación* of popular education

Despite the fact that the term pedagogy was not unusual in popular education discourse during the 1980s, pedagogy as a discipline was neglected until the mid-1990s. According to Colombian popular educator Mejía (1992), there are four main reasons for this. First, those who regarded pedagogy as specifically related to schooling considered it implicated in capitalist education. Second, many popular educators held the view that pedagogy consists basically of a range of participatory techniques developed by popular education processes. Third, some popular educators saw pedagogy as a completely new way to approach educational processes and therefore ignored mainstream educational studies. Many such studies had been the outcome of education research in the region, which had already made use of qualitative methodologies to understand social change taking place in education. However, a fourth vision put the emphasis on the social and political aspects of popular education, considering that pedagogical practice was a deviation, tending to depoliticise or neutralise popular education through a professional preoccupation with pedagogical knowledge.

At this stage, it was assumed that rather than a singular meaning, the concept of popular education was characterised by a number of constitutive elements (Ruiz, 2000). Those elements could be critical interpretations of the prevailing social order and the role of formal education, together with the aim of emancipatory politics, in which popular sectors were considered to be historical agents, protagonists of their own development. However, the recent constituents and practices of popular education projects have provided some elements for the grounding of a *popular pedagogy* (Torres, 1993). In this way, popular educators regard some of the main contributions of popular education to the construction of pedagogy as a discipline in terms of the widening of education as a concept and the recognition of the importance of cultural interactions in educational processes. *Refundamentación* of popular education has thus been considered to influence international agendas on adult education.

In the context of globalisation during the 1990s, it was acknowledged that the debate about pedagogy could not be carried on outside ongoing discussions between the education sciences and the social sciences in Latin America. According to Tábora (1995), the interest in debates about the epistemological status of pedagogy as a discipline emerged to consider its scientific status and the interdisciplinary construction of knowledge, as it had been conceived as an art for a considerable period of time. Pedagogy was then perceived as a 'young science', in the process of defining its theoretical frameworks, drawing on conceptualisations from more established disciplines such as psychology, anthropology and sociology (Zarco, 1996). It was only at this stage that pedagogy was perceived by some popular educators as ultimately responsible for the study of popular education processes. Thus, it was through this interest that popular educators engaged with the academy in terms of approaching debates around pedagogy.

Learning and methodologies

In the process of *refundamentación*, the Brazilian popular educator De Souza (1996) recognised some of the main challenges in trying to understand learning processes in popular education. This implied a critique of the iterative methodological formulation of popular education, framed as practice-theory-practice. A first acknowledgment was that there is no knowledge that comes directly from the political practice of popular groups, but only from the reflection upon such practice. Consequently, a basic reconceptualisation of learning within popular education processes was implied. Similarly, Ramírez (1996) pointed out that there have been at least three different conceptualisations of the relationship between learning and knowledge in popular education. The first was emancipatory knowledge, basically linked to militant practice. The second was an understanding of knowledge as the product of dialogue between 'knowledges' (*saberes*), characterising popular education as a communicative practice. A third understanding was that knowledges are rather a product of cultural negotiation, locating the identity of pedagogy beyond schools. It is possible to see that the recent relationship between popular education and pedagogy implied both the rethinking of social and political practices together with a reconsideration of pedagogical knowledge. Therefore, the consideration of knowledge and learning in popular education has created bridges to engage *refundamentación* in popular education with academic debates on pedagogy.

On the other hand, popular educators have also found fertile ground to explore recent developments of pedagogy drawing from educational psychology, as in the case of theorisations related to the work of Piaget and Vygotsky. This engagement is particularly relevant as both traditions have been highly influential on pedagogical approaches about educational planning, curriculum design and classroom didactics in education systems in Latin America since the 1980s. For instance, some studies have considered constructivism as compatible with popular education. This is the case in the work of Mariño (1993), who identifies similarities between magical, naive and critical levels of consciousness as proposed by Freire and Piagetian logical stages as steps in climbing the ladder of learning. However, a perceived limitation of this psychological approach is that it is centred on cognition; it therefore underestimates the emotional dimension and neglects the particularities of different cultural contexts, which are especially relevant in popular education. Another example is the importance of social and cultural dimensions in Vygotsky's approach to learning, despite the fact that the idea of a certain pre-fixed high point prevails. In this way, Mariño (1993) finds the development of a 'creative constructivism' necessary for popular educators, which might stimulate divergent thinking and enhance the construction of democracy in education. This is another example of the ways in which popular educators revalue pedagogical knowledge.

Amongst popular educators, there was also a consensus that learning takes place when people modify their ways of understanding and acting, and the previous structure of knowledge is changed. It was acknowledged that despite the fact that all social practice promotes the appropriation of new knowledge and the development of individuals, every social learning experience is not necessarily educational in a strict sense. Non-intentional knowledge is thus rather associated with the cultural sphere, and education is mostly identified as intentional learning actions. In this way, there is a distinction in popular education between non-formal practices such as 'schools of facilitators', where community activists take part in programmes on a regular basis, and the outcome learning of everyday tasks within organisations and social movements. Regarding the latter, popular education can enhance the practice of social movements that takes place in the cultural sphere of social life, towards the construction of social, cultural and political identity.

However, there are elements of popular education which persist despite *refundamentación*, such as the relevance of collective knowledge, the value of local knowledge as a starting point for learning, and the recognition of popular *knowledges*. In addition, the construction of collective identities remains an objective of this educational practice. Other principles of popular education practice are reaffirmed, such as valuing cultural diversity, social participation, the vision of change as involving qualitative processes, the agency and ability of popular sectors to decide for themselves, and the creation of identities through social movements (CEAAL, 1996).

Re-thinking education systems and social change

Through *refundamentación* the reconsideration of how to influence education systems in the region has overcome 'simplistic views in which everything which had to do with the state was intrinsically negative' (Zarco, 1996: 96). There was thus a reconsideration of whether pedagogical standpoints and their methods and topics were accessible to schools (formal education) or if those standpoints were only applicable to non-formal or semi-scholarly activities. The recognition of the need to understand official education systems in the region, and to engage popular education with them, was an outcome of this debate (Zarco, 1996). But this institutional recognition went along with a reconsideration of mainstream adult education, and the strategic links developed between them in the 1990s. An example of the latter were the links developed by CEAAL with the National Institute for Adult Education (INEA) in Mexico.

It is also worth noting in this context that educational reforms were carried out and some popular educators even occupied posts in Ministries of Education, like Fernando Cardenal in Nicaragua in the 1980s. For Osorio (1992), the two main political projects in which educational decentralisations were conceptualised were the neoliberal and the democratic. Both have in common a critique of the 'excessive centrality of the state'. Nevertheless, while the former privileges governability (instead of participation) and privatisation, the latter circumscribes educational decentralisation as a dimension of the democratic reorganisation of the state. Its objectives should thus be to provide autonomy at local levels for education management, based on a social (re)distribution of power. The mobilisation of new actors in Jomtien at the World Conference on Education for All (WCEFA) in 1990 thus 'opened the reconsideration of the role of popular organisations and social movements that popular education has worked with' (Osorio, 1992: 15).

Popular educators therefore considered that decentralisation did not consist in mere educational management. According to Cadima (1992), Bolivian educational decentralisation was faced with the challenge of responding to multicultural national identities, so that intercultural and bilingual education could be structured on the base of national pedagogies. Moreover, in the 2001 – 2004 period CEAAL has placed a strategic emphasis on influencing regional proposals about adult and young people's education, as well as strengthening national inter-institutional alliances which can affect education policy with regard to this population group. This has been interpreted as the active commitment of CEEAL to the recommendations of the the Dakar Education for All (EFA) Conference in 2000.

The debates within CEEAL in the 1990s on the reconsideration of schooling revealed a number of key themes. These can be grouped under three main heads: the contrast between the role of schools for democracy and participation and those in revolutionary contexts; the relevance of the recognition of bilingual education, multiculturalism and gender equity; and the relevance of exploring didactics within schools with a popular education orientation. Each will now be considered:

Democracy and participation in contrast with revolutionary contexts

Whereas it was argued that popular education had contributed to the transformation of schools in some cases, it was also considered that it had enhanced wider social democratisation, mostly in the context of transitional political regimes (e.g. after military dictatorships). The Argentinean researcher Rigal (1994) produced a report on a project called *Democracy, Public School and Popular Education*, carried out as a part of the systematisation programme of popular education in Latin America. In this project, the different relationships both within schools and towards society were considered. Similarly, Enríquez et al (1992) carried out research in the Dominican Republic, looking at schools as means for the configuration of democratic agents, for its potential in educational contents and the rather micro-processes of socialisation that take place in them. This research acknowledged that there was a raising of consciousness about the right to education for everyone within popular organisations and movements.

Progressive governments in transition provide particularly interesting cases of how popular education is re-considered within school systems. Lacayo (1992) found that the main achievements of the revolutionary strategy for education in Nicaragua were the National Literacy Crusade and the Adult Popular Education Programme, free access to public education and provision of texts in the context of land reform, together with the democratisation of health systems and social security. These elements appeared to have worked successfully in a coordinated way. In contrast, the implications of transitions of progressive groups into local government and the role that schools play in non-revolutionary contexts remained as a concern for further research.

Bilingual education, multiculturalism and gender equity

Concerns regarding ethnicity in education demonstrated the urgent need to recognise Latin America's diverse identities. Romero (1992) showed that bilingual education in Colombia was compatible with the political and ideological perspectives of popular education. This consideration relied on the fact that it validated relevant knowledges to forge distinctive linguistic and cultural communities in contrast with the universalising perspectives of teaching in Spanish only. In the same way, Azmitía (1992) described the project of the Indigenous Institute in Santiago as the first institution devoted to train indigenous teachers in Guatemala. Starting from the study of a 'normal' (teaching training centre), Azmitia pointed out that the main stages started from consolidating a cooperative to promote leaderships within students. The reconsideration of the cultural educational field, with its relative autonomy in Gramscian terms, was also contrasted with early understandings of schools as authoritarian and oppressive institutions (Rigal, 1994). Along with ethnic diversity, gender equity in education appeared as an important concern in reconsidering the role of schools in popular education. Rosero (1992: 25) showed that the Latin American Campaign 'Working for a human non-sexist education', promoted by the Popular Education between Women network in the 1990s, targeted the transformation of the dominant patriarchal ideology through the modification of attitudes towards the sexual division of labour.

Popular educators, teaching at schools and didactics

There was also an emphasis on didactics in *refundamentación*, as a discipline that brings about a good understanding for teaching, its mediations and the possibilities for learning (Tábora, 1995). In contrast to previous understandings of teaching as a non-guided horizontal process, discussions in this period were concerned with pedagogical approaches that explored teaching as an intentional activity. This can be considered as a breakthrough for popular education in the region. It was at the end of the 1990s when Freire himself reformulated his famous statement 'nobody educates anyone; men [sic] educate themselves mediated by the world' (Freire, 1984: 51). Some of his later formulations looked at the role of teachers in relation to pedagogy for autonomy (Freire, 1997). Indeed, Freire acknowledged that democratic authority is necessary for teachers/facilitators to practise a progressive pedagogy. In contrast to the pragmatic approach of applying didactics as an instrument, as in mainstream education, some developments emerged regarding the need to consider didactics in specific contexts to the practise of popular education in schools.

Refundamentación and pedagogies: from inside schools

Amongst the groups that we were working with here in the *colonia* [neighbourhoods], we started hearing that a secondary school was necessary. All *colonias* had their own school, but this one did not. Our principle was to start from people's needs, and in our grassroots organisation we used to work also on education . . . They said, 'We want a secondary school, our kids have to travel very early to other *colonias*, there are robberies and other problems to face!' We therefore struggled here to form one! We discussed in the assembly of the community, and everyone decided to form a secondary school, as a wider project of the grassroots organisation.

This quote comes from an interview with Elena, head teacher of a secondary school and member of the leadership of a radical organisation in the urban popular movement (UPM) in Ciudad Nezahualcóyotl, Estado de Mexico in November 2000. As part of a wider doctoral research project, I carried out 39 life history interviews between 2000 and 2001 with activists in the same grassroots organisation as that of Elena. Activists became teachers, head teachers and guidance teachers in popular schools in Ciudad Nezahualcóyotl, or Neza, on the outskirts of Mexico City. For a long time Neza had a reputation for being an urban development formed by internal migration in the 1960s under very rough conditions – poorly provided services, migration to the USA, as well as armed violence and gangs. Many radical grassroots organisations have proliferated in Neza since the 1970s, and their activists worked intensively with settlers. Some of them ran projects with a popular education orientation in the 1980s, and worked with groups of settlers linked with initiatives of organised women, transport and informal trade organisations, and also teachers. It is through their activism that various UPM grassroots organisations established popular schools.

Researching popular schools demonstrated the challenges of the diversity of practices that emerge while engaging popular education with schools. In my field research, the diverse origin or popular schools in the metropolitan area appeared to follow three main patterns. Popular schools were formed by grassroots organisations, run as cooperative schools with public funds and community participation, or managed by the teacher-leaders. Moreover, pedagogical orientations related to popular education in popular schools in Neza were unified. While head teachers had been involved in Maoist 'masses-line' groups, and more recently in left-wing party politics, teachers had been involved in activism, with cultural groups, anarchism, and more recently *Zapatismo*. These different ideological positions, inter-related with differences of gender, age and career, brought about different approaches to teaching and learning, mediations with the national curriculum and ways of understanding and implementing evaluation. Also, teaching related to activism at popular schools implied a variety of understandings of their links with the wider community.

Future directions

Popular education in Latin America cannot be equated exclusively with non-formal modalities anymore. To different extents, there is awareness amongst popular educators that schools are legitimate sites of struggle. However, this recognition presents some challenges in post-democratic transitions all over the region. On the one hand, grassroots groups, which practise popular education in schools, can get caught up with the agenda of the state at different levels, perhaps de-radicalising their pedagogical practice. On the other hand, teaching and learning in schools can also help to consolidate radical democracy, depending on how articulation with local communities and local government is achieved. Thus, researching popular schools as key sites of resistance seems to be relevant in exploring how popular education has been practised in schools in the region. It is strategically useful for popular educators to further engage with schools that have been involved in popular education and their struggles by researching their pedagogical debates and documenting the practice of teachers and head teachers with local communities.

Research approaches and methods of investigating popular education in schools need further discussion. Despite the fact that carrying out ethnographic research was often invoked in this period, there was little reference to how the study of learning processes using this research approach helped in *refundamentación*. Therefore, it is necessary to debate the politics of ethnographic research in schools with a popular education orientation, looking at their classrooms and links with local communities. In seeking to understand democratisation processes, issues of particular significance are power relations and the linkages with the wider projects of grassroots organisations and social movements.

Understanding popular education in schools has implications at both macro and micro levels. It appears to be of great importance to *refundamentación* to investigate how progressive social movements and grassroots organisations negotiate with the state at different levels (local, provincial, national). This would provide alternative ways to deal with education policy from the 'bottom-up' – and not necessarily by lobbying with international agencies and their agendas ('top-down'). In addition, it is important to study how progressive grassroots organisations and social movements articulate demands for the provision of public education, together with their contribution to teacher training. Further research on the learning of students and power relations in the classrooms of schools with a popular education orientation should also consider local and regional cultures in order to understand how didactics is linked in schools for social change.

References

Althusser, L. (1974), *Ideología y Aparatos Ideológicos de Estado*, Buenos Aires: Nueva Visión.

Azmitía, O. (1992), 'Educación popular y Escuela en Guatemala', *La Piragua*, 5, pp. 64-7.

Bourdieu, P. and Passeron, J.C. (1990), *Reproduction in Education, Society and Culture*, London: Sage.

Cadima, E. (1992), 'La descentralización educativa Boliviana', *La Piragua*, 4, pp. 19-20.

CEAAL (1994), *Educación Popular Para una Democracia con Ciudadanía y Equidad*. Documento de trabajo preparatorio a la III Asamblea Latinoamericana de Educación de Adultos, La Habana: CEAAL.

CEAAL (1996), *Nuevos escenarios y Nuevos Discursos en la Educación Popular. Memoria. Taller sobre Refundamentación de la Educación Popular*, Pátzcuaro: CEAAL.

CEAAL (2001), '*Qué es y qué hace el consejo de educación de adultos de América Latina?*' Unpublished CEAAL document.

De Souza, J. (1996), 'Perspectivas de una pedagogía de la educación popular, como ciencia social en América Latina' in CEAAL (ed.), *Nuevos escenarios y Nuevos Discursos en la Educación Popular. Memoria. Taller sobre Refundamentación de la Educación Popular*, Pátzcuaro: CEAAL.

Enríquez, A., Jimeno, C. and Mejía, M. (1992), 'Aportes desde la escuela a la construcción de sujetos democráticos', *La Piragua*, 4, pp. 43-5.

Freire, P. (1972), *Pedagogy of the Oppressed*, Harmondsworth: Penguin.

Freire, P. (1984), 'La importancia de leer y el proceso de liberación', México: Siglo XXI.

Freire, P. (1997), 'Pedagogía de la autonomía: saberes necesarios para la práctica educativa', México: Siglo Veintiuno.

Gómez, M. and Puiggrós, A. (1986), *La Educación Popular en América Latina*, México: SEP-Caballito.

Kane, L. (2001), *Popular Education and Social Change in Latin America*, London: Latin American Bureau.

Mariño, G.(1993), 'Constructivismo y educación popular', *La Piragua*, 7, pp. 60-73.

Mejía, M.R. (1995), 'Educación y escuela en el fin de siglo', Bogotá: Tarea-MEPB-CEBIAE.

Mejía, M.R. (1992), 'La pedagogía en la educación popular', *La Piragua*, 4, pp. 12-14

Mejía, M.R. (1998), 'Las metodologías en educación popular: una propuesta desde la negociación cultural' in CEAAL (ed.), *Procesos de Conocimiento en Educación Popular*, Santafé de Bogotá: CEAAL, pp. 54-90.

Nuñez, C. (1992), *Educar Para Transformar, Transformar Para Educar*, México: IMDEC.

Osorio, J. (1992), 'Educación y democratización: notas sobre la descentralización educativa', *La Piragua*, 4, pp. 15-18.

Ramírez, J. (1996), 'El problema de la construcción de conocimiento en las prácticas de educación popular' in CEAAL (ed.), *Procesos de Conocimiento en Educación Popular*, Santafé de Bogotá: CEAAL, pp. 7-23.

Rigal, L. (1994), 'Educación popular y escuela pública. A propósito de una investigación en marcha', *La Piragua*, 9, pp. 141-8.

Romero, F. (1992), 'Educación bilingüe: la alternativa cultural de la comunidad paez', *La Piragua*, 4, pp. 49-50.

Rosero, R. (1992), 'La educación básica desde las mujeres', *La Piragua*, 4, pp. 23-5.

Ruiz, M. (2000), Lo político y lo pedagógico: una mirada analítica a los procesos educativos de los sectores populares, PhD thesis, México: DIE-CINVESTAV.

Tábora, R. (1995), 'Pedagogía y educación popular: elementos para el debate sobre educación en América Latina' in CEAAL (ed.), *Nuevos escenarios y Nuevos Discursos en la Educación Popular. Memoria. Taller sobre Refundamentación de la Educación Popular*, Pátzcuaro: CEAAL.

Torres, A. (1993), 'La educación popular y lo pedagógico: evolución reciente y actuales búsquedas', *La Piragua*, 7, pp. 20-30.

Zarco, C. (1996), 'Repensando los fundamentos y horizontes de nuestras prácticas de educación popular en México' in CEAAL (ed.), *Nuevos escenarios y Nuevos Discursos en la Educación Popular. Memoria. Taller sobre Refundamentación de la Educación Popular*, Pátzcuaro: CEAAL.

Chapter 16

Social Movements and Free Spaces in Civil Society: The Case of the British Tenants Movement and Northern College

John Grayson

The tenants movement is an instructive yet under-researched example of organised self-education activity in British working-class communities. This chapter draws on the author's experience over many years of working with this social movement. It offers a unique insight into how changing state policy has influenced the struggle for justice in relation to public housing. This account is systematically related back to the history of radical adult education and the politics of class.

Northern College and adult education in the UK

Northern College, as one of seven adult residential colleges in the UK, represents a relatively late development of a particular tradition of adult education which has a meaning and resonance that goes well beyond the simple idea of older or mature students entering higher or further education. This is certainly the case in the UK where adult education has developed in a variety of ways, particularly since the Second World War. One powerful tradition within it has been a strand of popular adult education based on the idea of 'really useful knowledge'. What this means was, perhaps, best expressed in a letter to the *Poor Man's Guardian* newspaper in 1834 which stated: 'What we want to be informed about is – how to get out of our present troubles' (Clarke et al, 1979: 84). 'Present troubles' have remained at the heart of the popular adult education curriculum in the UK (see Hughes, 1995).

Social movements demanding 'really useful knowledge' have created 'in and against the state' educational innovations and institutions. These continue to exist precariously on the margins of the state, challenging official policies and contesting the orthodoxies of educational practice. The remains of this tradition, forged by class and social movements, are struggling to survive in the seven adult residential colleges in the UK.

Moments in history

A key feature of the UK residential colleges is that they emerged as a result of particular moments in history, conjunctures at which social movements and political groups were powerful enough to claim educational resources from the state in order to establish alternative counter-hegemonic spaces to work in relatively independent ways.

Historical moments when such spaces were prised open mark the periods when the residential colleges were created. Ruskin College in Oxford emerged in 1899 as a 'Labour' college, separate from the university, with trade unionists on its governing board and an overwhelmingly trade union-based student body. The small Plater College, also in Oxford, emerged in the 1930s through the Catholic Workingmen's Movement. The Cooperative College in Lough-borough (now in Manchester) was a wing of the once powerful British Cooperative Movement. Fircroft College in Birmingham was modelled by the unions on Grundtvig's Danish Folk High Schools. Certainly in the history and the current practices of Northern College, there is evidence of its creation at a particular moment in a free space created by the strength of organised labour and associated social movements – one of which was the tenants movement.

Formal educational institutions within modern capitalist states have always had difficulty relating to organised working-class movements. These institutions are patterned to respond primarily to dominant power groups – in Europe and North America, to middle-class or business interests. In this context, the adult residential colleges saw themselves as alternatives to mainstream state provision. But they also sought state funding and therefore placed themselves within the state system, giving 'access' a second time round for adults into higher education institutions. At the same time, positioned 'in and against the state', they sought to provide horizontal educational routes outwards to strengthen working-class self-organisation and the possibilities for change in society through collective action. Raymond Williams, himself a pioneer of popular adult education in the UK, put it this way:

> I remember the history of those without rights and without property demanding the means to understand and alter their world, of the complicated interaction between their own self-organising institutions and not only those who could control and buy them also those who knew, from direct experience, how hard, disturbing, and endlessly flexible any real learning is. (Williams, 1993: 243)

Northern College, the last of the existing colleges to be established, was created in 1979. Its staff represented a combination of a 1968 generation of Gramscian intellectuals and urban community workers, women's movement writers and activists, and trade union and university extension lecturers. Its students were trade union representatives and community activists. For the first time in a British adult residential college, half its provision was in the form of residential short courses ranging in length from a few days to six weeks. These were specifically intended to engage with the concerns of local community organisations and social movements in the declining industrial hinterland of the college, based on the steelworks and coalfields of South Yorkshire in the north of England.

Models of popular education and housing movements

Popular social movements since the Industrial Revolution have coalesced around major contradictions in the organisation of capitalist forms of social life. One of the central contradictions is that between landlord and tenant. Housing was a class battleground in Britain in the nineteenth century, and has remained so to the present. Tenants movements in the UK developed out of the proletarian labour cultures of the late nineteenth century and have survived into the early twenty-first century.

What is now being recognised is that social movements, particularly 'contentious social movements ... those involved in collective political struggle' (McAdam et al, 2001: 5) have a distinctive cultural and educational aspect. Tawney understood this clearly: 'If I was asked what is the creative force, which has carried forward educational movements, I should reply: the rise of new classes, of new forms of social structure, of new cultural and economic relationships' (cited in Jackson, 1995: 183).

In nineteenth century Europe it is also clear that in workers movements education was seen as a potentially transformative, even revolutionary, process. This kind of self-generated and autonomous popular education was a central feature of early artisan and working-class movements. The tenants movements that developed in the UK between 1910 and 1930 (as well as in Spain, France, Austria, Hungary, Denmark and Sweden) have to be understood as part of the organised labour movement and involved in worker education.

On the other hand, middle-class social movements with political influence, even control of state policies, developed to counter the threat from working-class movements. Such bourgeois social and political movements mobilised educational and cultural resources against and antagonistic to popular educational movements of the working classes. Their aim was

> ... specifically to influence the thinking of the then radical working and artisan classes, to draw them away from ideologies that led directly to radical or revolutionary conclusions, and to persuade the workers that their real interest lay in assisting, or co-operating with, the positive and active development of capitalism. (Simon, 1990: 17)

The threat posed by tenants movements as part of the broader challenge of organised labour was a real one in the early twentieth century. George Lansbury, a future leader of the Labour Party and founder of the *Daily Herald*, could write in an editorial in that newspaper in May 1912, at the height of the Syndicalist industrial strikes of 1911-14:

> Has not the time come for organising a strike against paying rents to slum landlords? .... We are of the opinion that the formation of Tenant Societies to resist the executions of landlords by all possible means might wring great benefits from that selfish class, even as Trade Unions

have extorted concessions from grasping employers … Such an organisation, powerfully directed, might make history.

In 1915 tenants groups in Glasgow, led by women, organised a successful mass rent strike, which forced the wartime government to freeze rents and mortgages until 1922.

In turn, ruling groups were roused to counter this powerful alliance of unions, tenants and socialism. To answer the challenge, they mobilised a morally charged, middle-class social movement around ideas of 'philanthropy' intent on both 'gentling the masses' and remoralising them into 'respectability'. Housing reformers identified strongly with this form of philanthropy. As one recent study has suggested, 'the goal of many early housing reformers was to improve standards of morality, as well as of mortality and morbidity' (Garside, 2000: 50). In Tawney's terms, philanthropy was a middle-class social movement, carrying with it a substantive educational agenda. It was not simply 'cold charity': with the money went a moral and political offensive. Housing for the working classes was a constant preoccupation, but at root this form of philanthropy was educational in character. As the editor of the *Working Man* put it, 'it is an education to live in a good house. A man may be bad in a good house: but he who is bad in a good house will be worse in a bad house' (Jowitt, 1986: 46). Establishing a unique form of working-class housing, 'council housing' with local authorities as landlords, was seen as an anti-revolutionary gesture. As one senior civil servant famously wrote to Lloyd George, the Prime Minister, in April 1919: 'the money we are going to spend on housing is an insurance against Bolshevism and Revolution' (Swenarton, 1981: 79).

Northern College, the distinctive moment of creation and, in particular, its work with the tenants movement have to be understood and located in this historical context.

In and against the state

In the late 1960s a new generation of student activists, militant women and civil rights campaigners coalesced with working-class tenants, who were by now deeply disillusioned with the quality of local state house building and wide-scale corruption amongst builders and architects and local politicians. Militant action and self-education took over. The rent strike returned, as did direct political action. For example, in 1969 Sheffield women activists fought as tenant candidates against the ruling Labour Council and removed it from office after thirty-six years in power (see Henderson, Wright and Wyncoll, 1982). In Northern Ireland housing issues became part of the civil rights struggle. In October 1971 the *Guardian* reported that:

> The civil disobedience campaign, which involves the non-payment of all rents, rates and bills to public bodies, has been running for seven weeks

... The Government reckons that local authorities have lost more than £400,000 in council rents alone ... Officials estimate that about 140,000 people living in council houses have been taking part in the campaign. (Moorhouse et al, 1972: 153)

In Derry the famous Civil Rights March of 5 October 1968 which is often seen as the beginning of the 'Troubles' in the North of Ireland, was organised by the Derry Housing Action Committee, 'which set out with the conscious intention of disrupting public life in the city to draw attention to the housing problem' (McCann, 1974: 27).

When the Conservative government attempted to increase council house rents in 1971, thousands of tenants withheld their rents or went on rent strike. Community workers and local activists started education and training courses aimed at developing campaigning skills. Tenants federations were revived in London, Newcastle, Coventry, Manchester and Glasgow. At Northern College some of the first 'short courses' offered in 1979 were organised for and with the tenants federations of Sheffield, Newcastle and Coventry.

Northern College and a moment of history

The original Northern College courses were designed for trade union activists, following on from a tradition of day-release classes for miners and steelworkers organised by the Universities of Sheffield and Leeds. These classes helped to develop a new militant leadership for the unions, a leadership which was to fight a three-month national steel strike early in 1980 and a year-long miners' strike from 1984 to 1985. Arthur Scargill, the miners' leader, was himself a student in these university classes. The first Principal of Northern College, Michael Barratt Brown, formerly of the University of Sheffield, was one of the moving forces behind these classes – himself an adherent of Guild Socialist or workers' control ideas. The first Vice-Principal of the College, Keith Jackson, came from a parallel tradition of radical adult education and community development at the University of Liverpool and was committed to developing work with community-based social movements – including tenants.

Thus a radical moment was exploited by a number of public intellectuals in alliance with powerful interests in the trade unions, women's organisations and tenants federations which were influential in local Labour Party politics. They put forward the idea of establishing a Ruskin-type college in the north of England. The national Labour government, however, rejected state funding, and it was an alliance of locals councils which eventually bought an eighteenth-century country house and established their own 'workers' university' with around thirty students on a full-time, two-year residential course and a range of short courses. The academy was invaded and occupied by deciding to mobilise a network of socialist intellectuals in universities to constitute the Academic Board. This would oversee educational standards and establish a new and independent Northern College Diploma – a qualification that was recognised both for work in trade unions, community organisations and local government and as a university entrance qualification for working-class students who had 'failed' in their first educational careers.

Tenants and the college

As one of the key social movements whose activists helped to create the college, tenants organisations worked closely with it in developing its education and training provision. This 'negotiating of the curriculum' became a trademark of Northern College's practice, which was quite different from the established practice of the academy in further and higher education. The assumption in mainstream practice is that work with social movements, particularly community organisations and tenants, is about working in a 'philanthropic' and 'top-down' way with 'disadvantaged' groups who 'need' education. Northern College always maintained an equal and non-patronising relationship with tenants organisations, working with their members and officers jointly to develop educational programmes.

This distinctive philosophy was documented in an early study of Sheffield community and tenant groups and their links with Northern College:

> They do not come to the college to acquire knowledge in some abstract sense, but to discover the knowledge they already have and to sharpen and develop it with a view to using it in their struggle to comprehend the world and to act upon it. The college then, seeks to practice a form of cooperative learning. (Cowburn, 1986: 192-3)

A 'sponsored' tenants movement and state training

In many parts of the UK the rent strikes and militancy of tenants organisations in the 1970s was met, not with philanthropy as in the early part of the century, but by direct concessions from the local state with offers of participation and tenant charters. Tenants were given rights to sit on decision-making committees and provided with financial grants to set up independent organisations and fund tenant management experiments.

Tenants federations began their own training programmes for members. Independent self-organised education and training was harnessed to activism. Links with trade unions were again forged: in Sheffield the 'Homes and Jobs' campaign organised joint meetings and training for shop stewards from the building industry and local authority landlords and tenant representatives. Northern College organised joint training for shop stewards and tenant representatives.

A regular Northern College course 'Housing in the Community' was designed to brief tenants organisations on political developments and to discuss possible responses. Ironically, the college had been founded in exactly the same year, 1979, as the Thatcher government came to power – the most right wing Conservative administration of the twentieth century. The government's first and biggest privatisation programme of the Thatcher era focused on the mass sale of council housing. In this context, a key element in the tenant education programme at Northern College was the links between the politically experienced staff and the leadership of the tenants movement. The same kind of self-organised and jointly controlled education also developed in other parts of the UK.

Eventually, in 1989 a National Tenants and Residents Federation was founded at Wakefield, partly on the basis of ground work done at Northern College. In effect, the state's programme of neoliberal reforms and privatisation had managed to mobilise a new tenants movement by 1990. But it was a movement the state was determined to control. Government and local council landlords developed a new management and educational offensive. Landlords appointed tenant liaison workers, and actually set up their own 'sponsored' tenants associations. These had to be non-political and conform to landlord-set rules in order to gain recognition and funding – a virtual incorporation of tenants organisations.

The Labour Party, after its landslide victory of the 1997 general election, simply continued and institutionalised this attempt to incorporate the tenants movement – now, in the language of New Labour, as depoliticised 'active citizens' to be 'consulted' as 'consumers' of a 'service'. The consequences have been predictable. As Lowe puts it, 'Much of what is labelled as 'tenant participation' is no such thing but rather an encounter of tenants in general with officially defined structures and approved forms of involvement' (1997: 153).

At the heart of this process of attempted incorporation was education and training. Large landlords set up training units for tenants. Training manuals were produced setting out the 'competencies' required by tenants to take on management responsibilities in community-based housing organisations. Voluntary tenants associations were to become part of the new 'enterprise culture' (Furbey, Grayson and Wishart, 1996) – tenants trained for their place on the conveyor belt of government policy. Just as the philanthropy movement had attempted to remoralise tenants, so the neoliberal state now sought to depoliticise them.

Northern College and the neoliberal agenda

The modelling and moulding of tenants organisations was mirrored in attempts to 'reform' the education system, simultaneously centralising power and deregulating control. There were still pockets of resistance, however. For instance, Northern College sought to build on collaborative work with the nearby Sheffield Hallam University which had pioneered housing courses in Sheffield, a city dominated by council housing modelled on social experiments in the 'Red Vienna' of the 1930s. Staff at both institutions worked with colleagues at the Universities of Durham and North London and, crucially, with tenants organisations to develop a National Certificate in Tenant Participation and Control (NCTP) which gained recognition by the Chartered Institute of Housing.

The NCTP, however, highlighted a fundamental ambivalence about accreditation and official qualifications. On the one hand, they can be seen as forms of regulation and control. On the other, they can be liberating and empowering – challenging the academy's traditional monopoly of what 'academic' means. As Mary Stuart argues:

> We need to fight for individuals and communities who are not considered to have the right to define their own knowledge . . . to enable them to investigate and explore their knowledge and to demand other forms of knowledge . . . It is about challenging the academy to allow active participation from a wide range of communities and individuals who will help to redefine the parameters of higher education itself. (Stuart, 2000: 33)

Northern College has also developed other accredited courses for tenants as well as a national qualification for volunteers in credit unions (local cooperative banks). These initiatives have recently culminated in the establishment of the first part-time degree in the UK, offered jointly with Sheffield Hallam University, in Community Development and Regeneration. This is specifically designed to attract community activists, unqualified workers and social movement activists working in the de-industrialised and re-industrialised areas around the college. The agendas of tenants and other social movements have thus continued to inform the work of the college.

But it has been, and continues to be, a struggle. Northern College was a target for government scrutiny and cutbacks in the 1990s. After a hostile inspection in 1983, the college managed to recover – only to lose its two-year diploma course with its independent status. It was forced to offer only one-year and short courses, and to have them externally accredited rather than retain control of its own self-accredited diploma. Its crucial links with local government, particularly Labour-controlled authorities, have also been weakened by the rapid erosion by central government of their educational and other financial powers.

Survival on the margins?

It could be argued that Northern College is a remarkable example of survival rather than a possible model for the future. It continues to operate within the inherent contradictions of state policy. David Blunkett, the former British Home Secretary and a politician with strong links to Northern College, emphasises the government's interest in both citizenship and order:

The central goal underpinning most potential reforms is the stimulation and development of a culture of active democratic citizenship . . . but a strong public authority which proves itself capable of defending social order is crucial. (Blunkett, 2001: 113 and 116)

It is perhaps in the free spaces between liberty and order that Northern College practice might survive and flourish. Certainly much of its work with community activists and social movements is now located in the spaces provided by 'projects' funded by regeneration or European Union (EU) support programmes. Ironically, therefore, EU social democratic approaches now support this kind of educational work on the margins.

Nevertheless, the college is still able to link with social movements, and it is important to recognise that the tenants movement in Britain never went away. Since the 1980s there have been two parallel strands of development: the sponsored tenants participation world of associations alongside the surviving self-organised campaigning and politically active tenants movement. A National Tenants and Residents Federation was established in 1989 – the first tenant-led national organisation since the 1940s. It should also be noted that between 1987 and 1991 the largest civil disobedience campaign in British history emerged: fourteen million people refused to pay all or part of a newly introduced flat-rate local tax. This Community Charge or Poll Tax became 'uncollectable', and eventually proved to be the undoing of the 'Iron Lady', Margaret Thatcher.

By 1989 there were a thousand local Anti-Poll Tax Unions in housing estates and suburbs throughout England, Scotland and Wales. Many of these campaigners were active members of tenants organisations, and their action included classic forms of popular education. For instance, when protestors and 'non-payers' were arraigned before the courts, 'throughout England and Wales over a thousand people were trained to do court support work and could quote the relevant legislation. This is unique in the history of popular campaigning' (Burns, 1992: 135-6).

Currently, tenants in Britain confront a national programme of 'large-scale voluntary transfer', or privatisation of state housing. This is the *same agenda* which now confronts working-class tenants across the European Union, and has already faced tenants in central and eastern Europe. In the UK a campaign called 'Defend Council Housing' has been organised. All the ingredients are present for another phase of the tenants movement. The powerful federations throughout Britain have found that state funding is easily withdrawn and they are now developing a campaign and training programme at Northern College based around 'conventions' or training weekends. Sympathetic academics are being mobilised to develop strategies with experienced activists. Some of these activists have stood at elections as candidates for the Socialist Alliance and Respect – politically left coalitions which have opposed the Labour Party in recent elections. Tenants are again linking up with such groups. The 'Defend Council Housing' campaign has won the support of UNISON , the biggest public service union in Europe, the GMBU, the third largest union in the UK, and UCATT, the union of the building and construction industry. The historic alliance between the tenants movement and the trade union movement has been resurrected. Northern College receives state funding but it also has other sources of support from the unions and EU programmes. Perhaps it still has enough space to resource, sustain and reinvigorate its long-standing work with the tenants movement.

Tenants of state housing in the UK are unique citizens because their political representatives are, at the same time, their landlords. Their movements are always political, always contentious, and always potentially at work within the contradictions of a market economy and marketised social policy. State intervention has so far failed to eradicate self-organised popular education in the tenants movement. Social movements of this kind have potential as agents of change because of their 'educational' character. This has enabled them to encroach on the academy and, in the case of Northern College, to occupy some of its territory and defend themselves against hostile state policies. Perhaps the real question now is: Can these footholds in the academy lead to the permanent occupation of free spaces and more pluralist and diverse forms of state provision? Hardly a revolutionary prospect, but we do live in hard times . . .!

References

Blunkett, D. (2001), *Politics and Progress: Renewing Democracy and Civil Society*, London: Demos and Politicos.

Burns, D. (1992), *Poll Tax Rebellion*, Stirling: AK Press.

Clarke, J., Crichter, C. and Johnson, R. (eds), (1979), *Working Class Culture: Studies in History and Theory*, London: Hutchinson.

Cowburn, W. (1986), *Class, Ideology and Community Education*, London: Croom Helm.

Furbey, R., Grayson, J. and Wishart, B. (1996), 'Training for tenants in an enterprise culture', *Housing Studies* II(2), pp. 251-69.

Garside, P. (2000), *The Conduct of Philanthropy: William Sutton Trust, 1900-2000*, London: Athlone.

Henderson, P., Wright, A. and Wyncoll, K. (eds), (1981), *Successes and Struggles on Council Estates: Tenant Action and Community Work*, London: ACW.

Hughes, K. (1995), 'Really useful knowledge: adult education and the Ruskin Learning Project' in Mayo, M. and Thompson, J. (eds), *Adult Education, Critical Intelligence and Social Change*, Leicester: NIACE, pp. 97-110.

Jackson, K. (1995), 'Popular education and the state: a new look at the community debate' in Mayo, M. and Thompson, J. (eds), *Adult Education, Critical Intelligence and Social Change*, Leicester: NIACE, pp. 182-203.

Jowitt, J.A. (ed.) (1986), (ed.), *Model Industrial Communities in mid-Nineteenth Century Yorkshire*, Bradford: University of Bradford.

Lowe, S. (1997), 'Tenant participation in a legal context' in Cooper, C. and Hawtin, M. (eds), *Housing, Community and Conflict: Understanding Resident Involvement*, London: Arena.

McAdam, D., Tarrow, S. and Tilley, C. (2001), *Dynamics of Contention*, Cambridge: Cambridge University Press.

McCann, E. (1974), *War and an Irish Town*, London: Penguin.

Moorhouse, B. (1972), 'Rent strikes: direct action and the working class' in Miliband, R. and Saville, J. (eds), *Socialist Register 1972*, London: Merlin.

Simon, B. (ed.), (1990), *The Search for Enlightenment: The Working Class and Adult Education in the Twentieth Century*, London: Lawrence and Wishart.

Stuart, M. (2000), 'Beyond rhetoric: reclaiming a radical agenda for active participation in Higher Education' in Thompson, J. (ed.), *Stretching the Academy*, Leicester: NIACE, pp. 23-35.

Swenarton, M. (1981), *Homes Fit for Heroes*, London: Heinemann.

Williams, R. (1993), 'Different sides of the wall' in McIlroy, J. and Westwood, S. (eds.), *Border Country: Raymond Williams in Adult Education*, Leicester: NIACE, pp. 242-6.

Chapter 17

Towards a Performance-based Pedogogy of Self-determination

Dan Baron Cohen

This account is based on the author's practical involvement, as a British arts-educator and researcher, with radical popular movements in Brazil. His particular concern is to demonstrate how curriculum and pedagogy can be developed to increase the creativity and critical autonomy of learners who have little or no experience of formal education. The argument is very much that the political struggle for emancipation must start with the personal struggle to liberate the self.

Situating this reflection

Should I write for Rubens?
Rubens withdraws into his coat. I hadn't anticipated this.
Rubens. How d'you usually remember?
A shrug. Eyes glaze.
I breakdance.
Ciru leans forward insistently. Earnest open palms.
He's learning to read. I'll write for him. It'll be in his notebook.
Rubens glances at Ciru. Uncomfortable gratitude. I interrupt.
What about your own responses, Ciru?
He straightens, tilting backwards almost imperceptibly.
We'll learn much more from him. Besides, Rubens' needs are more urgent.

In May of 2001 I worked with Rubens, Ciru and scores of popular educators and community activists as a pedagogical consultant to the department of education within the new Workers Party government of Rio Grande do Sul in southern Brazil. I was asked to coordinate five four-day 'capacitation workshops' to prepare university lecturers and community leaders for an educational programme designed to 'enable excluded communities to participate in the construction of a democratic society'. Quite apart from the big questions like 'What is democracy?' and 'How do people become skilled in practising it?' the workshops and the above fragment of dialogue (from one of the cultural literacy workshops I offered) revealed profound questions about how people from different social classes can work together without idealising or cultivating dependency in the other, and why we need to know our most internalised histories in order not to reproduce them.

During the past two decades, I have lived on the threshold between two worlds, as an activist within the academy and as a community-based arts-educator within popular struggles. I have been preoccupied by two recurring tendencies: the resistance in popular educators and leaders of social movements to include their own subjectivities within (educational) processes of transformation; and the mutation of radical movements into inert bureaucracies paralysed by internal conflict, authoritarianism and fear. In this chapter, I want to reflect upon these questions and preoccupations through my own experience in order to define what I call a performance-based pedagogy of self-determination and to demonstrate its potential for popular education and the cultivation of a new politics of empathetic solidarity and community democracy.

I am writing from my makeshift home within a landless movement *assentamento* (settlement) in southern Brazil, which I share with Manoela, my partner-collaborator. We are presently completing a one-year unwaged cultural literacy project with local youth – learning to *read ourselves in the world* critically in preparation for democracy – in exchange for the non-GM food which the young people collectively produce in their community school where we work, and evaluations with the families, community leaders and other educators who live nearby. These pedagogical conditions explain why in July 1999 I decided to resign my senior lectureship in drama at the University of Glamorgan in Wales to accept an invitation to extend my collaboration with *Movimento Sem Terra* (MST), the landless people's movement which emerged out of liberation theology and agrarian reform movements in the late 1970s to democratise Brazil (Branford and Rocha, 2002).

My decision to give up the security and precious resources of a permanent contract to work with the largest social movement in Latin America today was a decisive pedagogical response to three interwoven concerns. First, that in seeking to respond as educators to the new psychological and socio-cultural effects of the accelerating technological, information and media revolutions, social fragmentation, widening social inequality and global ecological threat, we need precisely what today's market-driven educational institutions deny: the opportunity to question and to experiment in a sustained and intimate way within a community of active dialogue. Second, that as a 'first-world' educator from the North, I needed to listen to and know the 'third-world' South in order to learn how to read peripherally – to see from the critical perspective of the excluded majorities. There is no other way to develop decolonised methods of community-based democratic change (Thiong'o, 1993). And third, educators need to study the educational models being developed by social movements struggling with the emotional and psychological legacies of centuries of exploitation and subjugation if we are to collaborate in the construction of a new society.

Based upon some three years of collaborations with MST, I believed their slow revolution – the organisation of the excluded to occupy and transform fertile unproductive land into autonomous, agro-ecological communities, consciously based on the educational methods of Paulo Freire – reveals important insights for activist-educators searching for an internationally-relevant *praxis* of self-determination. The invitation to participate in this young movement arose however because MST believes the pedagogy of community-based cultural action can contribute to resolving an increasingly urgent question: how to cultivate new, non-authoritarian, non-individualist, socialist subjectivities. The relentless political and economic discrimination and military violence the movement has been subjected to by successive federal governments has necessitated an uncompromising politics of survival and resistance. But certain significant ideological reasons also explain why it is struggling today to sustain any sense of community and to build a cooperative culture.

The question of subjectivity

Let me attempt to reveal these through the poem 'Within' which I wrote while contributing to the movement's national school for activists:

> In the national school for the formation of activists
>
> I met a black youth full of hope, struggling against himself
>
> being judged by his brigade for having eaten after the hour of silence.
>
> Why did he violate the collective discipline to search for bread
>
> when he wasn't hungry?
>
> I studied his *companheiros* as they evaluated him with angry certainty
>
> in the name of solidarity and the future.
>
> Why do people who have suffered so much injustice and deprivation
>
> themselves become involuntary oppressors?
>
> I studied another youth swallowing public humiliation
>
> for having unknowingly confused the word *intuition* for *institution*.
>
> Why was he directed to rededicate himself to the study of Lenin
>
> and not asked: what *is* intuition?
>
> Can we transform the histories inscribed within our bodies?

MST recognises that a 'cultural revolution' is required. The necessity which motivates land occupations and collective resistance to repression does not organically evolve into the choice or capacity to build cooperatives. But while the movement's leadership believes that unintentional authoritarianism or competitive individualism are simply ideological contradictions, it will not enable its political activists to understand and transform their own subjectivities. The most loved popular educators and activists are intuitively 'culturally and emotionally literate'. But while the predominantly male, formally educated leadership continues to understand subjectivity as bourgeois psychology, and culture as an effective weapon of propaganda or expression of popular identity, its activist-educators will neither be able to know themselves nor create anew communities.

The dynamic psychological and emotional structures that shape our subjectivity (our empathetic intelligence, ways of seeing, sense of integrity, community and identity) are acquired (often very violently) in our most intensely charged intimate and public relationships. For these reasons their origins tend to be deeply hidden from ourselves and they seem inexplicable and unchangeable. But they dynamically permeate all the spaces in our micro-social relations because they are inscribed within our bodies, in our very presence. We therefore need instruments which can reveal how centuries of violation and self-protection, authority and subordination are complexly inscribed in our body languages, our strategies of reasoning, our emotional structures, musculature, tones of voice, eye-expressions, in the very sensitivities of our skin. We need techniques which can illuminate how we influence and are influenced by, collude with or subvert the varying performance norms of all the public spaces we enter and exit (Kershaw, 1999); how the directed gaze of any collective space amplifies and focuses, shapes and is shaped by our presence (Boal, 1998); and how these cultural forces are used to pacify and direct or sensibilise and transform our social relations.

Without these instruments and techniques – what we might call a performance-aware pedagogy based in the constant practice of emotional and cultural literacy – how can we learn to consciously read ourselves and others or experiment with the sensitivities or strategies needed to develop democratic subjectivities and organisations?

Performance-awareness: the drama of being human

I will explain what I mean by 'performance-awareness' through various personal educational experiences. In the early 1980s I collaborated with the English educational dramatist Edward Bond and the Kenyan popular educator Ngugi Wa Thiong'o on several anti-imperialist theatre interventions. Despite the important ideological debate the productions provoked, what primarily remains in my memory are their *off-stage* conflicts, between performers. These were explained as class struggle, the effects of (neo)colonialism, the consequence of not having committed activist-performers. They were clearly all these things. But to keep the production intact, they needed to be resolved. Intuitively, I could see that the origins of these intensely personal confrontations were not 'personal', so I managed to ideologically 'depersonalise' and defuse them. But we all knew they had simply been diffused, deferred to an unspeakably-sensitive, unpublishably-dangerous 'place' beneath and beyond everything: a threatening, invisible presence in every debate and decision which cast its shadow across all our agreements, across the integrity of the very word 'collective', capable at any moment of reappearing centre-stage to mock and scandalously unmask our public declarations of 'democratic production'.

The conflicts appeared to divide into two crude categories: explicit confrontation (explosive and defensive), staged by the more 'oppressed' actors, and implicit demonstration (composed and offensive), staged by the more 'empowered' actors. I use the performance metaphor not to imply they were necessarily consciously staged or were in any sense fictional, but to underline two principal qualities: the *performativity* of the needs driving these conflicts (their sense of having not only been ideologically scripted and rehearsed, but of 'seeking an audience'); and their 'stage-consciousness', however intuitive, of the focusing and magnifying powers of aesthetic space generated by the directed social gaze of an audience (Boal, 1998).

In 1984 I entered Manchester's College of Adult Education, determined to solve this onstage/offstage contradiction. I established a *praxis* based upon dialogue, solidarity, care and respect for difference, focused upon the collective interpretation and production of a unanimously-selected play, within a democratised aesthetic space.

This pedagogical proposal generated immediate effects. Within three months my twice-weekly theatre production class had expanded into a part-time theatre-for-development collective. But though it was fulfilling the objectives of the college (rebuilding the self-esteem of primarily unemployed people), once it extended its collective, democratic practice through open rehearsals and performances beyond the walls of the college to stimulate impoverished working-class communities to re-imagine their future, the project was condemned as subversive and was closed by the academic dean.

In 1985 I entered Manchester University as a 'special lecturer in perform-ance'. Through the same *praxis*, the final year theatre production I was given to direct rapidly transformed itself into a theatre-as-education collective. My commitment to a dialogic culture of mutual support, uninhibited questioning and creative experiment again inspired unusual individual and collective motivation and critical courage. But though the department had canonised radical theatre practitioners like Piscator, Brecht and Boal, and taught political, feminist and gay theatre, when the collectively-prepared performance and project analysis gained a collective first class from its external examiner, the board of examiners rejected the grade as 'normatively impossible' and academically unacceptable. I was sent to the university dean who requested I individualise the grades. I explained I could not undo, and would not undermine, the pedagogical process that had generated an exceptional educational project. The collective grade was reluctantly accepted, but my contract was not renewed.

Both projects revealed the motivational force of our human need to determine and dramatise our own identity. Both projects' *praxis* demonstrated how this force can be harnessed to transform disciplined, self-doubting, individualised, limit-abiding and competitive subjectivities into organised, autonomous, cooperative subjects. Both projects were permitted to use this transformative potential onstage, within a world of fictional self-determination. But both institutions displayed ideological nervousness towards this *praxis* when it became linked to the marginalised needs of the neighbouring excluded community of Moss Side in Manchester, and zero-tolerance when it extended its critical questioning, desire and confidence beyond the stage. Because suddenly, all unaccountable authority and any trace of authoritarianism appeared transparent, unjust, intolerable and, significantly, transformable. I had learned the importance of 'mapping the resistances' of an institution. Today I ask: Are such resistances explainable and transformable *before* launching such a project?

Understanding the dialectical drama of resistance

Both projects had also experienced and documented offstage tensions, probably inhibited from developing into explicit confrontations by the part-time nature of the projects and the disciplinary power of the 'final grade'. To focus these methodological questions, I decided to leave formal education, and in August 1986, co-founded Frontline: Culture & Education with mainly local cultural workers from the earlier two projects. A month later, Asian teenager Abdul Iqbal Ullah was murdered in his school playground by a white teenager (Baron Cohen, 1996). Manchester City Council asked Frontline into the school in response to the inter-racial war that threatened. Our first decision was to replace text-based theatre with sustained, community-based, participant-centred improvisation workshops.

During four years of cultural education projects in Greater Manchester's post-industrial unemployed communities, young people dramatised the life-threatening questions they faced, framing their imaginable options within their own radical histories, to create profoundly inspiring educational theatre of community protest. However, the tensions from the ongoing conflicts within their homes and schools remained always only just contained by our workshop culture. Because we did not live in their communities, we believed we had neither the capacity nor the right to go beyond dramatising these contradictions. But while the young people were the subject of our workshops, these were contradictions within their lives – until we ourselves performed. First in workshop evaluations and then backstage, dedicated activists gradually encountered the same contradictions within ourselves, and found ourselves locked in conflict. The subversive needs of the more unresolved (and courageous?) identities in Frontline – exposed, agitated and asserted into 'voice' within our own democratised aesthetic space of affirmation, legitimation and hope – involuntarily provoked and were provoked by the more unself-aware identities. Our motivation was bruised but we now used the fictional space of the stage to dramatise ourselves.

We staged and theorised our subjectivities in terms of the *barricade*, identifying two often conflicting 'voices': the external, defensive, oppositional, rhetorical 'voice' of accusation, anger and collective resistance; and the internal, reflective, more poetic 'voice' of self-doubt, vulnerability, questioning, empathy and persistent individual need. The barricade enabled us to value and understand the two voices of resistance that live in a permanent state of tension, the contradictory, psycho-emotional intelligence of the victim that in an instant of danger, need, or excess of tension can ruthlessly and defensively attack its own, even wound, the very transformation it desires.

We began to identify how barricade reflexes – empathetic readings of danger and strategies of anticipation and self-protection – can rigidify into permanent somatic structures and gestures. And we came to understand all resistance – particularly the resistance of silence – as a critically important questioning and testing of authority, not to be massaged or expertly coordinated into quiescence but to be respected as a resource of radical scepticism, peripheral insight and emotional literacy. This became a defining insight and principle within our workshop method.

Understanding the dialectic power of community

Our cultural methods and interventions became known to republican community leaders in the North of Ireland and prompted the formation of Derry Frontline (Baron Cohen, 2001). During five years of 'anti-imperialist cultural struggle', republican working-class activists used community theatre, banners and murals to break the silences of censorship, but also more crucially, to hear and articulate the vulnerable, radical, self-censored voices behind the unified voice of resistance. In this extraordinarily politicised community of resistance, it was possible to imagine and attempt the coherent integration of our onstage cultural work into our offstage community lives.

However, it was precisely on this threshold – a personalised disagreement within the project in the gaze of the community – that another much more painful type of conflict emerged to bruise our collective processes. It demonstrates how a tiny incident or gesture – burdened with the weight of so much contradictory history, judgement and expectation – can suddenly become a conflictual drama of reactive and authoritarian judgement within communities mutilated by centuries of poverty, loss and subordination, to undermine the processes of constructing collectives and working collectively.

Our publicity coordinator – an experienced activist whose companion had been murdered by the British army during the 1981 hunger strike – had been called to an informal meeting to discuss our new play's collectively-conceived poster whose design accidentally affirmed the presence of the British army as mediators in the North of Ireland. The timely intervention should simply have prompted a revised design. But the flaw had been identified on the stage of the propaganda war in the focused scrutinising gaze of the community. The coordinator experienced the entire scene as a personal and political public criticism of her authority, and walked out of the project.

The incident dramatised a telling, intolerably painful contradiction between the political commitment to a deeply desired democracy and an emotional inability to practise it. But in the mind of the publicity coordinator and her closest friends, a fundamental pledge – that our intimate public space was safe – had been violated. Painstakingly, we tried to resolve the incident but significantly, it was resolutely dealt with by this activist and her small circle in a typically wounded way: it was *locked within the silence of the barricade* and, like an unexplained bruise, it drew to itself the inarticulate and conservative resistances among those within the community who had suffered and internalised the authoritarian violence of imperialism.

Try as we might, we co-ordinators were unable to avoid internalising this conflict as our own failing. But gradually we began to perceive what we came to call *resistance-to-liberation*: the fear of jeopardising the moral solidarity, unity and emotional security of the community; and the interwoven, intensely moral and explosively sensitive refusal to be judged, humiliated or rejected by the community, an inevitable risk in publicly confronting (let alone dismantling) *barricaded ways of being* to experiment with new identities and sensitivities. We saw how both are radically underpinned by the existential fear of isolation and loss of identity which, once activated, complexly (re)barricades itself behind silence, available rhetoric or within the most effective appropriate authoritarian strategy, even when the objective danger has withdrawn or long since dissolved. We named this moment the threshold between resistance and liberation, the intensely performative, psycho-emotional, cultural and aesthetic space that must be entered and lived to *decolonise the mind*.

Both concepts pointed to one significant untouched dimension within all our projects: the body. The war had never permitted us (and we had never permitted ourselves) to research the emotional histories inscribed within and upon this threshold, the vulnerabilities the body defensively barricades within its immunised self (Freire and Macedo, 1986), celebrated as impenetrable and policed by our popular cultures of survival and resistance.

Reading the drama of the body

At the University of Glamorgan, away from arenas of open social conflict, it was possible to research the body, its memory, intelligence and barricade reflexes, to propose and theorise the *decolonisation of the mindful-body* (Baron Cohen and King, 1996), the personal and collective memory 'recorded' in the gestures, reflexes, musculature, structures and 'voices' of the body, where social history 'meets' genetics. Three inter-related dialogue-based techniques emerged: the *intimate object*, an object of psycho-emotional personal value which – through the telling and questioning of its story – can be used to build democratic groups of empathetic solidarity; *empathetic body-sculpture*, an application of image theatre (Boal, 1979) in which the individual sees, hears and touches externalisations of his/her internalised history through the body of others, to build a self-aware and alert mindful-body; and *simultaneous interactive narration*, speaking through moving images while reading the intentions or voices of the moving body of the other, to reveal the dialectical relations between individual and collective, and between collective motivation and community. Though these techniques were effectively used within drama modules and popular education projects, it was impossible to develop them in a sustained, safe, community-based project.

However, throughout 1998, as visiting professor of drama in Brazil's University of Santa Catarina, I researched community-based drama-as-education with Marcia Pompeo-Nogueira. Our continuous bilingual coordination of her final year arts-education students in itself sensitised our research to the metaphorical, empathetic nature of non-verbal dialogue. But the integration of Sem Terra (the Landless People's Movement) into our project was decisive. It focused the mindful-body through the lens of a struggle in which the dispossessed transform their mutilated subjectivity into a new humanity through the collective democratisation and cultivation of the land. Our play 'Unearthing the Future' inspired not only a re-reading and systematisation of the *intimate object* as a *generative object* (Freire, 1972), and *empathetic body-sculpture* as an instrument to decodify the *immunised body*; it also critically articulated humanity in terms of a practical caring for and knowing of the land, and the tentative formulation of a *pedagogy of self-determination*.

Performing the mindful-body's contradictions

The pedagogy of self-determination took two new steps through the construction of a collective dialogical monument for a massacred community within the MST and the emergence of what became an emotional literacy workshop for a cluster of its 'illiterate' communities.

On 17 April 1996 nineteen landless peasants were murdered by military police on the motorway at Eldorado dos Carajas in the northern state of Para, while awaiting promised transport and food. The monumental sculpture of nineteen burnt and mutilated *castanheira* (brazil nut) trees – inspired by the survivors' use of their bodies as intimate objects to codify the massacre they had internalised, then decodified through image-theatre and an improvised trial – enabled me for the first time to visualise the dialectical relationship between the *internal* and *external* voices of the barricade. The space within the nineteen trees (arranged in the form of Brazil) functioned as a stage of internal dialogue, of radical questioning, intimate doubt, agonising self-reflection and confidential evaluation. The same space could be transformed into a stage to amplify the unified anger, accusation and demands of the massacred to a world beyond the trees.

This poetic visualisation – designed to provoke dialogue and reflection both in the 'reader' and its 'collective author' – enabled us to extend the sculpture into a self-transforming symbol for the massacred community and the entire movement. Immediately beyond the barricade of trees, nineteen saplings were planted. As the dead *castanheiras* disintegrate, new trees will grow, enabling the mutilated community to perceive its dialectical relation with its history and to visualise its victim-identity as changeable. It became a theatre of resistance and liberation.

In the state of Bahia, we adapted the *empathetic body-sculpture* to codify the two voices within the immunised mindful-body. The second part of my poem 'Within' documents the complex images of the barricade sculpted by rural activist-educators and their participants, and our collective evaluation of the emotional literacy workshop:

> We entered so many community schools of resistance:
>
> so many teachers struggling against their pupils
>
> sleeping with open eyes and inert bodies in regimented rows.
>
> Why are we using pedagogies of the pulpit and the courtroom
>
> to construct dialogue and motivation?
>
> We heard so many teachers discoursing equality and justice
>
> in accusing gestures with tortured expressions.
>
> Why are we using detached analysis and concluded argument
>
> to cultivate questioning and self-confident human beings?
>
> We felt the lust for life pulsing within our youth
>
> yearning for the human freedoms promised by our anthems
>
> to develop their own voices and independence.
>
> Why do we sing of love yet incarcerate it within self-sacrifice?
>
> What radical questions lie within our youth's silence?

The workshop had not only codified the mindful-body of MST's educators; it had revealed the immunised subjectivities of the Left political culture in general which, within threatening public (aesthetic) spaces of judgement, retreat behind or inhabit (however unconvincingly or ironically) the authoritarian subjectivity of the fortified, rationalised, mindful-body of invulnerable authority. Undemocratised public space was itself (re)stimulating inhibition and authority. The critical relationship between pedagogy, space and the mindful-body was becoming transparent. Not only were the limitations of ideological-debate-as-conscientisation now visible. The creation of a new humanity, the emergence of a new politics based upon principled, empathetic solidarity and confident, creative individual participation, *the very practice of dialogue itself*, could no longer be separated from the transformation of the mindful-body and the social spaces it enters and exits.

New questions emerged. The barricade-culture of resistance had become gendered. In the workshops that followed, thousands of MST activists responded passionately and creatively to the *sensibilisation* of their political culture of resistance. The landless movement's national anthem – sung with uniform rigid bodies and clenched fists – was danced into a waltz of diverse and smiling improvisation. Lucid anger was trembling into self-knowing laughter and an irrepressible carnival of dialogue. Key male leaders drew back.

Resistance to the *internal* is complex. It is always a declaration that a threshold of transformation and democratisation is close by. But whether resistance conceals itself behind an ideological dismissal of the subjective or – as in the case of Ciru – a focus upon 'the more urgent' subjectivity of another, it always has *immunised* and *rationalised* interests. For the internal is both the hidden realm of intolerable, shameful, even painful contradiction *behind* the barricade (Baron Cohen and King, 1997), vivid in its contrast to the idealistic rhetoric of resistance, and/or the unrevealable realm of fear and self-hatred, locked behind the impenetrable composure of the fortress. Who chooses to confront and unravel the entangled histories of sexual, emotional and psychological abuse – caused by violation, humiliation, isolation and rationalisation – that they have inflicted upon or suffered from their loved ones, let alone others? Who chooses to admit their complicity – however unconscious or compulsive – with the abuse of power and ultimately unjustifiable violence? Who, in the absence of a community of understanding, skilled support and unconditional commitment, will risk certain condemnation and exile?

The emotional literacy workshop therefore focused on three priorities: the building and sustaining of new *communities* of intimate solidarity; the *sensibilisation* of the mindful-body to release our subjective intelligences and mobilise our intuitive knowledges; and the development of *pedagogical forms* to re-learn how to listen and to question, to learn how to dialogue without judgement.

It may now be possible to understand the opening fragment of dialogue between myself, Rubens and Ciru. The emotional and cultural literacy workshop we developed together revealed the unconscious complicity between the *excluded* and the *included* in reproducing the very social relations we want to change. Rubens – a homeless 'illiterate' leader learned to use his *immunised* mindful-body as an analytical metaphor and pen to begin to transform his psycho-emotional history into instruments of radical community education. Ciru – a popular education university lecturer – learned to use his *rationalised* mindful-body as a canvass to critically read his own authoritarian temperament and coercive *praxis*. I learned I need to understand both, within myself, and how both need to 'dialogue' within the same space to open the possibility of creating new, self-aware and democratic subjectivities.

Rubens' and Ciru's courage is the courage of the hundreds of people who have contributed to define this pedagogy which challenges the academy and social movements alike. You will judge whether it might be relevant and useful for where you work.

References

Baron Cohen, D. (1996), 'Resistance to liberation: decolonising the mindful-body', *Performance Research*, 1(2), pp. 60-74.

Baron Cohen, D. (2001), *Theatre of Self-Determination,* Derry: Guildhall Press.

Baron Cohen, D. and King, J. (1996), 'Dramatherapy: radical intervention or counter-insurgency?', in Jennings, S. (ed.), *Dramatherapy 3: Theory and Practice*, London: Routledge, pp. 269-83.

Boal, A. (1979), *Theatre of the Oppressed*, London: Pluto.

Boal, A. (1998), *Legislative Theatre*, London: Routledge.

Branford, S. and Rocha, J. (2002), *Cutting the Wire*, London: Latin American Bureau.

Freire, P. (1972), *Pedagogy of the Oppressed*, Harmondsworth, Penguin.

Freire, P. and Macedo, D. (1987), *Reading the World, Reading the Word*, London: Routledge and Kegan Paul.

Kershaw, B. (1999), *The Radical in Performance,* London: Routledge.

Thiong'o N, Wa (1993), *Moving the Centre*, London: Heinemann.

Chapter 18

Learning from the Women's Community Education Movement in Ireland

Bríd Connolly

This chapter draws on the author's experience of working in the women's community education movement in Ireland. It maintains that this now constitutes a social movement which has radically transformed the lives of its participants. Women's community education has also been very influential in the development of theory, policy and practice. However, the power of the movement is restricted by a panoptic effect that limits its radical potential and dilutes its impact in other milieux. It is the responsibility of progressive adult educators to resolve the tension between the radical agenda of women's community education and its adoption and dilution in more liberal and neoliberal arenas.

Introduction

The search for the right words to grasp the quintessential qualities of the women's community education movement in Ireland are difficult to find. Attempts to characterise it range over aspects of it like wholeness (Parsons et al, 2003), the 'hidden' nature of the phenomenon (AONTAS, 2000), its creativity and innovation (WERRC, 2001), and the ephemeral and oral qualities of its embodiment in communication between participants as suggested in the notion of 'listening to voices' (Connolly, 2003). All are attempts to encapsulate the meanings and processes that have developed in women's community education, autonomously, outside of mainstream and conventional educational theory and practice.

Women's community education in Ireland is remarkable from many perspectives. For participants, it often bridges the gap between the personal and political in a tangible, experiential way. Generally, research finds that participants have had negative prior experiences in education (WERRC, 2001; Parsons et al, 2003), despite the widely accepted myth that the education system in Ireland is excellent. Education, as a central institution in Irish society, is regarded as the key route to the redistribution of resources and the provision of equality of opportunity. Policy makers increasingly see adult and community education as the way in which the benefits of education can be spread over the entire lifetime of the population. In particular, it is successful in reaching those who have not been able to avail themselves of early education. The White Paper *Learning for Life* (DES, 2000) places particular emphasis on the role of adult education in addressing the social and economic needs of Irish society, especially given Ireland's lower levels of education and qualification in comparison with most other OECD countries. Adult education also has a role in enriching lives by encouraging learning for its own sake and mobilising the not-for-profit and social enterprise sectors to foster creative and innovative development.

In this chapter, I draw on my experiences within women's community education to explore the underlying thinking in terms of both pedagogical approaches (Connolly, 1999) and the concept of 'really useful knowledge' (Thompson, 1996). I then consider the implications of this account for educational provision in the academy.

Women's community education

Women's community education has, to use Linda Connolly's (2003) phrase, 'mushroomed' to become a measurable, influential force in Irish society. This constitutes the engagement of ordinary women with the women's movement, extending the ownership of the movement from purely academic and public arenas into women's everyday lives. It has enabled women to see themselves as active citizens in Irish society, women who might otherwise perceive themselves as operating within the private sphere only. It has emancipated women to a level of citizenship they had hitherto been denied, in spite of the legal and social changes emanating from the 1971 Commission on the Status of Women and Ireland's accession to membership of the European Union (EU) in 1973.

Reflecting on my experience, mainly as an educator, I realise that the women's community education movement has enabled me to be active, reflective and to develop a sense of social purpose. This is an approach I subsequently identified with bell hooks' (1994: 13) notion of 'engaged pedagogy':

> To educate as the practice of freedom is a way of teaching that anyone can learn. That learning process comes easiest to those of us who teach who also believe that there is an aspect of our vocation that is sacred; who believe that our work is not merely to share information but to share in the intellectual and spiritual growth of our students.

Community education and community development

AONTAS, the National Association of Adult Education, in its policy document *Community Education* indicates the strong inter-relationship between community education and community development. Both share much the same underpinning philosophy, but, while community development is perceived as an alternative political process, it lacks a clear vision of how to enable people to work collectively as citizens. Community education, with its focus on methods and processes and emphasis on 'really useful knowledge', has incorporated the 'how' and 'what' with the 'why' (AONTAS, 2004).

The Irish government's White Paper *Learning for Life* highlights the non-statutory nature of community education. It locates it firmly within the community, emphasising its flexible, problem solving, process-orientated focus, and the promotion of participative democracy, leading to the transformation of society (DES, 2000: 113). Community education is founded on Freirean principles of *praxis* and 'conscientisation' (Freire, 1986). AONTAS identifies two interconnected outcomes: first, the personal acquisition of skills and knowledge; second, social and community advancement and empowerment. Also, by adopting Freirean principles, it considers that education can become a force for redistributing power and privilege. The pedagogical approach is dialogical and reflexive. Conscientisation and consciousness raising are primarily experiential processes encompassing emotional, psychological and cognitive dimensions (Connolly, 1996). Emancipatory education is a process that enables people to raise awareness, to reflect and to bring about change.

In addition, it develops the microcosmic experience of inclusion and influence (Rogers, 1967). Relationship or person-centred process is at the heart of social analysis and education for politicisation. Freire (1986) sees it as pivotal to the task of overturning oppressive relationships. Hope and Timmel (1995) take the view that this is a vital part of adult education, vital in the building of unity and commitment. The women's community education movement became part of the general inclination towards community development as a way of reaching marginal people in order to provide them with an accessible political process. It provides participants with the tools and resources to exercise their own influence. It also helps to overcome the problems of shared leadership: stagnation, disunity, lack of accountability, and simply running out of steam. Elsewhere (Connolly, 1999), I evaluate this process from a feminist perspective, but the point here is that person-centred group work has been significantly refined and enriched by practice in women's community education.

Key features of women's community education

First, the participants own women's community education. It started when key women set up day-time classes in their own communities, sometimes with help of the statutory agencies but retaining ownership of the process. Second, it is underpinned by the notion of agency. The need for outside intervention is reduced, and self-reliance is enhanced. In this way, women have been able to manage the process in the way they wanted. Third, participants are focused on themselves as subjects. The curricula and processes are women-centred, making their own experiences, interpretations and insights the basis of all the learning. Consciousness raising, beginning with the analysis of lived experience and subjectivity, is a distinct shift away from the principle that knowledge is established through logical objectivity. Ryan (2001) points out that women's ways of knowing are not essentially different from other ways of knowing; rather, women have different experiences and ways of learning and knowing because of social factors. Women's lives are different because they are socially constructed as different. The fourth distinctive feature is the way in which the facilitation of the group remains in the hands of the group. While the content of courses may be determined, to some extent, by academic and other factors, the way in which learning is developed remains in the control of the participants. The development of human-centred, empowering methodologies derives from these processes.

Another outcome is the way groups identify with each other. This identification of common interests and the development of collectivity highlight the social, political and cultural impact of the phenomenon. The failure of representational, traditional democracy has allowed room for this type of political activity, evident also in grassroots responses to globalisation and development. Women's community education is part of the wide spectrum of community-based developmental organisations in which people, encompassing difference and diversity, organise to meet their own needs, based on ethical principles and shared values.

Popular education, community education and 'really useful methods'

The concept of popular education is somewhat underdeveloped in Ireland. Community education has a long history, but it is in the past twenty years that it has developed a distinct identity, based on the growth of women's community education as a movement. There is certainly some overlap with notions of popular education which, according to Crowther et al (1999: 4-5), has the following characteristics:

- it is rooted in the real interests and struggles of ordinary people
- it is overtly political and critical of the status quo
- it is committed to progressive social and political change
- it is based on the clear analysis of the nature of inequality, exploitation and oppression
- its curriculum comes out of the concrete experiences and material interests of people in communities
- its pedagogy is collective, focused primarily on group as distinct from individual learning and development.

The main point of departure is the concept of the individual. In community education in Ireland the person is perceived as the agent of social change in collective activity. It is understood that consciousness raising enables the individual to identify and connect with others within the same group, class and/or gender. Personal change is necessary in order to overcome the constraints of socialisation and of passive, unquestioned acceptance of the status quo. Popular education is aimed at all oppressed and exploited members of society, while women's community education works for change primarily of and through women.

Many people perceive feminism as negative, oppressive and extreme. The backlash has made deep inroads into the Irish psyche, with anti-feminist voices gaining ground, particularly in men's groups. O'Donovan and Ward (1999) found that women involved in the women's community education movement were reluctant to describe themselves as feminists, because of an ambivalent attitude to feminism. While it was felt that feminism was good for women, individual feminists gave women a 'bad name'. This is a very complex issue. It strongly indicates that social movements can be perceived as the work of individuals. Their collective nature is overshadowed by the influence of strong personalities, especially those who can be pilloried by the popular media. Community education grapples with this. The connection between the personal and the political is facilitated by an equal focus on each.

At times and in some circumstances, the personal is elevated at the expense of the political. This is particularly the case in the liberal discourse, and it has implications for education provision in other contexts, as will be discussed below. The key issue is the place of the individual: emancipatory education is facilitated when agency is central. Collective action is not sustainable unless individuals perceive themselves as having influence and power. Democracy is contingent on individual power and it seems that effective forms of political activity rest on the assumption that people are acting on their own behalf. Participative democracy, which I argue elsewhere is the logical outcome of community development (Connolly, 1996), is based on the premise of empowered, knowledgeable individuals working collectively towards social change.

Communitarianism is a concept that is very influential in Irish community education. The core idea is that people in society have responsibility for and to one another. This is essential when linking the local with the global, and underpins the recent demonstrations against the negative effects of globalisation. In many ways, women's community education is part of this overall grassroots activity (Connolly, 2003). Again, in O'Donovan and Ward's (1999) account women recognised that they should be involved in campaigning, for example, for a cleaner environment or in solidarity with women of the Third World. Interestingly, this was not perceived as 'political activity', indicating a negative attitude towards politics: political activity was something that politicians did, rather than women like themselves. Thus, while popular education and community education have this large overlap, in Ireland there is still a distinct lack of work on what Thompson (1996: 23) calls 'really useful knowledge' or 'popular education for democracy'. Indeed, this reluctance to engage in politics is matched by a distinct push to shift adult and community education's 'really useful methods' (Connolly and Ryan, 2002) away from the political sphere and into mainstream education and training.

Anne Ryan and I have developed the notion of 'really useful methods' in our work – that is, emancipatory, transformative pedagogies which are the pedagogical equivalent to 'really useful knowledge' – in order to articulate the type of politicising pedagogies we believe are derived from women's community education and can be transferred to the academic arena to great advantage. We developed this idea in response to the unease we feel when we work in academic environments. This unease comes directly from our experiences as learners as well as teachers, and we use the metaphor of the lighthouse in the bog, 'brilliant but useless', to encapsulate our argument.[1] In particular, we feel that the practice of flooding students with information is counter-productive, and it reinforces what Freire called the 'banking method' of education. In contrast, 'really useful methods', as developed in women's community education, can challenge participants fundamentally, without reducing their dignity or confidence. This is the key area of influence of women's community education in other educational provision.

Implications for other educational provision

The influence of women's community education on adult and community education has been widely significant. Its methodologies have been adopted by training agencies, in secondary schools and in the academy because 'community education is viewed as an approach rather than merely a system of provision' (DES, 2000).

However, there is often confusion about the bottom-up nature of community education. A top-down approach creates consumers rather than participants or agents. For many trainees – people with disabilities, unemployed men, travellers and other groups who lack social power – education and training are provided through a top-down approach. Thus, the training agency determines the needs of the target group and designs a programme to meet these needs. Community education is radically different in this respect, educating the participants to become agents of their own learning and to develop a critical awareness of structures, systems, assumptions and knowledge. In contrast, groups subjected to a top-down approach are not encouraged to participate as the equals of their tutors or to become agents of their own learning. The top-down approach may use active learning methods, but stays firmly within the dominant discourse of liberal education which, as Kathleen Lynch (1989) has convincingly shown, ensures the continuance of the status quo.

A glass fence separates community education from mainstream education and training. This, in effect, creates a panoptic, allowing the observation and replication of methodologies, while remaining disengaged from the underpinning philosophy. The mainstream can look in through the fence, see the participatory pedagogical approaches and then adapt them to their own environments and purposes. Likewise, those involved in community education can be encouraged by the apparent adoption of participative methodologies by the mainstream. However, the glass fence keeps the groups apart and ensures that the influence of participative methodologies on the mainstream is only superficial. Furthermore, the fence isolates community education and makes it easy for the mainstream to scrutinise and control its development.

This glass fence is also a constraining force against which social movements may collide. It has been erected by dominant discourses, representing the aims of existing privileged interests and ensuring that the dividends of belonging to the dominant groups remain intact. Inside the fence, the empowering process provides the wherewithal for critical analysis and the deconstruction of traditional social relations. But it also ensures that these developments are seriously circumscribed. The continuance of deep divisions in Irish society, despite profound changes, shows that the formidable forces that oppose emancipatory change remain in control. In spite of the explicit agenda of education as the route to the redistribution of resources, the glass fence systematically reduces its impact.

These processes are sometimes applied in other contexts where there is no radical agenda at all. It should be possible for marginalised individuals and groups to use community education to relocate themselves in Irish society. However, while local issues may be addressed in this way, it is very difficult to tackle questions of national significance. In addition, feminism has so many implications for personal relationships and for traditional roles that women have to overcome stubborn resistance from disparate and suspicious individuals and groups where they might otherwise have expected to find allies.

Community education for community development

Community education has proved itself to be vital for community development. The pedagogical approach in community education identifies the group as the key resource. Person-centred group work is pivotal to the process and has potential for wider applications. My work in education for community development is premised on the concept of group work as an emancipatory adult education methodology. Process-orientated community development is also dependent on group work as a methodology, especially in the light of the work of the Community Action Network (Kelleher and Whelan, 1992; Prendiville, 1995). This process-orientated approach contrasts with other models of community development, in particular economistic or structural models.

As a practitioner, some of my work entails organising community education programmes for people who wish to consolidate their skills in community development. This programme is funded by Area Based Partnerships – the mechanism put in place to disburse EU funding for development – and some voluntary agencies. The groups are mixed, comprising men and women of all ages and backgrounds. Working in an academic department, we endeavoured to gender proof the course modules and to create an environment suitable for emancipation. That is, the entire curriculum and the learning process were non-sexist and based on egalitarianism. It was underpinned by community development principles, people coming together to provide for their own needs, thereby aiming to bring about change in the institutions at cultural and social levels. The self-selecting participants were both the subjects and the authors of the whole process.

The evaluation of this programme highlighted a number of interesting gender issues. It is very striking that, of all social inequalities, gender has remained the most contentious. Two strands, in particular, throw up this gender aspect. Traditional rural development, which is largely about modernisation and bringing the benefits of technological and economic development to rural Ireland, is a force for dominant political and economic development in more conservative rural communities. While the position of women may shift from the traditional role of private, unpaid labour to a more public, waged role, the fundamental gendered social divisions are not addressed. In addition, it is perceived that the aspiration to equality undermines those facets of rural life that the development seeks to retain as foundational precepts. For example, farming is perceived as a male occupation whereas the 'farm home' is the female sphere of influence.

The second strand of community development, based on the urban labour movement, sees class as the fundamental inequality and perceives feminism as a middle-class phenomenon and therefore part of the problem. Gendered divisions are secondary to those of class. Feminism, according to this view, undermines efforts to seek fundamental change. In some cases, initiatives set up by women have been colonised by groups espousing such views.

Another factor emerging is the anti-feminist backlash. The powerlessness which many men feel because of economic and social change is attributed to the women's movement. The anti-feminist men's movement voices these concerns, blaming the women's movement for the changing role of men in family life. Further, it holds that women's employment and the demand for childcare are strengthening capitalist economic values in Irish society, over-looking the role that successive governments, financial institutions and social policy have played in establishing the neoliberal economic policies which prevail. This thinking is percolating through to some men's groups who are using group work, community development and adult education to build a men's movement which aims to counter the progress made by the women's movement. Of course, not all men's groups are anti-feminist, but this thinking confirms the anti-emancipatory practices current in some community development and education (Connolly, 1998). This phenomenon needs a fuller analysis in future research.

In most of the research conducted on women's community education, the focus has been exclusively on the impact that it has had on the participants. However, educators have carried the pedagogy from the beginning, through the process of development, and continue to allow it room to grow. These educators have embodied the political positionings and contributed the critical edge to the process of learning. Even as equal partners in the learning 'duologue', their prior learning, their idealism and the strength of their ideological commitment are central to the transaction. They make the difference in the educational environment, in community education and in the academy. Adult educators are the emissaries for the emancipatory processes which promote personal change and equip participants to engage with those cultural and social discourses antithetical to emancipation. The philosophy of women's community education has an implicit feminist agenda, and the women's community education movement in Ireland has ensured that all thinking on adult education and lifelong learning is influenced by its creativity and innovation. In particular, emancipatory transformative pedagogies, or 'really useful methods', embody a critical feminist dimension, without which women would find themselves in subordinate roles – yet again. As such, it is necessary for radical adult educators to continue to challenge the appropriation of their processes and methods for purposes of depoliticisation in order to maintain their role as advocates and agents of social change.

Note

1. A bog refers to peaty land where turf is extracted for fuel. The title of the input was 'Lighthouses and bogs: really useful methods', and it was derived from an observation of the Irish intellectual and politician, Conor Cruise O'Brien, that he was like a lighthouse in a bog: brilliant but useless.

References

AONTIS (2000), *Invisible Movement*. Video, directed and produced by Anne Daly and Ronan Tynan, Dublin: Esperanza Production/AONTAS.

AONTAS Policy Series (2004), *Community Education*, Dublin: AONTAS.

Connolly, B.M. (1996), 'Community development and adult education: prospects for change?' in Connolly, B., Fleming, T., McCormack, D. and Ryan, A. (eds), *Radical Learning for Liberation*, Maynooth: MACE, pp. 27-44.

Connolly, B. (1998), *Evaluation of Community Development and Leadership Programme: 1996-1997*. Unpublished report.

Connolly, B. (1999), 'Groupwork and facilitation: a feminist evaluation of their role in transformative adult and community education' in Connolly, B. and Ryan, A.B. (eds), *Women and Education in Ireland* Vol 1, Maynooth: MACE, pp.109-30.

Connolly, B. (2003), 'Community education: listening to the voices', *The Adult Learner*, pp. 9-19.

Connolly, L. (2003), *The Irish Women's Movement: From Revolution to Devolution*, Dublin: Lilliput Press.

Connolly, B. and Ryan, A.B. (2002), 'Lighthouses and bogs: really useful methods'. Paper presented at the Second International Conference of the Popular Education Network, Barcelona.

Crowther, J., Martin, I. and Shaw, M. (eds), (1999), *Popular Education and Social Movements in Scotland Today*, Leicester: NIACE.

DES (2000), *Learning for Life: White Paper on Adult Education*, Dublin: Government Publications Office.

Freire, P. (1986), *Pedagogy of the Oppressed*, Harmondsworth: Penguin.

Hooks, B. (1994), *Teaching to Transgress: Education as the Practice of Freedom*, London: Routledge.

Hope, A. and Timmel, S. (1995), *Training for Transformation Book 1*, Gweru, Zimbabwe: Mambo Press.

Kelleher, P. and Whelan, M. (1992), *Dublin Communities in Action*, Dublin: CAN and CPA.

Lynch, K. (1989), *The Hidden Curriculum: Reproduction in Education: A Reappraisal*, London: Falmer.

O'Donovan, Ó. and Ward, E. (1999), 'Networks of women's groups in the Republic of Ireland' in Galligan, Y., Ward, E. and Wilford, R. (eds), *Contesting Politics: Women in Ireland, North and South*, Oxford: Westview Press, pp. 90-108.

Parsons, S., O'Connor, J. and Conlon, C. (2003), *A Whole New World: A Feminist Model of Community and Lifelong Learning*, Dublin: WERRC.

Prendiville, P. (1995), *Developing Facilitation Skills: A Handbook for Group Facilitators*, Dublin: CPA.

Rogers, C. (1967), *On Becoming a Person*, London: Constable.

Ryan, A.B. (2001), *Feminist Ways of Knowing: Towards Theorising the Person for Radical Adult Education,* Leicester: NIACE.

Thompson, J. (1996), ' "Really useful knowledge": linking theory and practice' in Connolly, B., Fleming, T., McCormack, D. and Ryan, A. (eds), *Radical Learning for Liberation*, Maynooth: MACE, pp. 15-26.

WERRC (Women's Education, Research and Resource Centre) (2001), *At the Forefront: The Role of Women's Community Education in Combatting Poverty and Disadvantage in the Republic of Ireland*, Dublin: AONTAS.

Chapter 19

Emancipatory Organisational Learning: Context and Method

Griff Foley

Globalising capitalism puts constant pressure on both organisations and individuals to increase performance and 'output'. This is a hostile climate in which to sustain a commitment to emancipatory educational work. Drawing on twenty years' experience of working with people in organisations, the author demonstrates how organisational change issues can be addressed through a strategic learning approach which seeks to foster more democratic, accountable and flexible workplace practices.

Introduction

The fundamental problem with many organisational change efforts is all too familiar to us. Globalising capitalism puts pressure on organisations and individuals to continually increase their performance. Various means are tried: downsizing, performance management, quality circles, self-managed teams, training. Frequently, managers confuse structural and cultural change, believing that the former (which almost always involves staff reductions) will automatically lead to the latter. Often, attempts at organisational change simply increase the workloads of those who are left, exhausting and embittering them. Deeper problems remain, and quite frequently people do not learn from their experience, but keep on with behaviour which is no longer functional.

In this chapter I will discuss what people with an interest in emancipatory organisational learning might do in such a seemingly unpropitious environment. I worked in the continuing university professional education of adult educators for more than twenty years. For much of that time the people I taught were wrestling with organisational change and learning issues. Many of my students were responsible for managing organisational change. Increasingly, I became interested in how they might work with organisational change issues in more critical and productive ways.

Context: organisational life and globalising capitalism

Our starting point was the broader political and economic context of workplace change, a dimension that is frequently neglected. The contemporary global scramble for market share is the latest manifestation of the logic of capitalism, which creates an unwinnable competition among producers, and which in turn generates periodic crises, and massive inequalities within and between nations. This logic also generates what appear to be radical changes in the organisation of production. But the way work is organised does not really change – it still rests on the attempts of capital to control the work process. Worker resistance is endemic in this intrinsically exploitative labour process, and this resistance has a learning dimension. If they are going to act effectively and in accordance with their espoused values, change facilitators need to understand the capitalist political economy and labour process, and both the resistance and the learning they generate.

What we do in work is shaped by the logic and development of the capitalist political economy and labour process. But these broader economic and political processes are worked through in distinctive ways in different workplaces. It is this particularity that people involved in facilitating workplace change must understand if they are to act effectively. Analysis of the experiential learning of workers and managers provides a way into this deeper understanding. The question we need to ask is: What do people actually learn in work?

Method: strategic learning

So, to understand the complexities of workplace learning we need a way of analytically connecting everyday informal learning in particular workplaces to both the micro-politics of those workplaces and to their wider political and economic contexts. In particular, we need to focus on the stories people tell of their work experience, and to locate those stories within an analysis of the capitalist labour process.

In organisational settings, most significant learning is informal and inciden-tal. Yet this is rarely recognised or acted on. Nor can we assume, as much educational theory does, that all learning is constructive. A moment's reflection on one's own work experience demonstrates that much learning in organisations is negative and disabling. Further, in the last twenty years the very notions of 'adult education' and 'adult educator' have dissolved. Today, few people identify with those labels. Rather, they see themselves as managers, human resource people, activists, teachers, change agents, and as working with learning in a broader sense that can be captured in the notion of 'education'.

As I look back, one of the most striking things about the past twenty years has been the growth of dissatisfaction with the shaping of organisational life by a globalising capitalism. I have worked with computer company executives, Christians and family men, who met on weekends to first deal with their pain about, and then to critically analyse, their firm's abandonment of lifetime employment and its adoption of harsher forms of performance management. I have worked with police who felt devalued and abused by their organisation's drive to change its culture. I have worked with vocational educators who had developed a Russian-style black humour to deal with the endless restructuring of their organisation (the biggest provider of adult education in its state) over more than a decade, a process that had no function other than justifying and masking the expansion of a management cadre and its perquisites. In all this I have been struck by the spread of critical analysis among people previously content with the system, and their adherence to use values in the face of pressures to put an exchange value on everything.

Strategy becomes more important than ideology in this context, because people are looking for ways to act successfully, to win something for their side, their values. So the challenge for left intellectuals like me has been to devise a method that enables people in workplaces to understand and act on their situations in critical and emancipatory ways.

Grand words, 'critical' and 'emancipatory' – perhaps, in these times, even grandiloquent-sounding. So I had better explain what I mean, which is something quite humble and ordinary, and a continuation of a long tradition of progressive work. 'Critical' is from the Greek *krites*, to make judgements. When we think and act critically we make judgements about injustices, and attempt to rectify them by addressing their fundamental causes, their deeper dynamics and determining factors. Emancipatory education and action (from the Latin *manus* [hand] and *capare* [take]) aims to free people from some oppression, to free them to take control of their lives. There is, of course, a great tradition of critical and emancipatory adult education. The challenge for those of us who have been shaped by this tradition is to bring it alive in new times. And at the heart of radical adult education, in any era, has been a method.

The method I outline here is nothing new or original. It has many familiar elements: the action research cycle, the ethnographic account, the organisational audit, the discussion method. What is new about it, perhaps (and even here I won't be surprised if someone else has already thought of this), is its emphasis on the learning dimension of organisational life and change – on all forms of learning, formal and informal, constructive and destructive, instrumental and critical. Needing to give it a name, I've called it the strategic learning method.

This method can be summed up in a few propositions:

- Workplace life and learning are complex, contextual and contested
- People in workplaces learn all the time, experientially and informally
- This learning can be positive or negative, productive or unproductive (it is often the latter)
- In attempting to change workplaces it is essential to understand the dynamics and outcomes of this informal, experiential learning
- Change projects should be treated as learning experiences, capable of being learned in and from
- Each organisational change project requires a deep analysis, that is, an analysis that is at once contextual, ethical and strategic
- Change strategies must be:
  - democratic: all participants should be able to influence the process and outcome, but none dominate

- explicit and transparent: there should be clear processes and proce-
    dures, visible to all
  - accountable: they should be continually monitored and evaluated
  - flexible: they should be able to change, in orderly and equitable ways
- Change projects should be treated as long conversations, which follow
  procedural rules for discussion groups – reasonableness, truthfulness,
  freedom, equality, respect for persons, peaceableness and orderliness
- Change agents need to develop skills in: consultancy, negotiation, political
  mapping, facilitation of group process and facilitation of discussion.

Teaching strategic learning

These prescriptions slide off the tongue easily. It is, of course, much harder to
make them a reality. But my experience is that many people are keen to try.
And, of course, the method only comes alive in concrete situations.

Energising discouraged teachers

John is a newly appointed deputy principal in an inner-city primary school. He
finds the staff disheartened, feeling besieged by disruptive students. He asks:
What have these teachers learned, in their daily work, to make them feel like
this? He finds that the students carry the wounds of their home life into the
school. They fall asleep in class after being kept awake all night by drug-taking
and abusive parents. They come late to school and don't bring their lunch.
When the teachers raise these issues, parents react aggressively, or don't
respond at all. But the teachers are not just responding to what the students
bring with them; their attitudes are also shaped by the *laissez-faire* culture of the
school. Traditionally in this school, leaders have not led, and staff, individualised and fragmented, have shut the doors of their classrooms and survived the
best they can.

  John calls a meeting in which staff, for the first time that they can
remember, share experiences and concerns. He takes a record of this
discussion to the district office and asks for help. A team of consultants visits
the school, and finds quantitative data on negative student behaviour, kept at
the suggestion of the local union organiser. The consultants use this
information to successfully argue for the appointment to the school of a
full-time specialist in behaviour disorders.

Participatory performance management

Paul is a human resource manager in a large federal government department.
He spends much of his working time explaining change initiatives. He notes
considerable staff resistance to a new performance management system.
Investigating further, he finds that staff are worried about having to evaluate

their peers and their managers, and concerned about having their own behaviour judged against designated corporate values. Many also fear that the proposed introduction of performance pay will bring salary reductions.

Management responds to these findings by agreeing to take more time to introduce the performance management system, and by making a concerted effort to allay people's anxieties about pay. In his own unit, Paul organises discussion sessions on a work team basis, 'to talk through and agree on some approaches to giving and receiving feedback'. Staff are now better informed, they have some evidence of being listened to and are demonstrating the beginnings of involvement in and ownership of the performance management process. Paul himself has learned that implementation of such a system is necessarily time consuming. He also observes:

> I've yet to experience a 'magic wand' effect with any change. Steady, ongoing effort, using genuinely participative processes, is the only approach that comes close to succeeding in my particular workplace. People aren't stupid. They want answers to their questions, are quick to spot inconsistencies, and if they sense something less than the truth, are quick to distance themselves from whatever bosses are trying to do to them.

More especially, they want an honest answer to the question, 'Why?'

When I worked with them, John and Paul were students in a Masters programme in adult education at the University of Technology in Sydney. When they enrolled neither saw themselves as an adult educator, and even now that is not their primary identification. But they are fostering adult learning. More specifically, they are identifying negative learning (the teachers learning to be discouraged, the public servants learning to distrust and resist attempts to evaluate their performance), and they are fostering productive learning (the teachers learn that they can act on apparently intractable problems, the public servants learn that they can influence how their work is evaluated).

For John, Paul and their colleagues this is ordinary yet radical learning. It is ordinary in that it is embedded in their daily work, and it is not remarkable. Yet in the context of the contemporary workplace, where suppressing awareness of what is actually going on and what people are actually learning is the norm, to name the negative learning and change it to more productive learning is radical. It is radically educational, for the 'educators' (the managers) as much as for the 'learners' (the workers).

Doing progressive work in capitalism involves looking for spaces among constraints and contradictions. Paul, for example, is a manager and a union representative. He is disturbed, but not daunted, by the decline in union membership and influence in his workplace. He sees this decline as symptomatic of something deeper: a strategic failure of the labour movement. Labour, Paul argues, has tried to accommodate to a globalising capitalism, offering to manage it better than conservative governments and corporations.

In doing so it has abandoned many of its core commitments – to such things as secure, full-time employment, and centralised wage-fixing. Unions have become bureaucracies providing services to largely passive memberships. While this worked well enough when jobs were plentiful, tighter times require a return to more creative and activist strategies. Unions, Paul argues, need to mobilise workers to tackle issues currently alive in their workplaces. This will often involve small actions, like the following one, described in Paul's own words.

> Last month, with enterprise bargaining at an unsatisfactory stage, many members supported an action that called for everyone to commence work at 10.00am on a particular day. While some people crossed the picket line, many others chose to congregate outside the building from about 9.45am onwards. As some of us went around, thanking people for their support, about two hundred members munched on doughnuts and drank coffee provided by union funds – their funds. We then had a loud, ten second countdown before people entered the building *en masse*, causing massive congestion in the lift lobby and inconveniencing people coming out of lifts – ironically, on their way to buy a coffee! It was a good feeling, even (especially ?) when someone asked me if I'd been 'trained in Vladivostock'. It had been a long time between drinks. Too long by far.

In another case study, Mhairi, the training manager of a community worker peak organisation described how she had come to understand that what appeared to be worker burnout was actually an internal struggle (within the organisation, and within individuals) triggered by changes in the political economy. The ten staff in her section all had a background in community work and a commitment to critical and emancipatory forms of education. But to access funding in the government-created training market, these educators had to adapt to a competency-based curriculum, which Mhairi and her colleagues saw as 'a domesticated form of education which can be easily packaged and does not offer effective tools for change to workers in the sector who are struggling with the impact of inequity and injustices'. The tension this forced adaptation set up turned colleagues against each other. Instead of focusing on structural factors like economic pressures, workloads and inappropriate work practices, workers turned on each other and on management. It was only when Mhairi, having recognised the problem, set aside time in the week when colleagues could talk issues through, that they were able to name the structural problem and to discuss how they might adapt their radical educational ideology and practice to the new environment.

A strategic learning approach rejects attempts to recast organisational learning, and education and learning more broadly, simply as instruments for improving performance and productivity. It sees learning as complex, contested and contextual. It assumes that critical and emancipatory learning is possible and necessary. It asserts that a first step to their realisation is an honest investigation of what people are actually learning and teaching each other in different sites – workplaces, families, communities, the mass media, social movements. It insists on rigorous analysis while offering a practical way of linking analysis, strategy and skill.

Case studies analysed in context are central to this approach. Ethnographic accounts of learning in social action, located within a broader economic, political and cultural analysis, enable us to see the warp and weft of emancipatory and reproductive learning that occurs as people struggle against various forms of oppression. The broader political, economic and cultural context sets the scene for local social action, but for this action to occur, something must happen to the consciousness of the people involved – they must see that action is necessary and possible. Further, any social action occurs in a local political- or 'micro-political'-context.

In any particular workplace then, everyday informal and incidental learning involves something happening to people's consciousness, and this 'something' is connected to broader social and local micro-political factors. These connections are represented in the following figure:

A framework for analysing workplace learning and change

Political economy	Labour process
(Implications for educational interventions)	Workers' informal & incidental learning
Micro-politics & culture of particular workplaced	Worker subjectivity & consciousness

Extensions

But much remains to be done if we are to understand the what, how and why of informal learning in everyday life and popular struggle. I think that the best way to document this learning would be a variation on Henry Glassie's (1982) fine ethnography of Ballymenone, a small community in Ireland, where he endeavoured to represent the whole life of a people – their work, their food, their entertainment, their religion, their politics, their stories, their connection to the land. I would like to see a similar study, with the learning dimension added. This would be the truest way to understand the experience and learning of any group of people anywhere.

Two central issues in such a study would be:

- the extent to which everyday experiential learning reproduces relations of exploitation and oppression, and the extent to which it does, or can, resist and help to transcend, such relations

- the extent to which everyday experiential learning is implicit and embedded in other activities, and the extent to which it is, or can be, deliberately fostered.

Some indications of where these questions might lead are found in an interesting ethnography of by the American anthropologist Christina Turner (1995). Turner studied two groups of Japanese workers involved in union-directed takeovers of bankrupt small businesses in the late 1970s. Such takeovers were common during this period, when rising oil prices and revaluation of the yen were affecting the viability of smaller Japanese firms. Turner examined two of these, a camera company (Unikon) and a shoe manufacturer (Universal Shoes). Both firms were declared bankrupt in 1977, and in each case workers waged long and ultimately successful campaigns to take over the businesses. In the mid-1990s both firms were still operating profitably, Unikon as a conventional capitalist enterprise, Universal Shoes as a worker cooperative (Turner, 1995: 12-18, 239-42).

Turner examined relationships of workers' consciousness and action in the campaigns to take over the companies and their aftermath. She concluded that the formation of consciousness involves interaction between three processes: explicit argument, implicit knowledge, and action, the last 'itself a perform-ance and experience of social relatedness' (249). In the two cases Turner studied, direct experience and discursive argument were each important in forming the ideas and feelings that guided workers' actions. 'Unspoken assumptions and nonverbal actions [were] as critical ... as ... direct discussion, debate, reading or intellectual pondering. Furthermore, all social experiences matter[ed], from daily life routines like those of a usual workday or chatting over tea or sake, to periodic events like union meetings or company outings, to exceptional occasions like demonstrations, formal parties or internal union conflicts' (237-8).

Action and consciousness, thought and feeling, says Turner, are interde-pendent and formative. She also sees participants as actively thinking through and taking decisions about their situations. This insistence on agency connects with a great tradition in literature and social science, typified in literature by George Eliott (1866, 1871-2), in history by E.P. Thompson (1968), in cultural studies by Raymond Williams (1958), and in anthropology by Clifford Geertz (1973, 1983). While this approach recognises that agents are continually constrained and ultimately determined by wider economic, political and cultural forces, it also tracks, in convincing detail, the dialectic of agency and structure, action and consciousness that is forged as people live and work together. This perspective, then, is realistic and strategic: it enables us to understand more clearly 'how things actually are', and thus informs subse-quent action. It also helps us to understand the learning dimension of organisational and social life.

We learn as we act, and our learning is both tacit and explicit. This is indeed a complex tapestry, difficult to unpick. But just to know that it is complex and needs to be unpicked is important for those of us concerned with understanding and facilitating organisational and social learning and change. We can then let go of formulas that promise quick results, and get on with the difficult and rewarding work of trying to understand what people are actually learning in the places where we work and live. And, of course, considering the implications of that learning for what we do next.

Connections

The connections between this 'strategic learning' approach and the focus of this book should be readily apparent. 'Strategic learning' engages with the realities of changes brought about by a globalising capitalism. This approach is popular, critical and emancipatory. It works with the concrete experience of workers and managers. It subjects existing workplace relationships to critical scrutiny. It fosters democratic, transparent, accountable and flexible workplace change strategies. The pedagogy of the strategic learning process is politically engaged. It uses the time and autonomy provided by university study to help learners to critically understand and act on their work situations.

Further reading

The argument of this chapter is further developed in Griff Foley (2001) *Strategic Learning: Understanding and Facilitating Organisational Change,* Sydney: Centre for Popular Education, University of Technology, Sydney. (For orders: e-mail: cpe@uts.edu.au; fax: (612) 9514 3939; or write to Centre for Popular Education, UTS, PO Box 123, Broadway NSW 2007, Australia).

References

Eliot, G. 1866 (1965), *Felix Holt The Radical,* London: Panther.

Eliot, G. 1871-2 (1965), *Middlemarch,* Harmondsworth: Penguin.

Geertz, C. (1973), *The Interpretation of Cultures,* London: Fontana.

Geertz, C. (1983), *Local Knowledge: Further Essays in Interpretive Anthropology,* London: Fontana.

Glassie, H. 1982 (1995), *Passing the Time in Ballymenone: Culture and History of an Ulster Community,* Bloomington: Indiana University Press.

Thompson, E.P. (1968), *The Making of the English Working Class,* Harmondsworth: Penguin.

Turner, C. (1995), *Japanese Workers in Protest: An Ethnography of Consciousness and Experience,* Berkeley, University of California Press.

Williams, R. (1958), *Culture and Society, 1780-1950,* Harmondsworth: Penguin.

Index